IMAGES
of America

WOOD COUNTY
WEST VIRGINIA

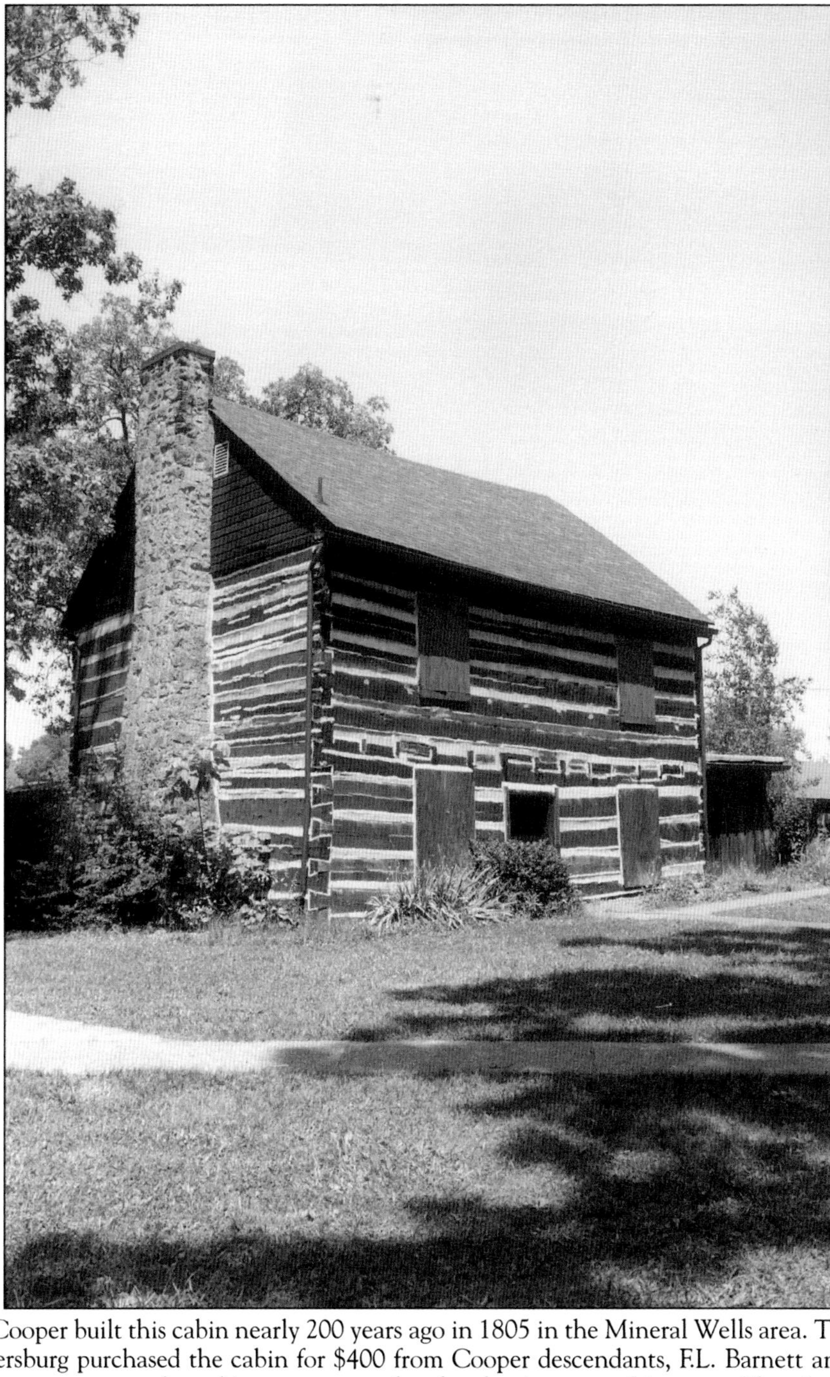

Henry Cooper built this cabin nearly 200 years ago in 1805 in the Mineral Wells area. The City of Parkersburg purchased the cabin for $400 from Cooper descendants, F.L. Barnett and M.L. LeMaster, to preserve the cabin as an example of early pioneer architecture. The city moved the cabin in 1910, log by log, to the City Park where it stands today. The Daughters of the American Pioneers own and maintain the cabin. It is open on Sundays from 1:30 to 4:30 p.m., from Memorial Day through Labor Day. (Photo taken by the author.)

IMAGES
of America

WOOD COUNTY
WEST VIRGINIA

Betty Leavengood

ARCADIA
PUBLISHING

ISBN 978-0-7385-1478-9

Published by Arcadia Publishing
Charleston, South Carolina

Printed in the United States of America

Library of Congress Catalog Card Number: 2002110805

For all general information contact Arcadia Publishing at:
Telephone 843-853-2070
Fax 843-853-0044
E-Mail sales@arcadiapublishing.com
For customer service and orders:
Toll-Free 1-888-313-2665

Visit us on the Internet at www.arcadiapublishing.com

Contents

ACKNOWLEDGMENTS

This glimpse into Wood County's past would not have been possible without the help of many people. My heartfelt thanks to Ken Gilbert, editor of *Parkersburg High School History*; Rae Brown, curator of Sumnerite Museum, and her sister and assistant, Fran Davis; Ray Swick, historian of Blennerhassett Island Historical State Park; James Measell, associate historian, Fenton Art Glass Company; Robert E. Enoch, president of the Wood County Historical and Preservation Society; James Miracle, chairman of the Wood County Landmarks Commission; Paul A. Borrelli, Artcraft Studio; Trinity Episcopal Church; Parkersburg Fire Department; the good folks at Kramer's Photo Supply; Ed Hicks, photographer, West Virginia State Archives; Jon Leavitt of Leavitt Funeral Services; Edwin L.E. Dils, former chairman of Dils Brothers and Company; Betty Shreve, West Virginia Extension Services; Fred Shreve, principal, McKinley Elementary School; Greg Smith, Camden Clark Hospital; Jill Parsons, St. Joseph's Hospital; Felice Jorgensen, artistic director, Smoot Theater; Mountain State College; Jack Parrish, Boy Scout Troop Three; Brenda Paden, Mullen Motors; Kim Miller. Antique Automobile Club of America; Esther Carroll, New Era School; and Lilly Library, Indiana University.

I am also deeply grateful to many individuals who shared their private collections with me, including Nadine Hofmann, Charles D. Alden, Darrell Deem, Clarence Hackett, William Hackett, Pat Peters, John King, Leta Dunlap, James W. Murphy, Ruth Gearhart, Mark Mondo, Jacquelyn Goodman, Sally Wyatt, Mike Naylor, Kathleen Smith, and Walter Taitt. Thanks also to Bill Bee who loaned me books on Wood County history and edited the final manuscript.

Two people deserve a special thank you. My mother, Gladys Marshall, sorted through 60 years of photographs to find several photos I could use. She also helped research many of the photos I located. Also, my friend, Fred Cornwell, drove around the county taking photographs and still found time, as my deadline approached, to shop for groceries, cook the meals, and generally support my efforts.

INTRODUCTION

Driving through Wood County today, it is hard to believe that these rolling hills and peaceful rivers have been the scene of so many conflicts.

Mingo, Shawnee, and Delaware Indians claimed the land that is now Wood County as white settlers moved into the area in the 1760s. Clashes between the two groups were inevitable, as were conflicts between the two nations—England and France—who claimed the land. And, when those conflicts were resolved, Wood County divided against itself in the War Between the States.

In 1487, John Cabot discovered the Atlantic coastline of North America and claimed the entire continent for the king of England. Rene Robert Cavalier La Salle established French claims in 1682 when he buried a leaden plate at the mouth of the Mississippi, claiming all the lands drained by the river for the king of France. Captain Bienville de Celoron reinforced France's claims in August of 1749 by burying leaden plates at intervals along the Ohio River proclaiming, "We have buried this plate as a monument of renewal of possessions which we have taken of the said river Ohio and of all those which fall into it, and of all the lands on both sides as far as the sources of said rivers."

To make certain the English understood their position, France announced its intentions to build a line of forts all along the Ohio River in 1753 and promptly began building Fort Le Boeuf on the headwaters of the Allegheny River. The governor of Virginia responded by sending Major George Washington later that year to warn the French to cease building forts and to vacate English land. To emphasize the point, the governor sent William Trent and a party of 40 men to build a fort on the site of present-day Pittsburgh. When the fort was partially constructed a large French and Indian army forced Trent and his men to return east and the French and Indian War began.

When men did not rush to enlist in a war that meant little to them, Gov. Robert Dinwiddie of Virginia issued his Proclamation of 1754 promising land east of the Ohio River to "such persons, who by their voluntary engagement and good behavior in the said service, shall deserve the same." Enough men enlisted to create an army to dispel the French, and England's claims on the American continent were acknowledged in the Treaty of Paris in 1763.

The king of England issued a proclamation acknowledging the American Indian's ownership of the land west of the Allegheny Mountains. He ordered the settlers already in those areas to leave, and he gave the army the right to burn their homes.

Contrary to the proclamation, the settlers in the area did not move and more settlers came to the Ohio Valley. Many claimed that the land was owed to them for their services in the French and Indian War, and others moved to be near other family members. To resolve the situation, England negotiated the Treaty of Fort Stanwix on November 5, 1768, in which American Indians relinquished all lands west of the Allegheny Mountains to the Ohio River.

The numbers of settlers coming to Wood County increased every year, as did the number of conflicts with the American Indians, who did not follow the Fort Stanwix Treaty agreements. In 1773, Robert Thornton, Parkersburg's first white settler, made a tomahawk claim on the area around the confluence of the Little Kanawha and Ohio Rivers. Three years later the General Assembly of Virginia passed an ordinance employing 400 men to defend the western frontier. Emigration continued until the outbreak of the Revolutionary War.

In 1783, shortly after the Revolutionary War ended, Parkersburg's namesake, Capt. Alexander Parker, purchased 1,350 acres from Thornton for a small amount, thought to be $10 or $50 or a horse and a gallon of whiskey. Parker died in 1791 without ever having been to Parkersburg. He did send Capt. James Neal to survey his purchase, and Neal became the first permanent settler of Parkersburg. Neal came to Parkersburg in 1785 and built a blockhouse on the south side of the Little Kanawha River to protect himself and his neighbors from the American Indians.

Neal's blockhouse provided refuge on several occasions. Between 1789 and 1795, at least 45 people were killed in the area that is now Wood County and Washington County in Ohio. The Indians joined forces to fight for their land. It was not until Mad Anthony Wayne and his army decisively defeated the American Indians in the Battle of Fallen Timbers in August of 1794 and the subsequent Treaty of Greenville that relative peace came to the frontier and Wood County.

With peace at hand, the leaders of what would become Wood County turned their attention to forming a new county. Currently, they were part of Harrison County. All courts, elections, and legal records were at the Harrison County seat of Clarksburg, too far for most people to conduct their business, attend court, or vote.

In 1798, 146 inhabitants of the area around the Little Kanawha and Hughes River petitioned the General Assembly of Virginia for a division of Harrison County into a new county along the Ohio River. They cited as their reason "the distance from the center of our settlements to the courthouse of seventy-four miles, the way mountainous and many dangers (and) no comfortable accommodations." The general assembly passed an act creating Wood County, named for the current governor, James Wood, on December 21, 1798. The act took effect May 1, 1799.

Before he left office, Governor Wood appointed a court of nine justices to organize the new county. A lengthy battle between two factions over the location of the courthouse ensued. One faction proposed that the courthouse be located south of the Little Kanawha River on property belonging to Hugh Phelps, Neal's son-in-law. A second faction, led by Dr. Joseph Spencer of Vienna, argued for the county seat to be in Vienna. Finally, on November 11, 1800, the justices voted unanimously on a compromise. The courthouse would be built at Newport, chartered by the General Assembly of Virginia on January 6, 1800, on land owned by John Stokely at The Point, where the Little Kanawha River and Ohio Rivers meet.

This compromise led to more controversy. Stokely's property was claimed by the heirs of Capt. Alexander Parker, who purchased the land from Robert Thornton in 1785. When Parker died in 1791, his daughters challenged Stokely's claim.

It was not until September of 1810 that the claims were finally settled in favor of the Parker family. The town was renamed "Parkersburgh" in honor of Captain Parker. (In 1894 the United States Post Office removed the "h" in "burgh" nationwide. Pittsburgh fought the order and remains Pittsburgh today.)

The town of Parkersburg grew slowly. The railroad reached the town from the east in 1857. There were the first discoveries of oil and gas around the county.

With the outbreak of the War Between the States, growth halted. Wood County families split—some favored the North and others the South. Cannons were placed on Fort Boreman Hill to protect the city. Wood County leaders led the fight to break away from Virginia and form a separate state. West Virginia became a state on June 20, 1863 and a Parkersburg man, Arthur Boreman, became the first governor. After the war, the oil boom started and Parkersburg became the center for the refining and distribution of oil. Newly rich oilmen built large, elegant homes in Parkersburg. Businesses started, organizations formed, schools and hospitals were built. Wood County was on the move.

Betty Leavengood

One

BEGINNINGS

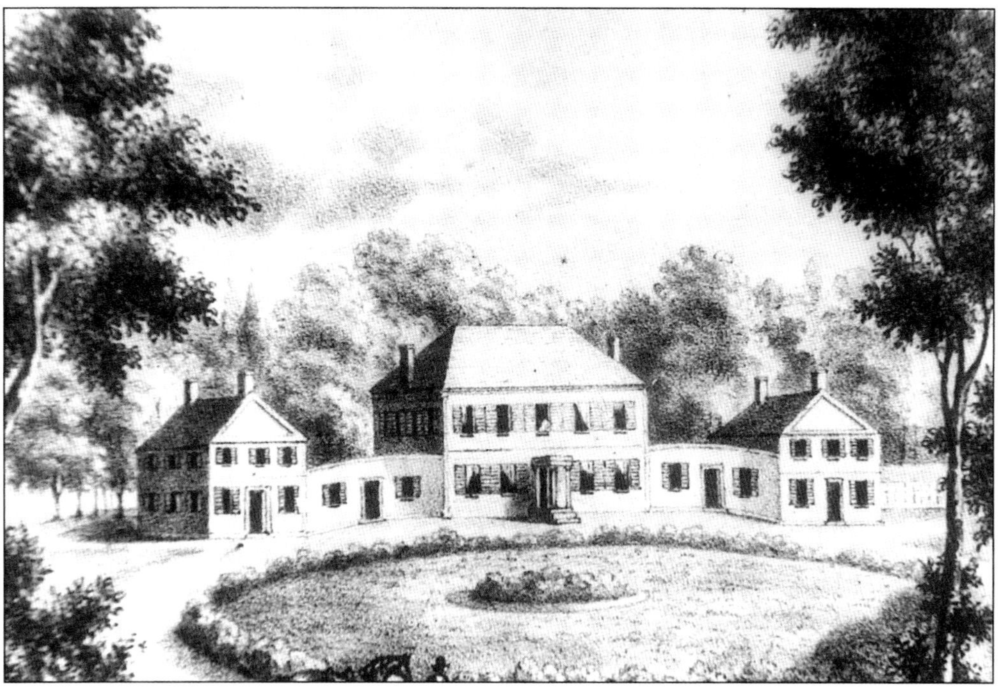

Harman Blennerhassett and his wife, Margaret, left Ireland in 1796 to settle in America. They built a mansion on Backus Island in the Ohio River near Parkersburg from 1798 to 1800. Built in the Palladian style of architecture with a central house and two dependencies connected by curved porticos, the Blennerhassett Mansion was one of the most beautiful private homes in America. (Courtesy of Blennerhassett Island Historical State Park.)

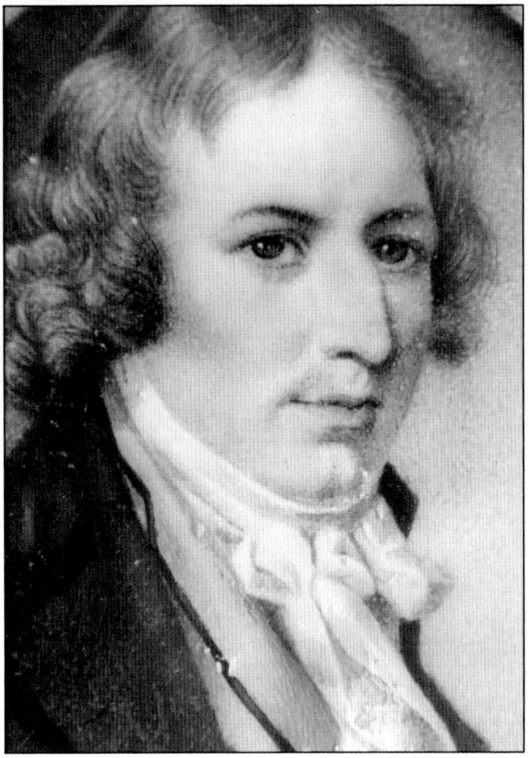

Fearing possible charges of treason for his involvement with the Society of United Irishmen and facing harsh criticism for marrying his niece, Harman Blennerhassett and his wife Margaret left Ireland in 1796 to begin a new life in America. The Blennerhassetts built an elegant mansion on an island near present-day Parkersburg, West Virginia, where they lived from 1798 to 1806, when Harman's support of Aaron Burr's alleged scheme to create a new nation in the Southwest forced the Blennerhassetts to flee. (Courtesy of Blennerhassett Island Historical State Park.)

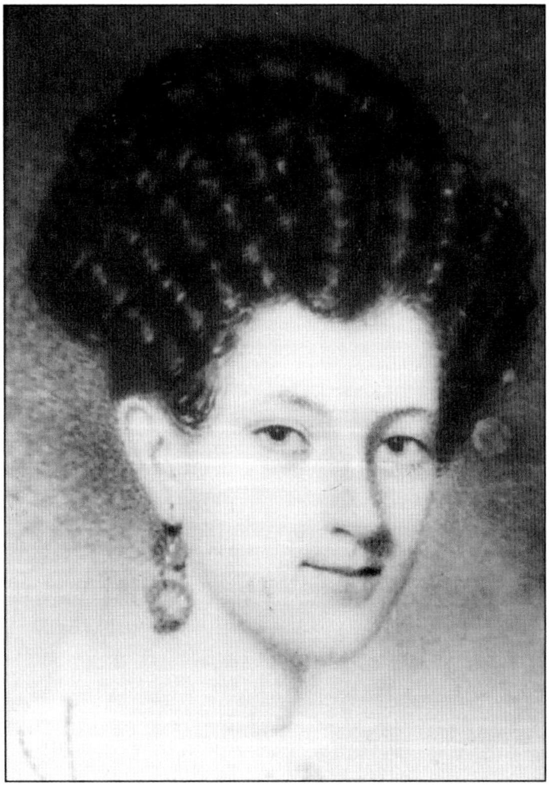

Margaret Blennerhassett made her Blennerhassett Island estate the showplace of the Ohio Valley. She filled her home with fine paintings; furniture brought from England, Baltimore, and Philadelphia; and oriental carpets. She supervised a 2.5-acre garden planted with both exotic and native flowers and shrubs. After leaving the Island in 1806, Margaret never returned. In her poem, "The Desert Isle," she wrote, "Oh why, dear Isle, art thou still not my own? Thy charms could then for all my griefs atone . . ." In 1996 her body and that of her son, Harman Blennerhassett, Jr., were returned to the Island from New York and interred between the mansion and the site of her flower garden. (Courtesy of Blennerhassett Island Historical State Park.)

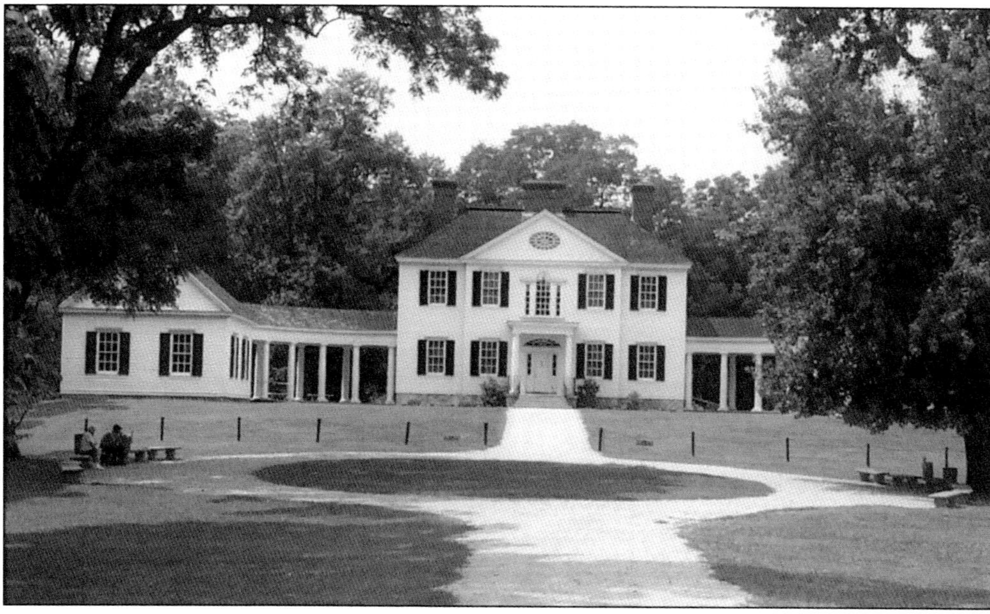

In 1975, the West Virginia state legislature established the Blennerhassett Historical Park Commission to preserve Blennerhassett Island's history. The island opened to the public in July 1980 as Blennerhassett Island Historical State Park. Visitors came from all 50 states and 40 foreign countries. Many suggested reconstructing the mansion. Due to this demand the State of West Virginia decided to rebuild the mansion. Construction began in 1984. The kitchen wing opened to the public in 1987; the north wing, Blennerhassett's study, in 1990; and the main part of the mansion on July 4, 1991. Today volunteers and staff attired in period dress conduct tours of the mansion from May through October. (Photograph by Fred Cornwell.)

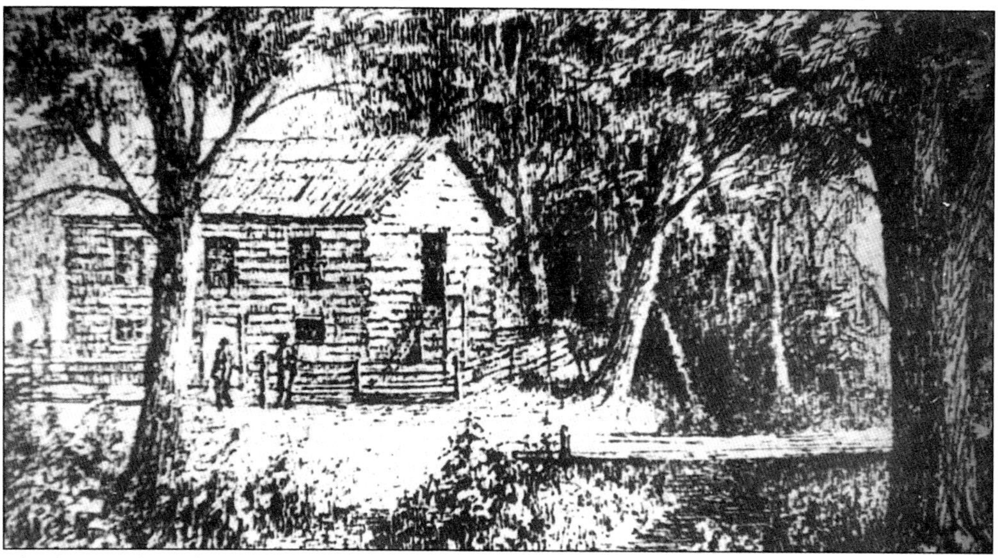

The home of Hugh Phelps, located on the southside of the Little Kanawha River near Squire Run, served as Wood County's first courthouse from 1798 to 1800. Hugh Phelps, son-in-law of the founder of Parkersburg Capt. James Neal, came to Neal's Station in 1787 from Pennsylvania. Phelps was active in the formation of Wood County and served at different times as head of the Wood County Militia, sheriff, and presiding justice. (Courtesy of Mike Naylor.)

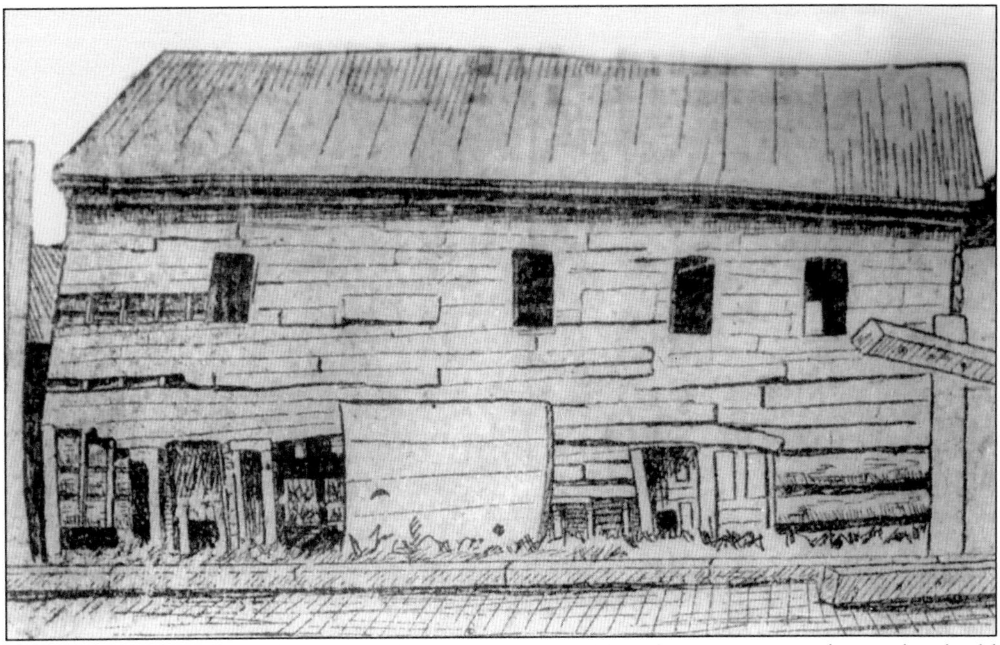

On November 10, 1800, the Court of Wood County held its first meeting and agreed to build a courthouse on land belonging to John Stokely, near the junction of the Ohio and Little Kanawha Rivers. Stokely donated two acres to the county and the courthouse was built at what is now the corner of Second and Juliana Streets. It was used as the courthouse until 1817. After that the building was occupied as a residence until the flood of 1884. Later the Rex Hardware Company occupied the building. (Courtesy of Paul A. Borrelli, Artcraft Studio.)

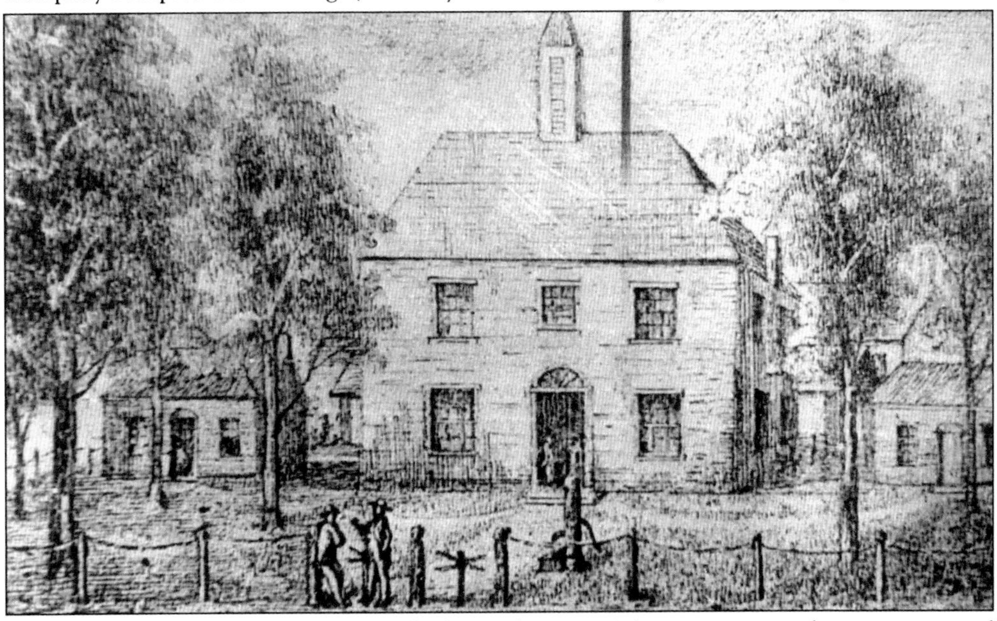

Wood County's third courthouse was built on the site of the present courthouse square and stood from 1817 until the fall of 1860. A $400 bell hung in the steeple. It was in the third courthouse that 13 votes were cast for Abraham Lincoln at a time when only the bravest dared stem the tide of Virginia opinion. (Courtesy of Mike Naylor.)

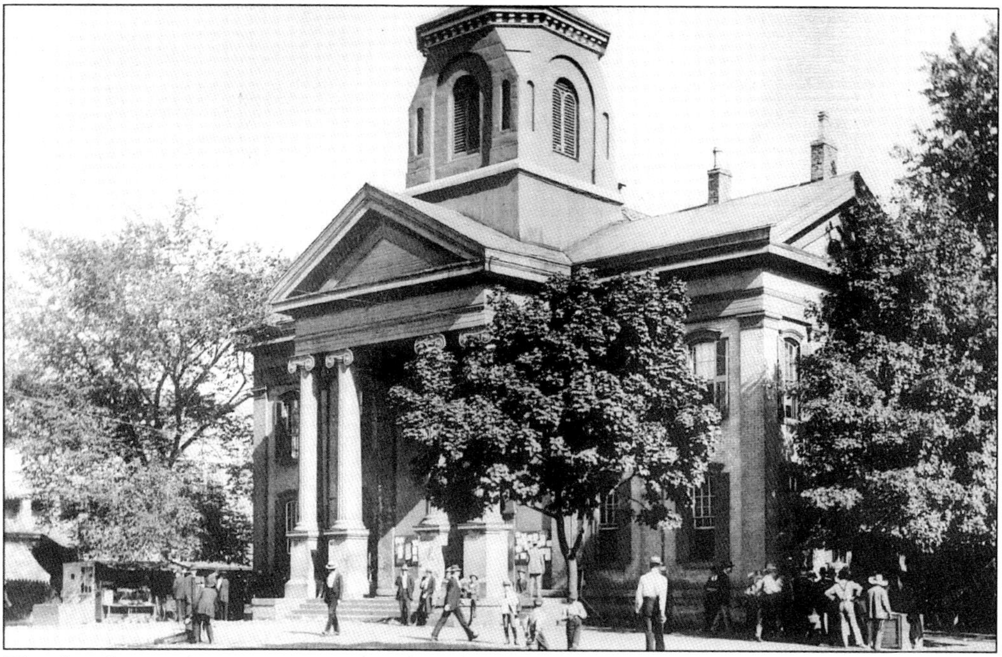

The fourth courthouse was completed and ready for use in 1860. Little is known about the fourth courthouse. Troops were mobilized in the courthouse during the Civil War. Lightning struck its steeple around 1873 and the steeple was replaced with a large cupola. (Courtesy of West Virginia State Archives.)

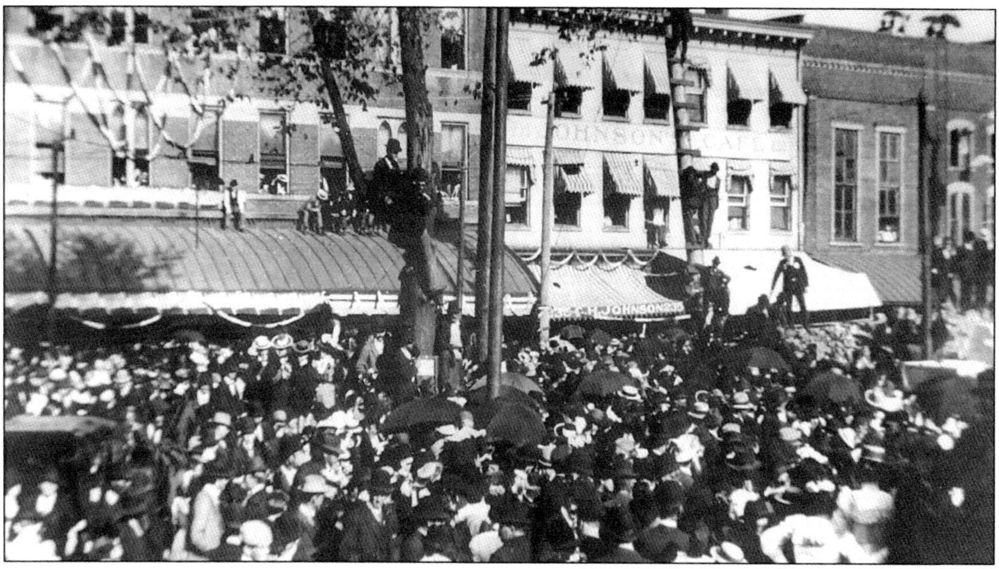

On October 5, 1899, Wood County culminated a three-day celebration of its centennial with a parade that included 100 floats, musical entertainment, fireworks, and the laying of the cornerstone for the new courthouse. A tremendous crowd gathered on Court Square as the eight-ton cornerstone was eased into place. Judge J.M. Jackson, grand orator of the Grand Lodge of Masons, addressed the crowd, dedicating the new building to the "preservation of society and the promotion of morality and public decency." A box containing over 200 items, primarily business cards, was embedded in the cornerstone. (Courtesy of R.E. Enoch.)

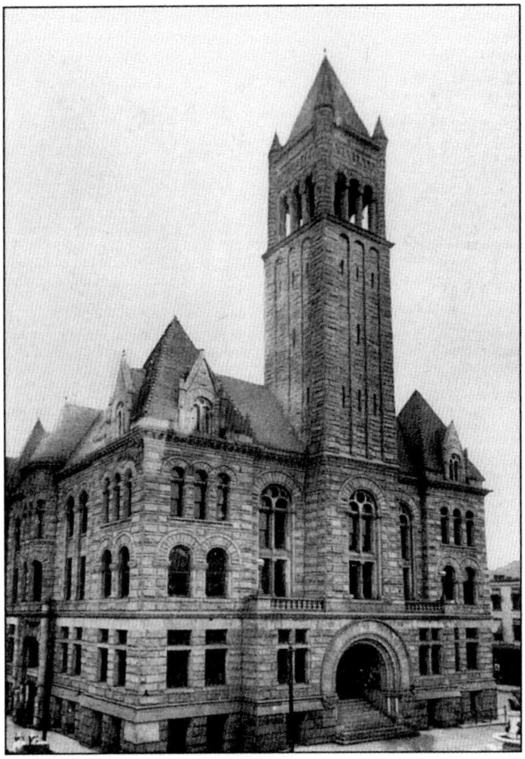

Wood County's fifth courthouse was the third to be built in the public square donated by heirs of Alexander Parker. Construction began in 1899 and was completed in 1901. The building was made fireproof with stone and steel used entirely for the walls and terra cotta for the floors. Wood was placed on the floors of the offices to make standing easier. The stilted arches and other embellishments were hand carved. Efforts by the city to demolish the courthouse in 1978 were thwarted by a citizens campaign, spearheaded by Snowden Kesterson, to "Save the Courthouse." (Collection of B. Leavengood.)

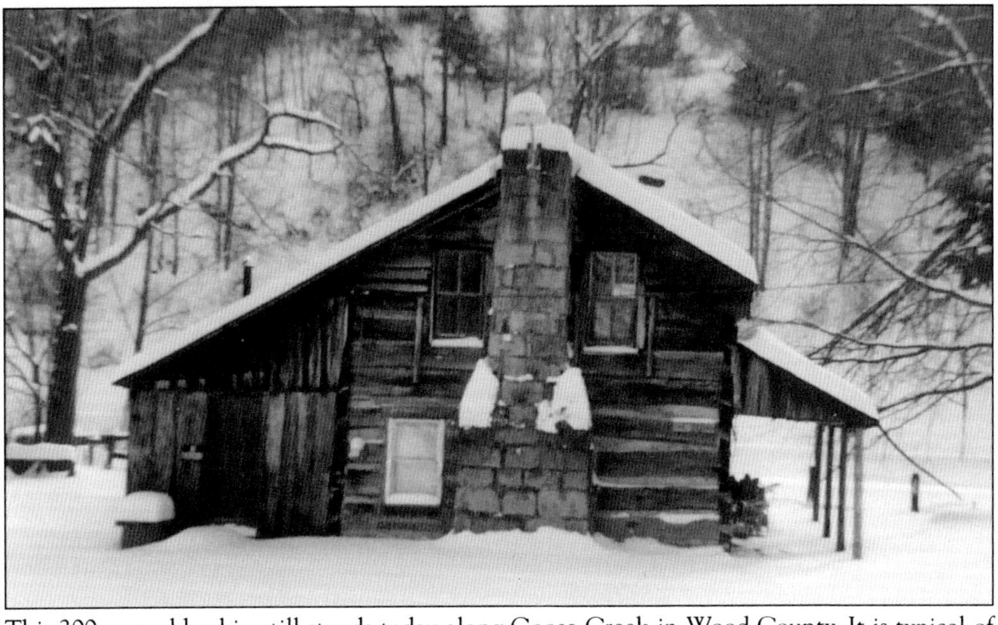

This 200-year-old cabin still stands today along Goose Creek in Wood County. It is typical of early pioneer cabins. Small trees were felled and the logs cut to the needed lengths. Cracks were chinked (filled) with mud and clay. Heat came from the fireplace and cook stove. The current owners found a diary in the house kept by Silouee Dilworth from 1872 to 1918. He wrote about smallpox, train wrecks, serving on the jury, illness, death, and always—the weather. (Courtesy of Gary and Darlene Willis.)

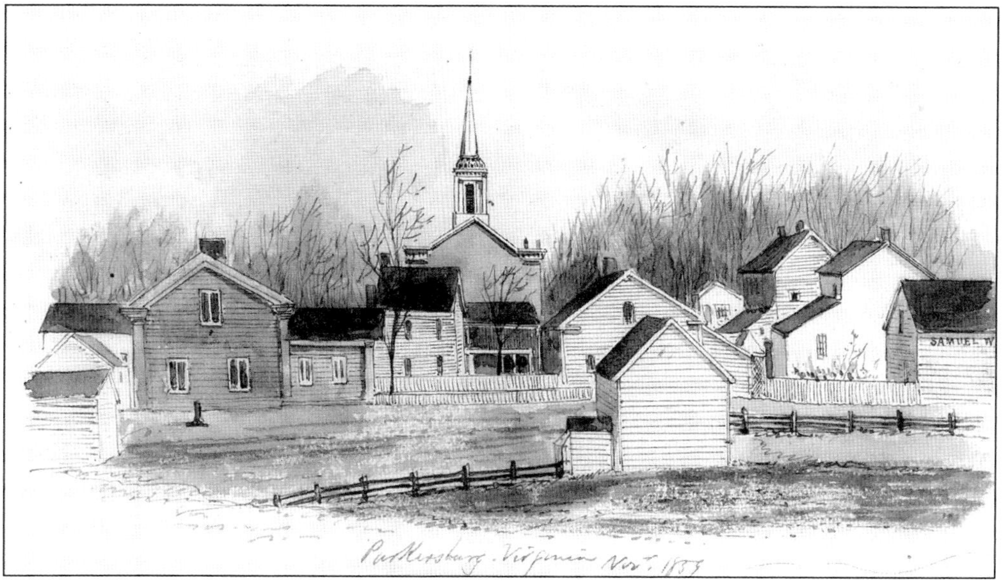

Lefevre J. Cranstone, an English artist, toured the United States from 1859 to 1861. He kept a record of his travels by making detailed sketches. This sketch depicts Parkersburg as it was in 1859. (Courtesy of Lilly Library, Indiana University, Bloomington, Indiana.)

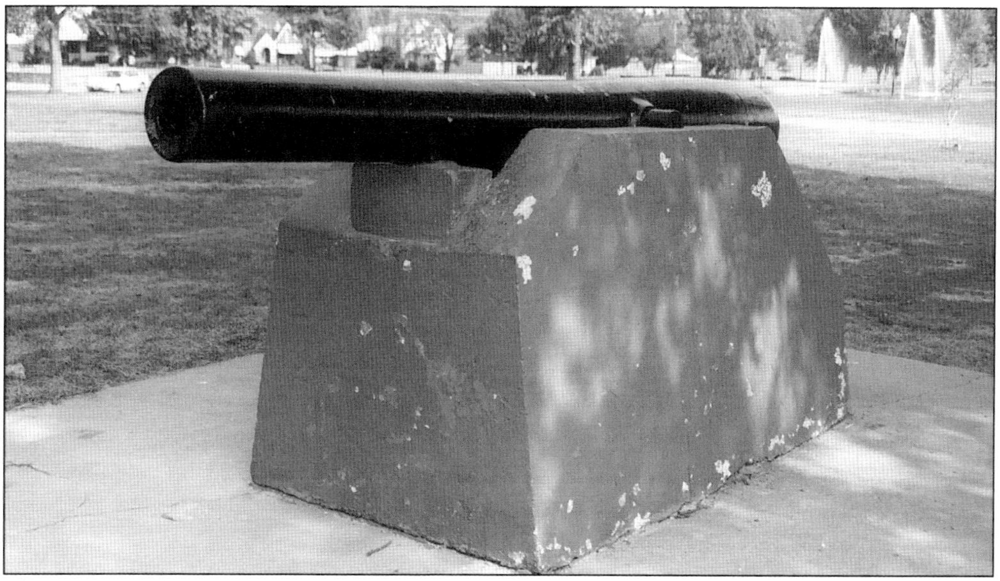

The cannons placed on Fort Boreman Hill during the Civil War were sent to a United States arsenal after the war. In the 1890s the Andrew Mather Post of the Grand Army of the Republic obtained the cannon pictured from the United States government. Six teams of horses hauled the cannon, called "Long Tom," to Fort Boreman. There, it was fired on ceremonial occasions and holidays causing the residents near Fort Boreman Hill to complain about the noise and broken windows. The protests led to the sale of the cannon to the Parkersburg Junk Company. The Kiwanis Club rescued the cannon just in time—it had been hoisted on a crane 110 feet high and was about to be dropped and broken into pieces of scrap iron. The Kiwanians quickly struck a deal to save the cannon. The city donated a plot and mounted "Long Tom" in the City Park where it sits today. (Photograph taken by Fred Cornwell.)

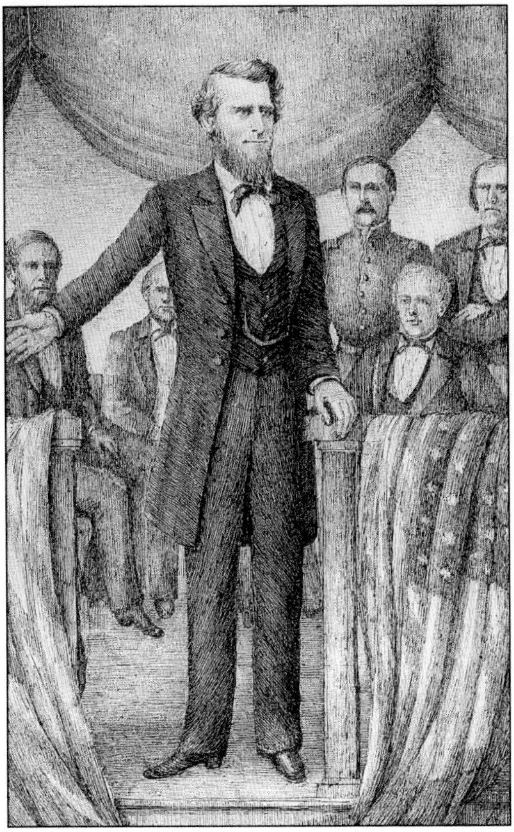

Arthur I. Boreman, a prominent Parkersburg lawyer, served as a delegate from Wood County to the Virginia House of Delegates from 1855 to 1861. He later played a decisive role in the western Virginia drive for statehood. After President Abraham Lincoln signed the bill making West Virginia a state, 235 delegates met in Parkersburg on May 6 and 7, 1863, to nominate offices provided under the West Virginia constitution. Arthur I. Boreman, sketched by Joseph Hubert Diss DeBarr, became the first governor of the State of West Virginia on June 20, 1863. (Courtesy of the West Virginia State Archives.)

The United Daughters of the Confederacy dedicated this monument in the City Park in 1908 to Confederate soldiers. Although a similar monument has not been erected in memory of Union soldiers, a post of the Grand Army of the Republic was organized by 16 Union veterans on September 1, 1882. These events show that long after the close of the Civil War there were still sharp divisions in Wood County. (Photograph by Fred Cornwell.)

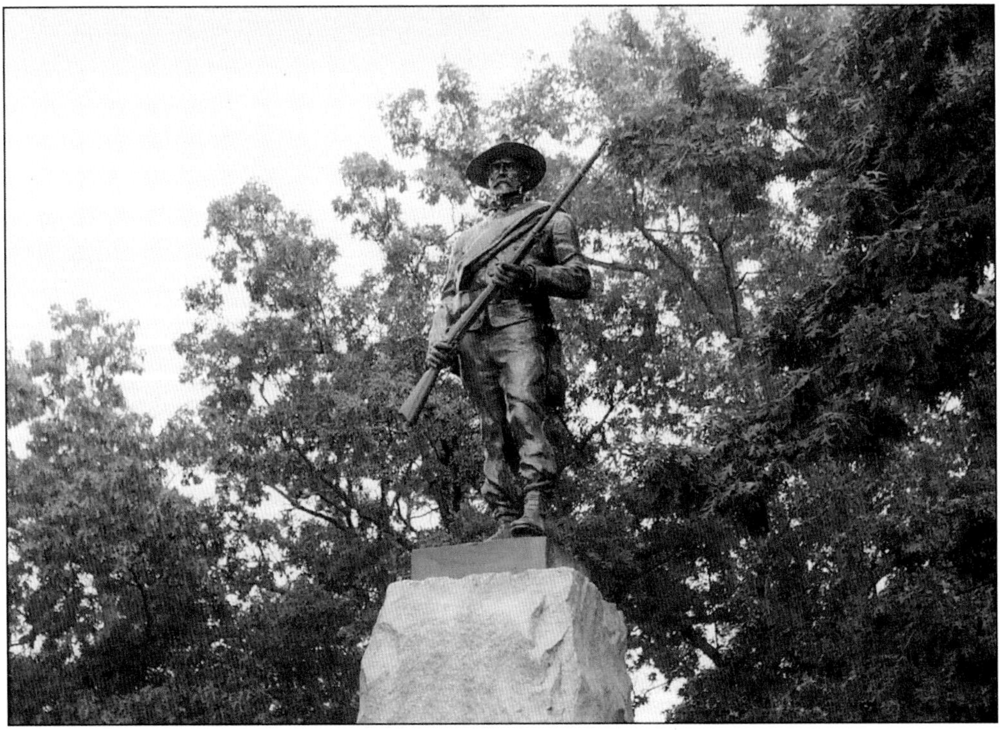

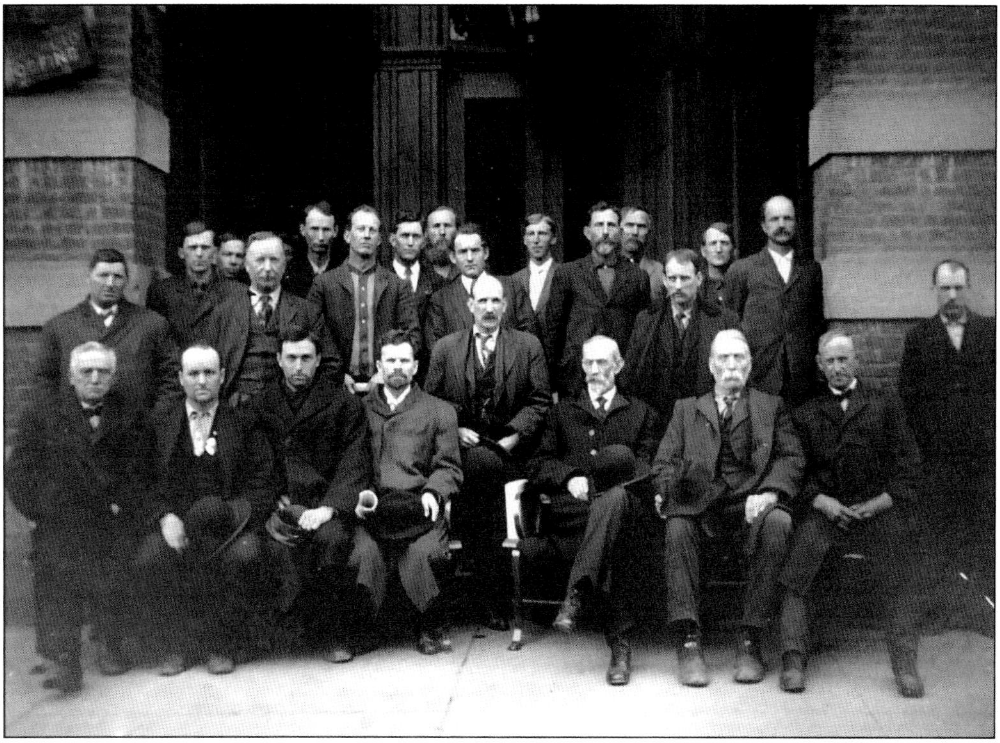

The Civil War divided Wood County families. The first mayor of Parkersburg, James Cook, supported the Union, his brother Paul, the Confederacy. Churches split over the issue. Baptists and Methodists divided into Northern and Southern branches. It was not until long after the war ended in 1865 that the bitterness healed enough for Union and Confederate soldiers, pictured above, to have a joint reunion. (Courtesy of James Miracle.)

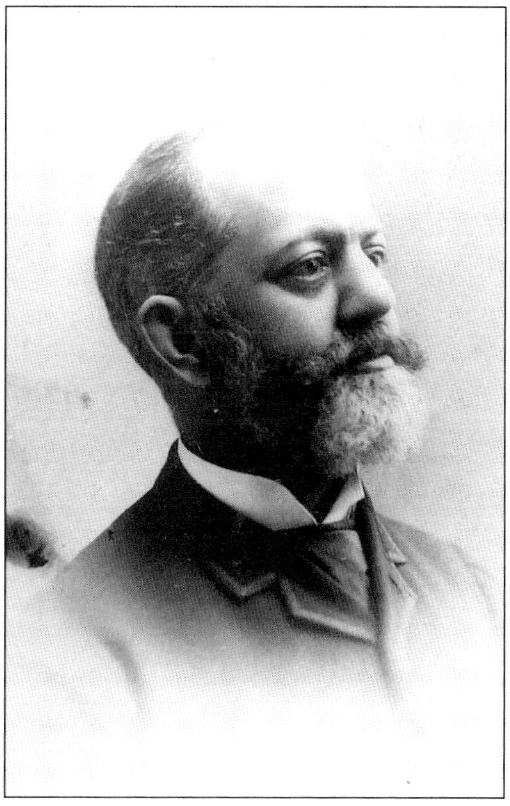

William Cooper Stiles Jr. came to Wood County in 1857 to investigate the potential of the oil field near White Oak on the eastern border of what is now Wood County. He returned in 1864 to form the Volcanic Oil and Coal Company. Stiles purchased 2,000 acres, began drilling, and laid out the town that by 1870 was called Volcano. In its heyday Volcano had nearly 4,000 permanent residents. Stiles died in his Volcano home on December 17, 1896. (Courtesy of Blennerhassett Island Historical State Park.)

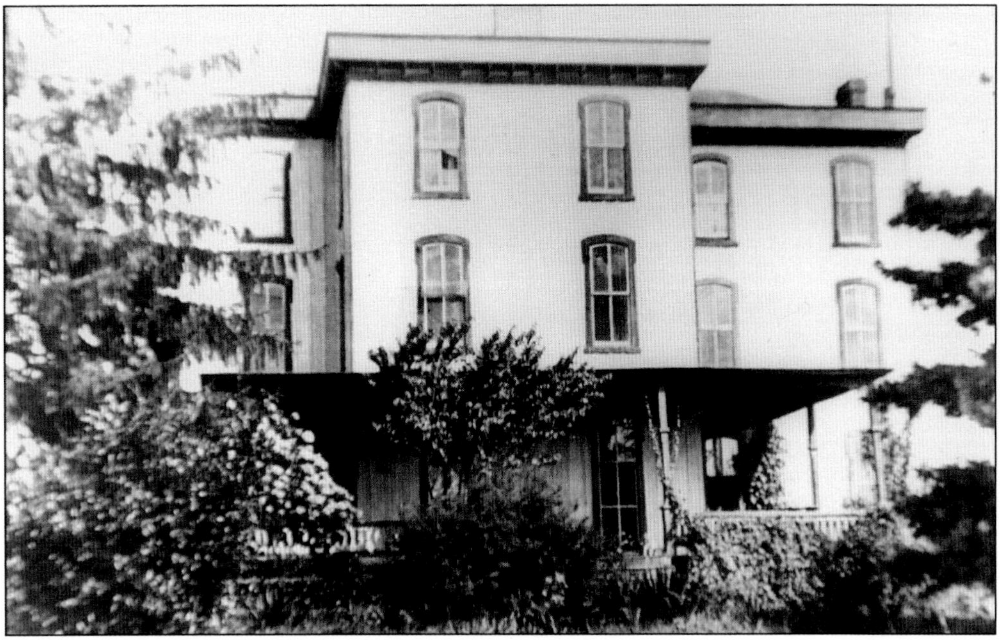

William Cooper Stiles Jr. built his mansion, Thornhill Farm, on a hill above Volcano. Shaped in the form of a Maltese Cross, the 25-room mansion had extensive flower and vegetable gardens, stables, and a wine cellar. After his death in 1896, the mansion slowly deteriorated until today only the foundation remains. (Courtesy of Blennerhassett Island Historical State Park.)

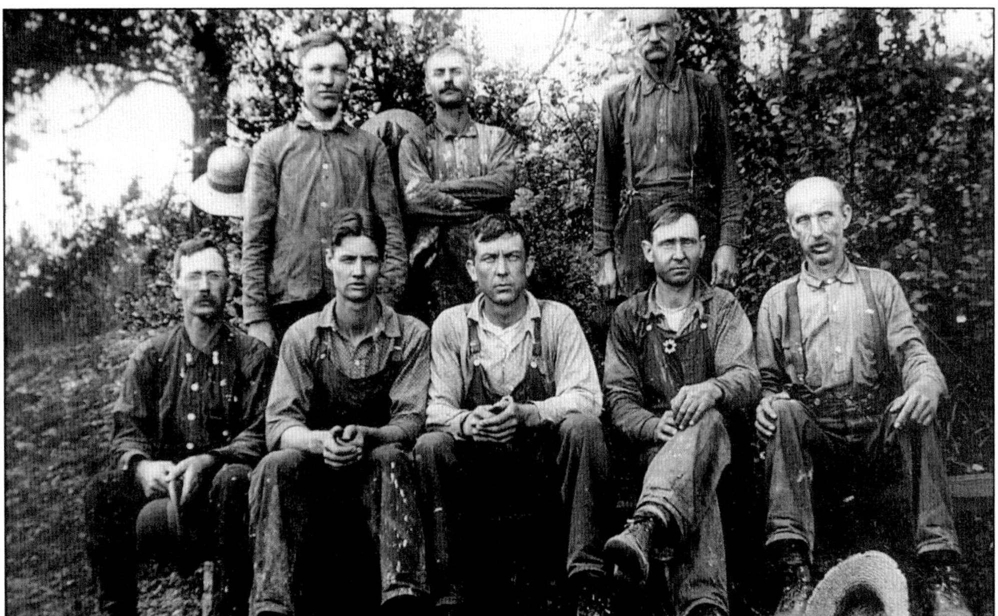

These men look like they have put in a hard day's work. The photograph, taken on July 10, 1907, shows the workers of W.C. Stiles Jr. in the Volcano oil fields. During Volcano's heyday men came to work in the oil fields, bringing their wives and children. The town grew to an estimated population of 4,000 at the height of production. (Courtesy of the family of Mary Reece Dunlap.)

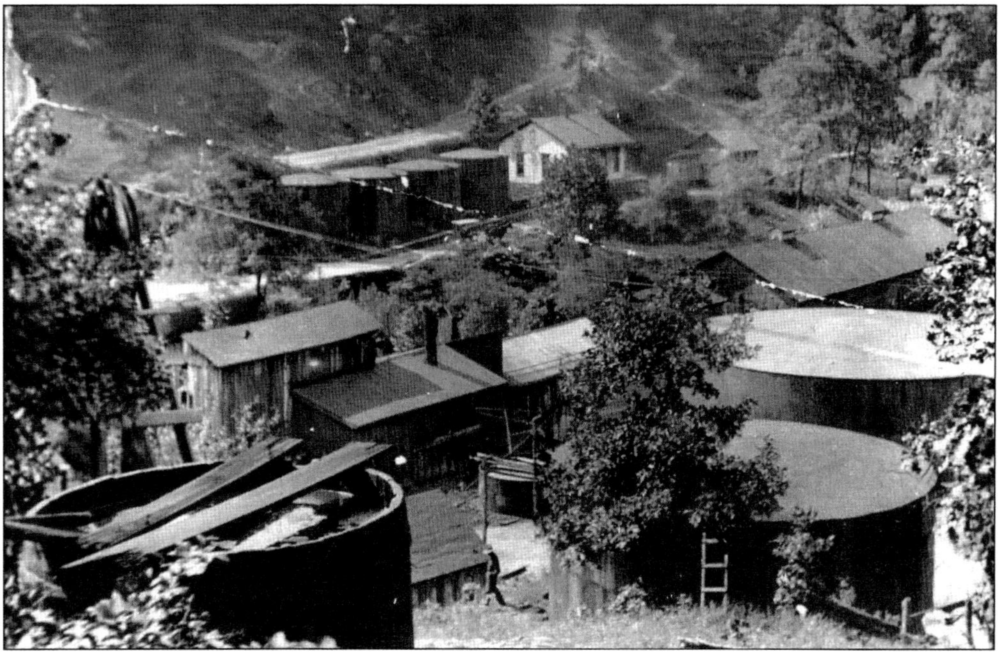

The tank farm in Volcano stored oil waiting to be shipped to refineries in Parkersburg. At first barrels of oil were hauled by horse and wagon to the Baltimore and Ohio Railroad. In 1866 the Laurel Fork and Sand Hill Railroad built a track into Volcano. When the Laurel Fork and Sand Hill Railroad ceased operation, a pipeline carried the oil to the railroad station. (Courtesy of the West Virginia State Archives.)

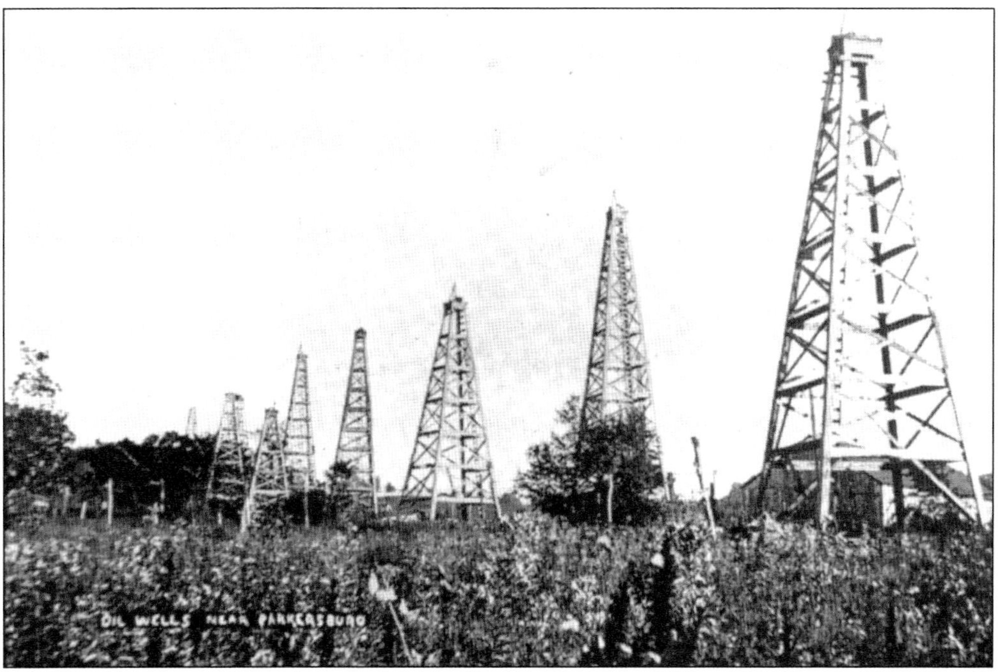

After the Civil War oil fields developed in several locations in Wood County. The Boaz field, pictured above, was located between Williamstown and Parkersburg. (Courtesy of Mike Naylor.)

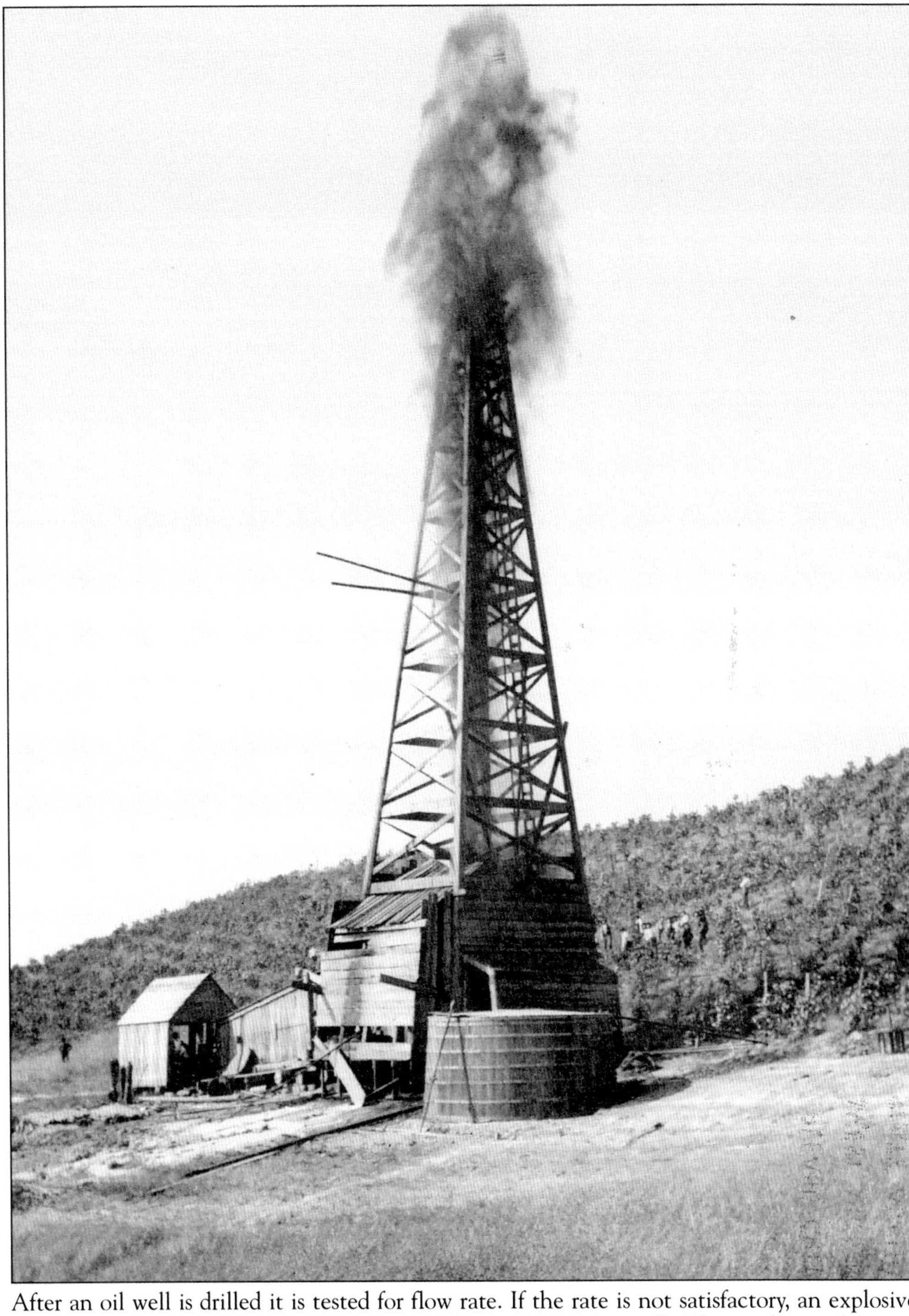

After an oil well is drilled it is tested for flow rate. If the rate is not satisfactory, an explosive called a torpedo containing nitroglycerin is dropped into the well. The explosion fractures the rock at the bottom of the well, which allows the oil to flow more freely. Sometimes the oil shoots out of the well propelled by natural gas pressure—thus the term, "shooting a well." (Courtesy of the West Virginia State Archives.)

Two

Getting From Here to There

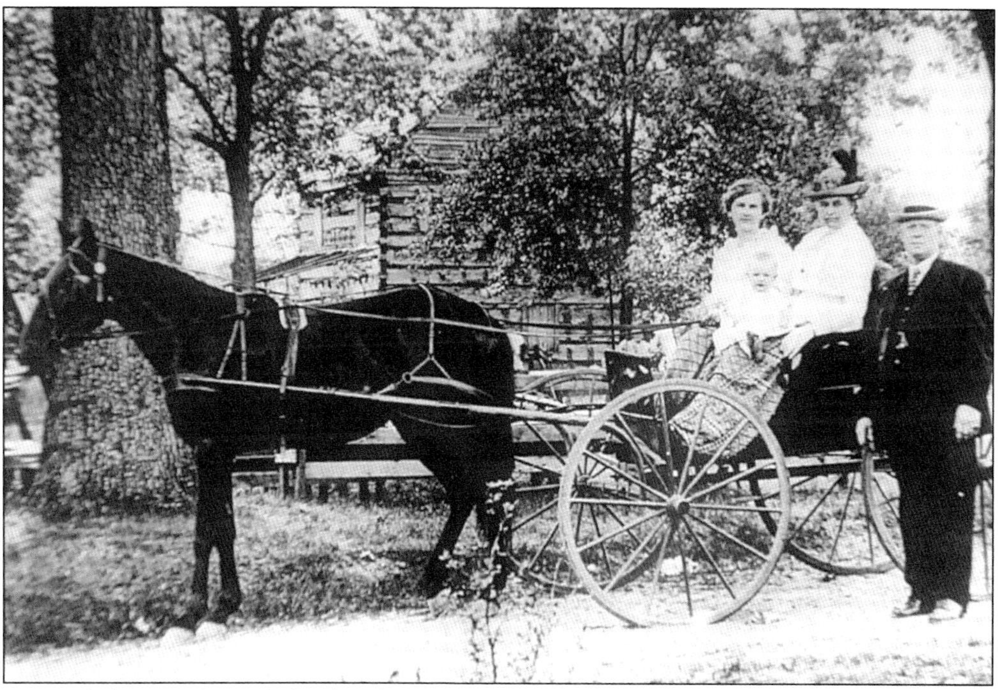

Pictured above is the Kirk family of Parkersburg taking a Sunday buggy ride in the City Park, c. 1910. The cabin in the background is the Cooper Cabin, built in 1805 in the Mineral Wells area. Today the Daughters of the American Pioneers own and maintain the cabin, which was moved to the park as an example of early pioneer architecture. (Courtesy of R.E. Enoch.)

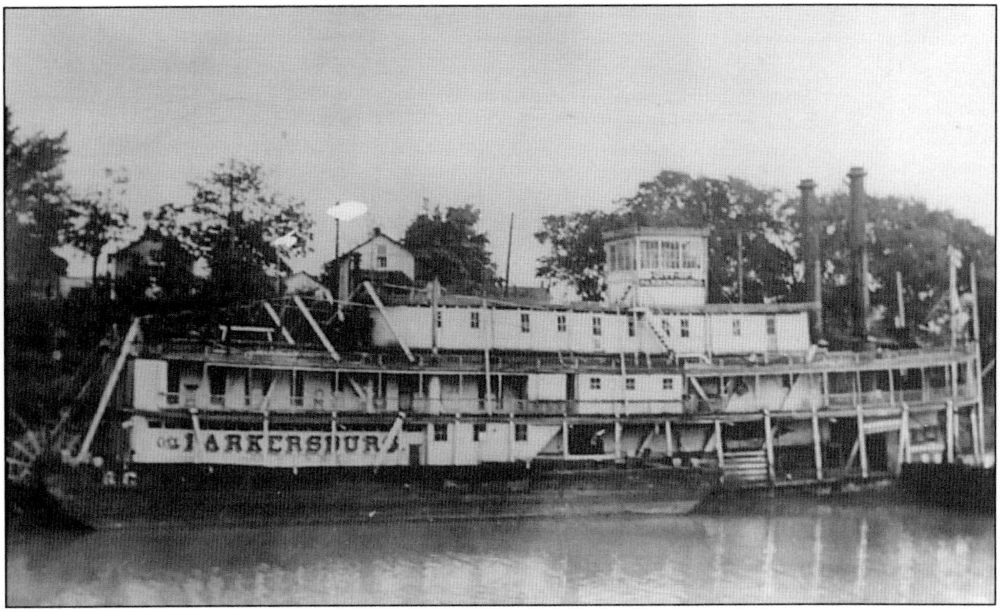

The *City of Parkersburg* packet boat was built in 1899. At that time, it was called *Liberty*. In 1912, John Hubbard of Pittsburgh bought the *Liberty*, altered it extensively, and renamed it *City of Parkersburg*. In the winter of 1913 the boat began running the Pittsburgh-Cincinnati route. On its second upbound trip, the boat hit a cofferdam at Dam 26 and sank. It was raised, repaired, and put back in service by October on the same route. On March 25, 1915, the *City of Parkersburg* hit an obstruction and was towed to Point Pleasant for repairs. That summer the boat towed a floating water circus to the Upper Mississippi. Back on its regular route early in 1918, the boat hit a half-sunken barge and sank for keeps. (Courtesy of R.E. Enoch.)

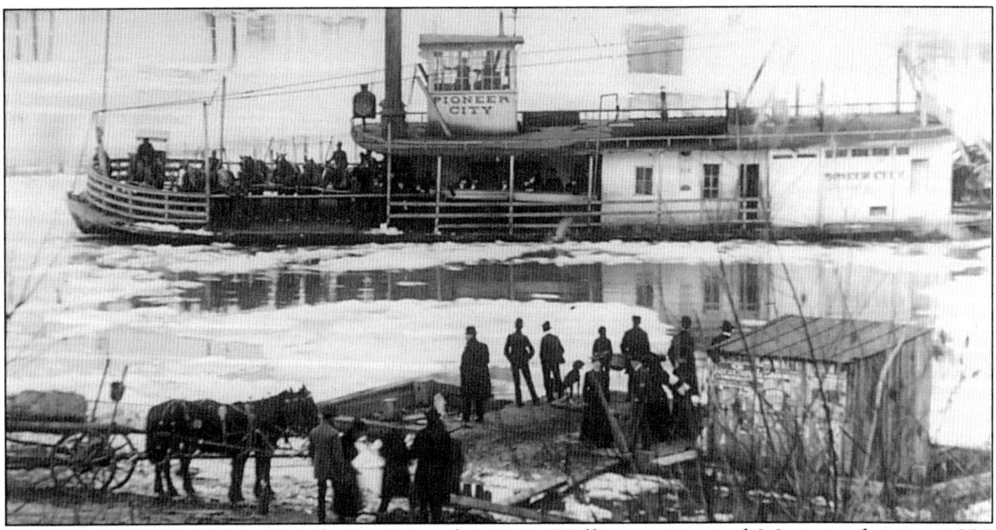

The Pioneer Ferry transported passengers between Williamstown and Marietta from c. 1889 until the Williamstown-Marietta bridge opened in 1903. The ferry made regular trips from 6 a.m. until 10 p.m. After 10 p.m. the night watchman transported passengers across the river in a skiff that seated 32 people. In the winter the skiff was used all day when the river was icy. Four extra men were needed to keep the ice pushed away while the oarsman rowed. (Courtesy of Charles D. Alden.)

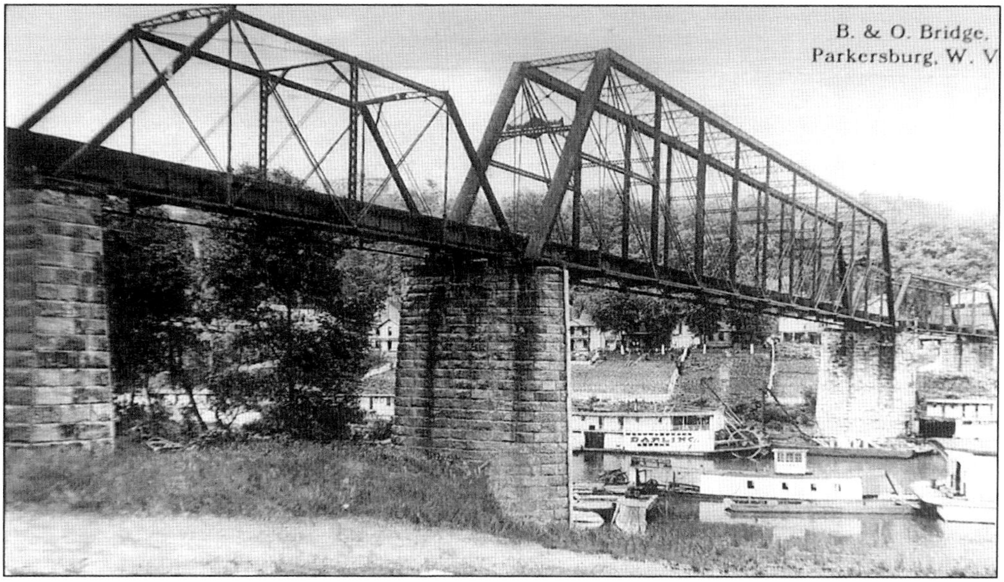

This postcard image shows the railroad bridge across the Little Kanawha River, which was built in 1885. The buildings in the background are Newtown, infamous center of beer, wine, and whiskey production in Parkersburg. (Collection of B. Leavengood.)

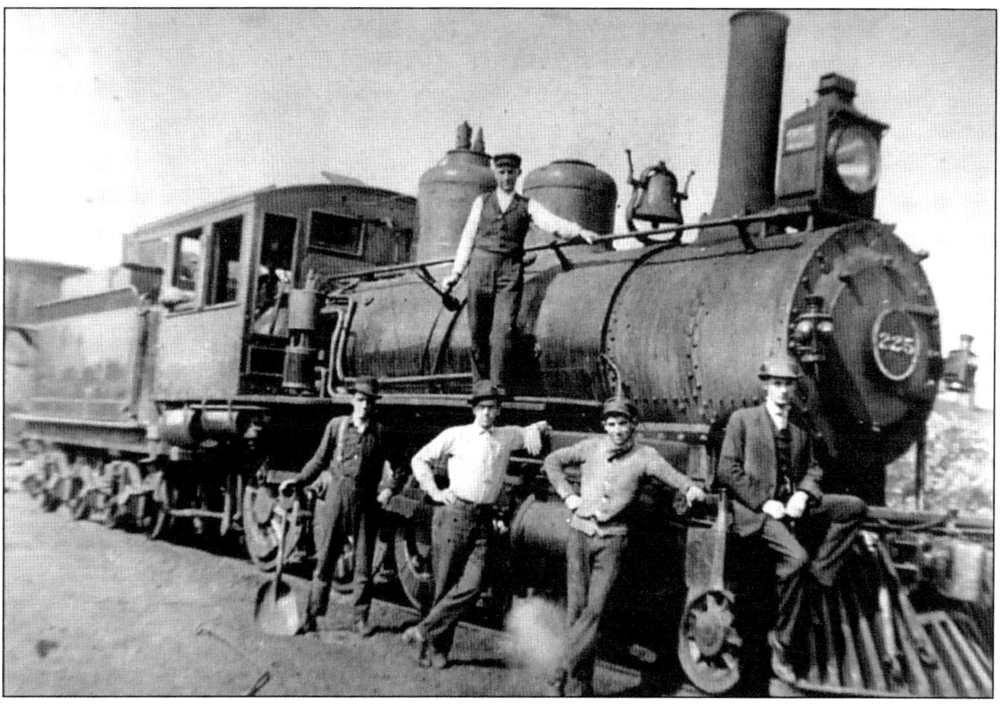

This 1906 steam engine number 225 is sitting in front of the square shed that housed four engines in the Parkersburg railroad yard. The shed burned down in late 1906 and was replaced by a roundhouse that housed six engines. The train required a five-man crew—the engineer, conductor, fireman, a front brakeman, and a rear brakeman. (Courtesy of John King.)

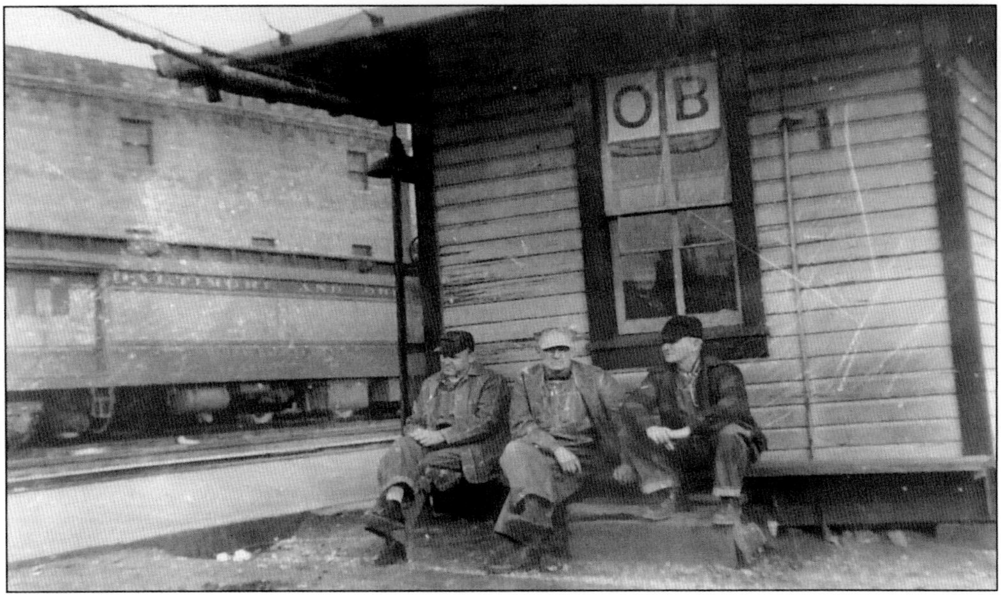

Pictured from left to right, fireman "Cub" Dils, engineer Harlan James, and yard foreman K.B. Howard take a break at the telegraph office. Nearby, according to retired engineer Clarence Hackett of Parkersburg, is where Jim McClinton kept his private railroad car. "The car was fully equipped," Hackett said, "down to the best silverware and china. It had two bedrooms, a living room, kitchen, and dining room. When they went on a trip, McClinton hired a chef from Cincinnati to do the cooking." (Courtesy of Clarence Hackett.)

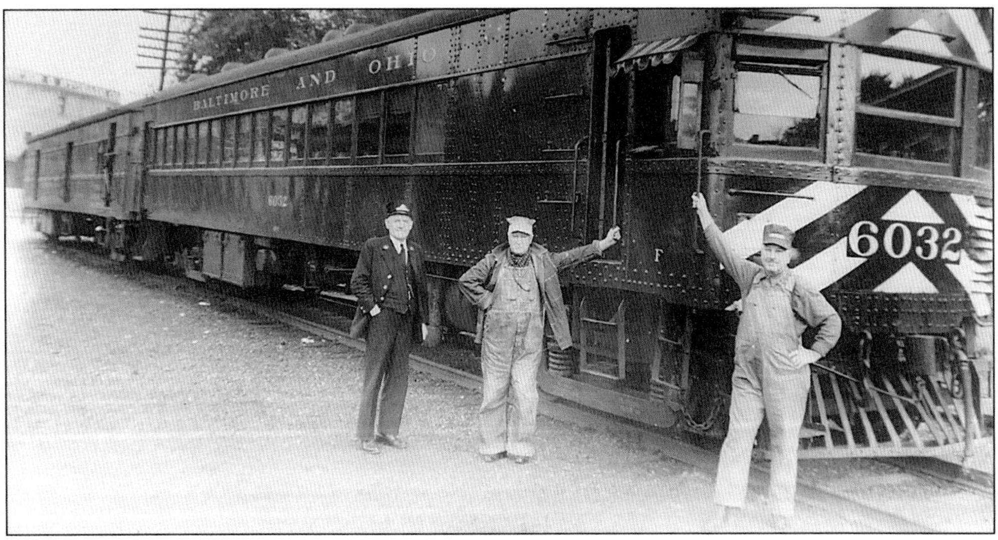

The Brill Company manufactured the "Doodlebug" pictured above. Although it looked like a streetcar, it was actually a railroad engine that ran on gasoline-generated electricity. The Doodlebug pulled a trailer, which was half post office and half baggage car. The Baltimore and Ohio railroad had 20 built because they were economical to operate. The Doodlebug pictured ran a regular route from Parkersburg to Zanesville and, later, on to Portsmouth. Doodlebug enthusiasts meet once a year to enjoy rides and share information. According to former railroad engineer Clarence Hackett, one Doodlebug is still operating in Cuba. "I wish we could get it back," Hackett says. (Courtesy of Clarence Hackett and Paul A. Borrelli, Artcraft Studio.)

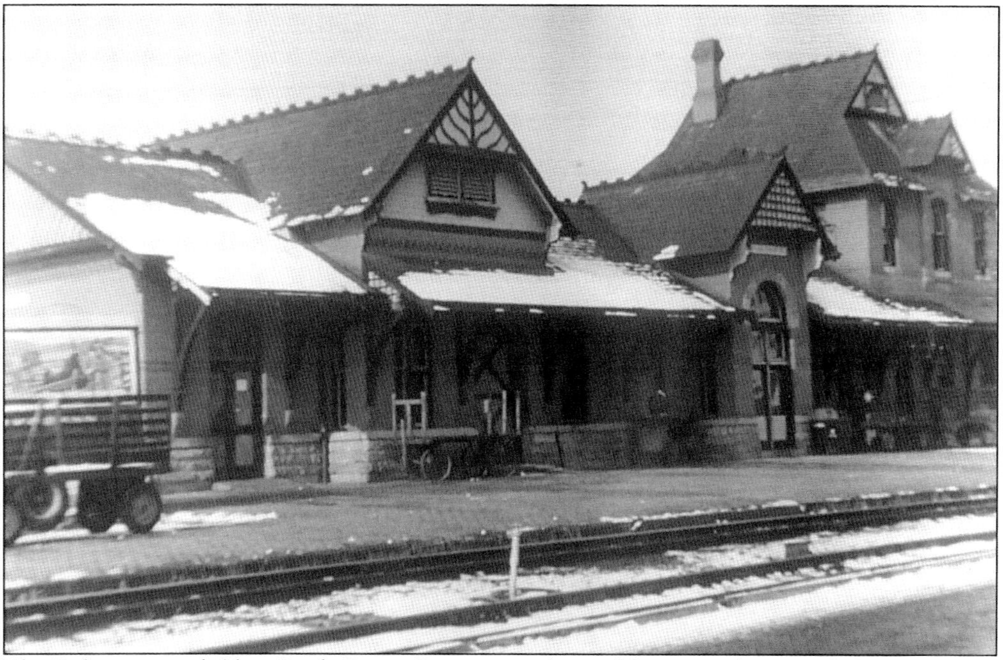

The Baltimore and Ohio Sixth Street Station was located between Avery and Green Streets. The depot was built in 1883 to accommodate passenger traffic after the building of the Ohio River bridge, which opened in 1871. The bridge, with a total length of 7,140 feet, was once the longest in the world. The picture above was taken by William Corey, head brakeman, the day before the depot was demolished in 1973. (Courtesy of Steve Corey.)

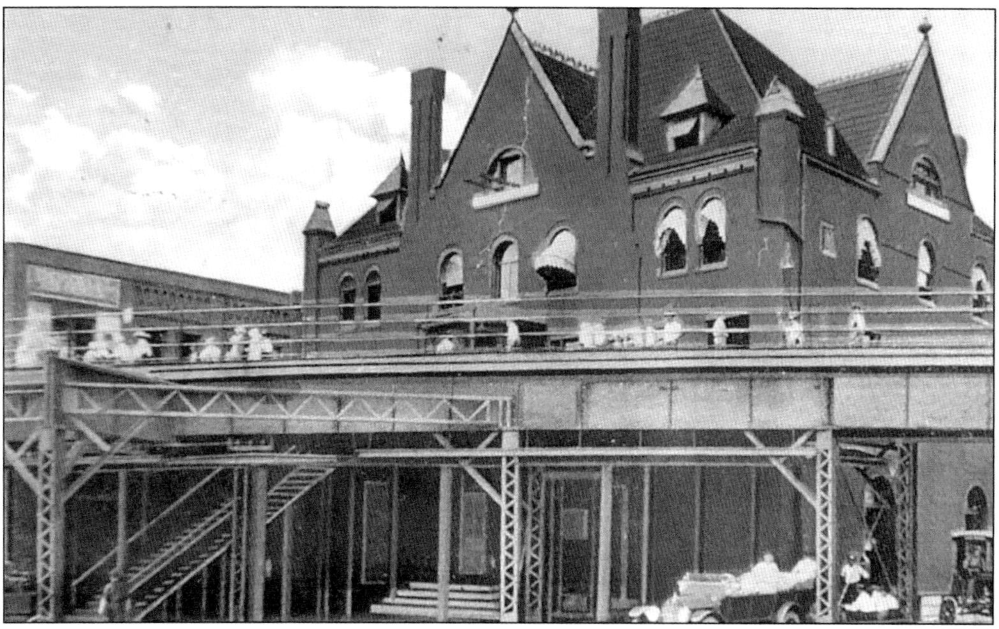

The Ann Street Station was built in 1887 to service the Wheeling-to-Huntington train route. A four-foot-high grandfather's clock hung on the wall on the third floor. The water level from the 1913 flood came almost to the ceiling of the first-floor baggage room. The building was demolished in March of 1972. (Courtesy of Paul A. Borrelli, Artcraft Studio.)

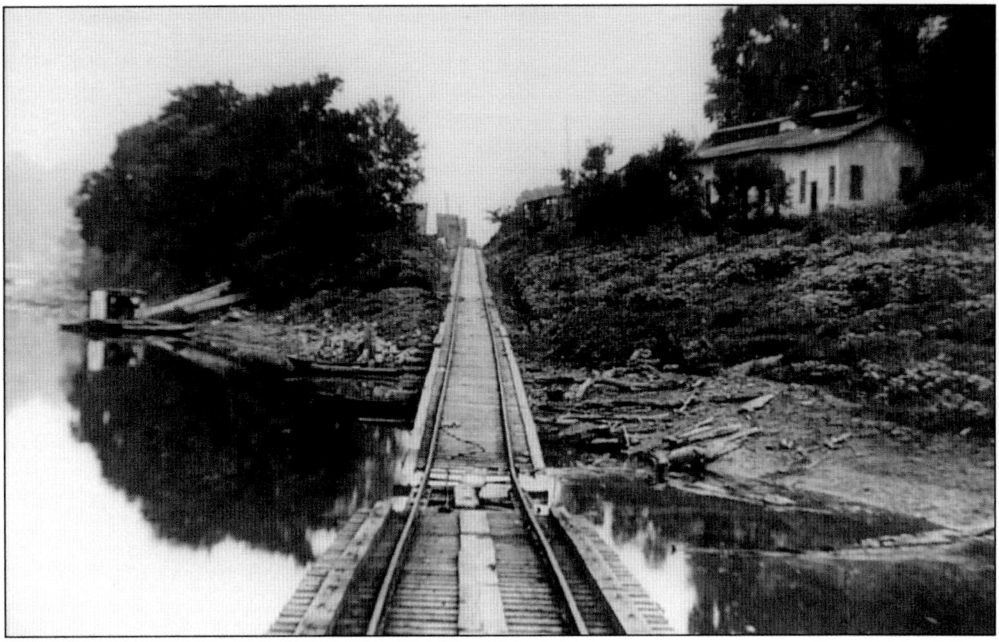

Since there was no bridge across the Little Kanawha River, trains were taken down this incline off Fifth Street, put on a ferry, and taken up river to Johnson Station (behind the Viscose Plant). Once there, the trains were hooked onto tracks that went 33.1 miles to Owens Port, now called Palestine. The building on the right in the picture is still there today. (Courtesy of R.E. Enoch.)

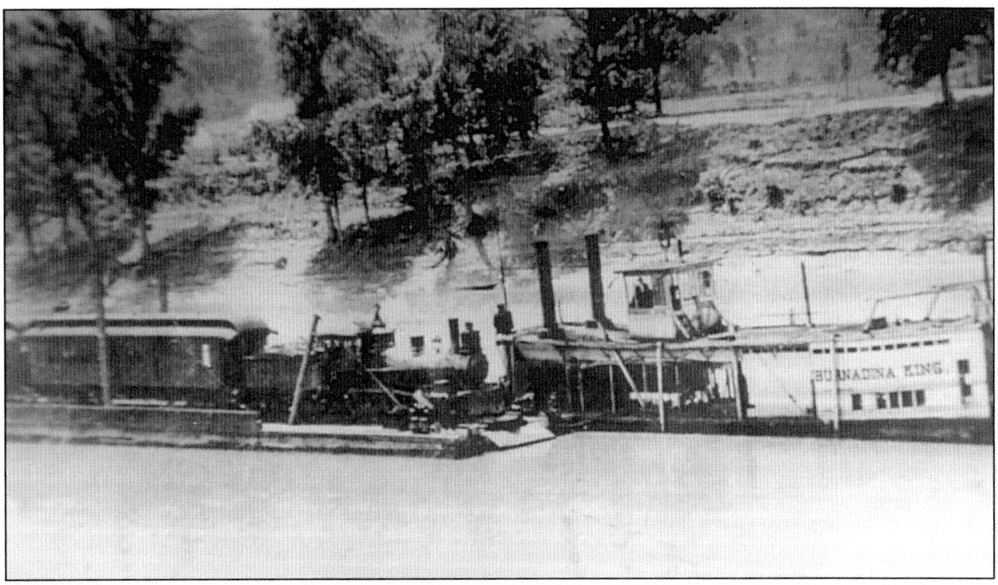

The *Burnadina King* is shown ferrying an engine and two cars from the incline at the bottom of Fifth Street to hook-up with the track that went to Owens Port, now called Palestine. From 1857 to 1860 similar ferries took railroad cars, but not engines, from Parkersburg across the Ohio River to Scots Landing, now Moore's Junction, south of Marietta to hook up on the Marietta-Cincinnati route. In 1860 a hook-up was established at the foot of Fourth Street in Belpre. (Courtesy of R.E. Enoch.)

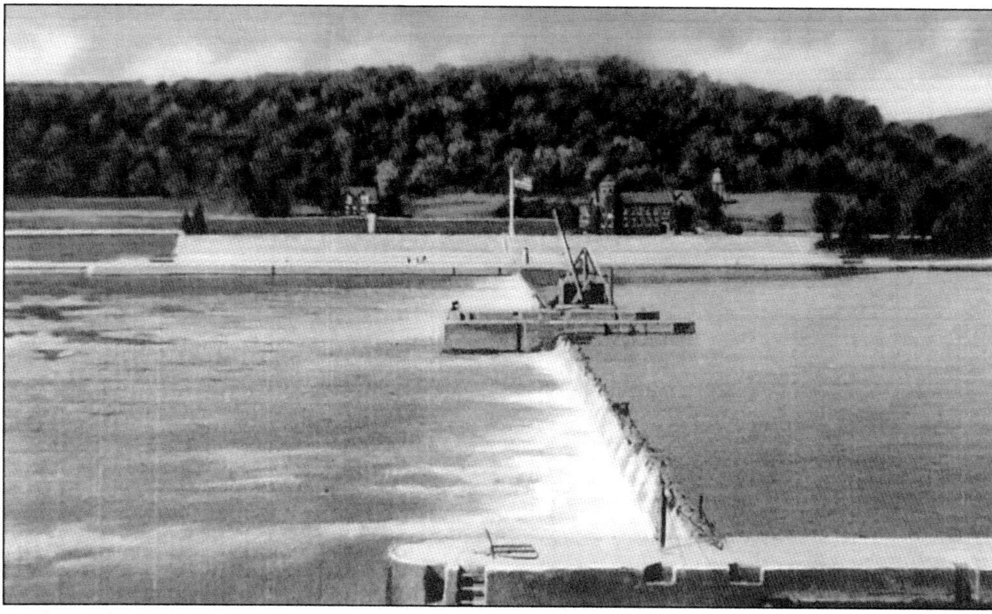

Lock 18, between Parkersburg and Marietta, was completed in 1910 at a cost of $1,250,000. The lock was part of a system of locks and dams that transformed navigation on the Ohio River. Until the lock system was completed, the Ohio River was shallow enough to ride a horse across at many points. Lock 18 was demolished *c.* 1967. (Collection of B. Leavengood.)

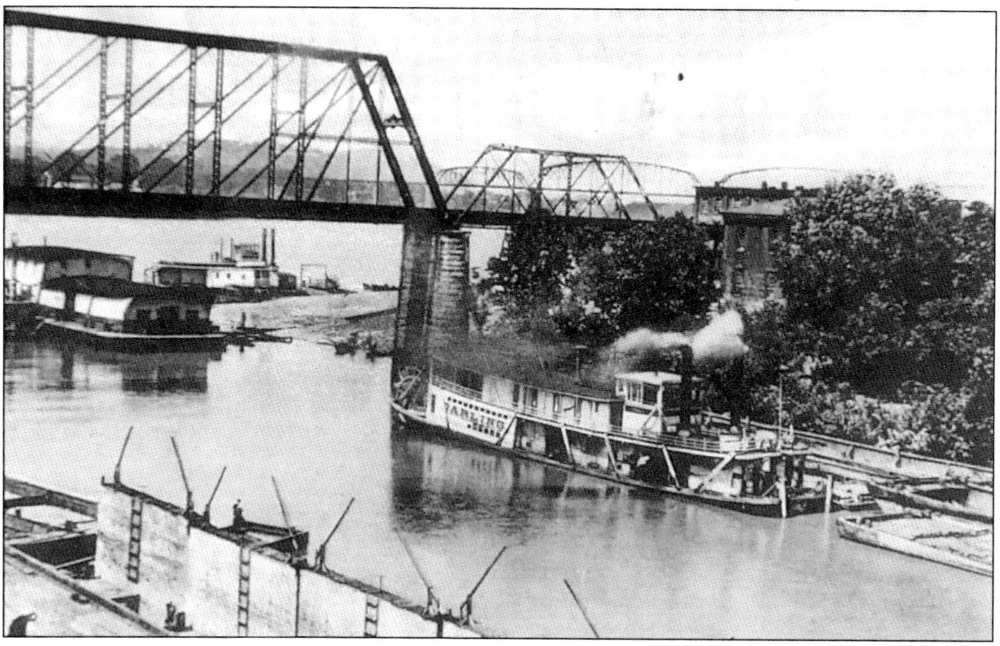

This postcard scene at The Point around 1900 shows advances in the transportation system in Parkersburg. In the foreground is the railroad bridge built across the Little Kanawha in 1885. The railroad bridge constructed in 1871 across the Ohio River can be seen in the background. The Point is crowded with docked boats doing business in Parkersburg and up the Little Kanawha River. At that time, unlike today, there were five locks on the Little Kanawha River, making it navigable as far upstream as Creston. (Collection of B. Leavengood.)

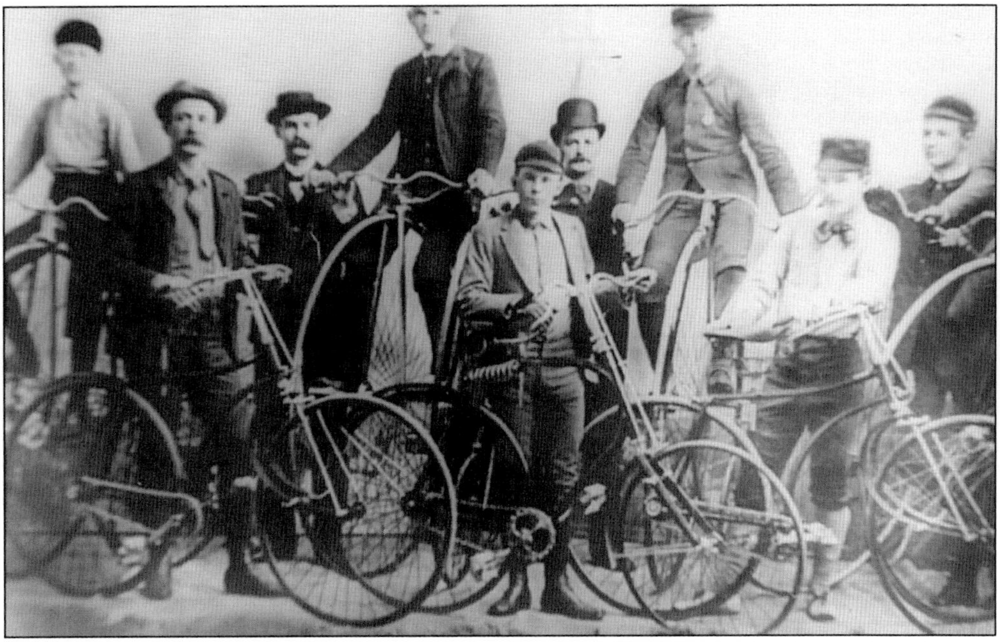

Bicycles first appeared in Parkersburg in the late 1800s and were immediately popular. A group of male cyclers formed the Blennerhassett Bicycle Club, seen here in 1889. Members compared notes on the mechanics of their vehicles and took group rides around the county. The March 24, 1899 issue of *The Parkersburg Sentinel* advertised Monarch Bicycles for sale at Boreman's for $25. The bicycles were "guaranteed against defects in any way." (Courtesy of Paul A. Borrelli, Artcraft Studio.)

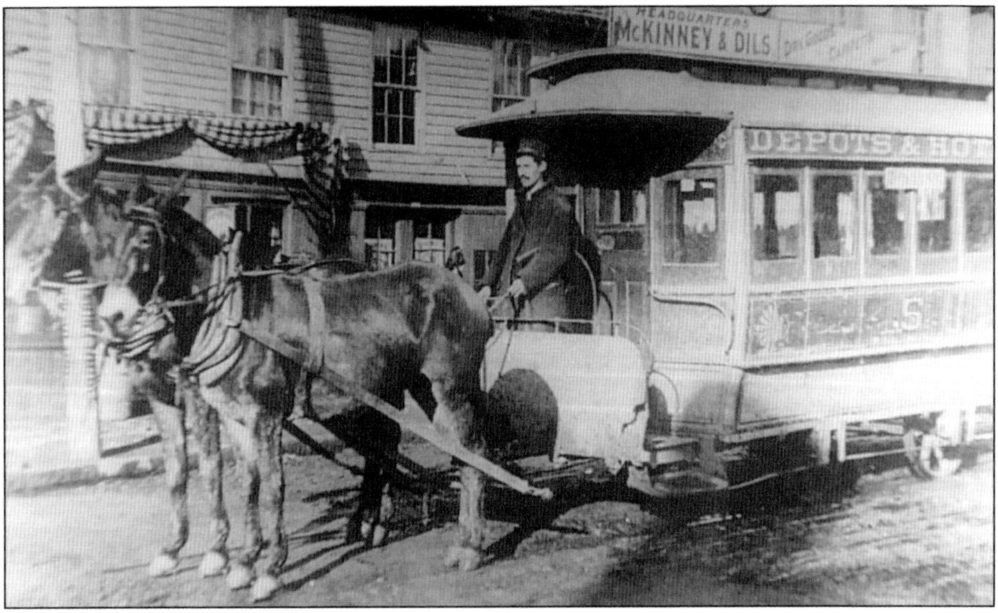

This horse-drawn streetcar was operated by the Park City Railway company from 1889 until the City of Parkersburg installed an electric cable car system in 1898. The advertisement on top of the car is for McKinney & Dils, forerunner of the Dils Brothers and Company Store. (Courtesy of Edwin L.D. Dils.)

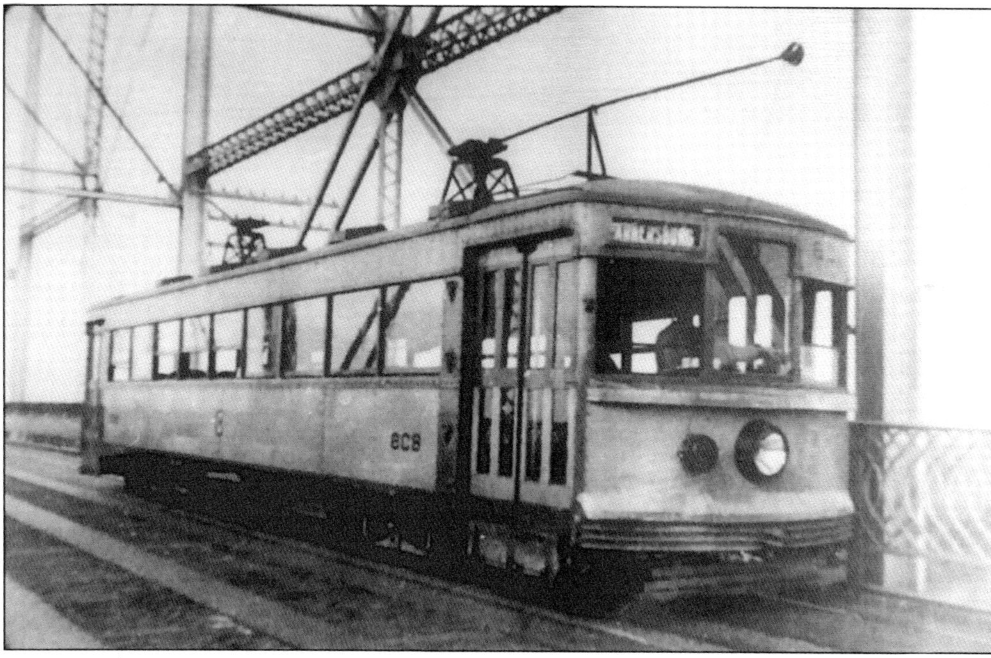

In 1902 the streetcar companies of Parkersburg and Marietta consolidated to form the Parkersburg, Marietta, and Inter-Urban Railway Company. After the bridge between Marietta and Williamstown was completed in 1903 hourly service began between the two cities. As more people owned automobiles, streetcar ridership declined. The Williamstown-Marietta route was discontinued on April 27, 1947. (Courtesy of Pat Peters.)

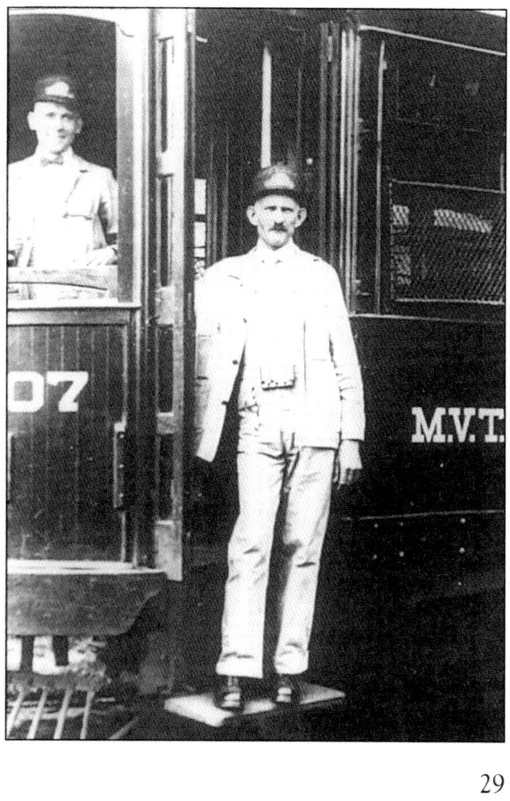

Henry Dayton, pictured to the right, worked as a conductor of the streetcar for nearly 30 years. In 1897, the Parkersburg City Council granted a franchise to the Parkersburg Gas, Electric Light, and Street Railway Company to install and operate an electric cable car system. The streetcars began operating on July 2, 1898. The inner loop, with green cars, traveled along Spring, Gould, and Lynn Streets. The outer loop, with red cars, went from Gould Street to City Park. Other routes were opened as passenger demands increased. Streetcars were the main mode of local transportation in Parkersburg until most people had automobiles. The last working route ceased operating on May 25, 1947. (Courtesy of Jim Miracle.)

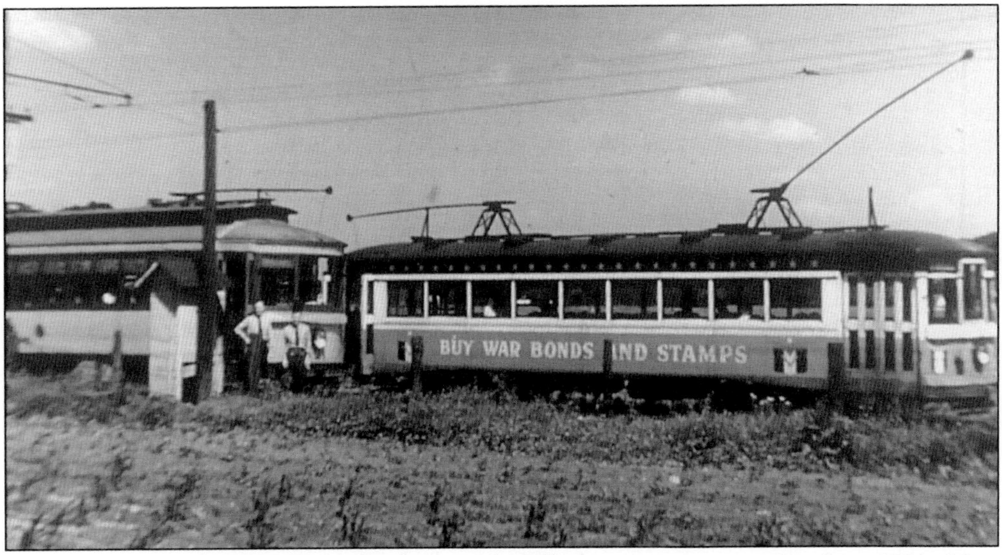

The streetcar track between Parkersburg and Williamstown was completed in 1901. Now farmers in Boaz could pick their produce in the morning and have it on the market by early afternoon. In 1902 the streetcar companies of Marietta and Parkersburg consolidated to form the Parkersburg, Marietta, and Inter-Urban Railway Company. When the Marietta-Williamstown Bridge was finished in 1903, regular streetcar service began between Marietta, Williamstown, and Parkersburg. The streetcar pictured above is stopped in Boaz. The service was discontinued in 1947. (Courtesy of Pat Peters.)

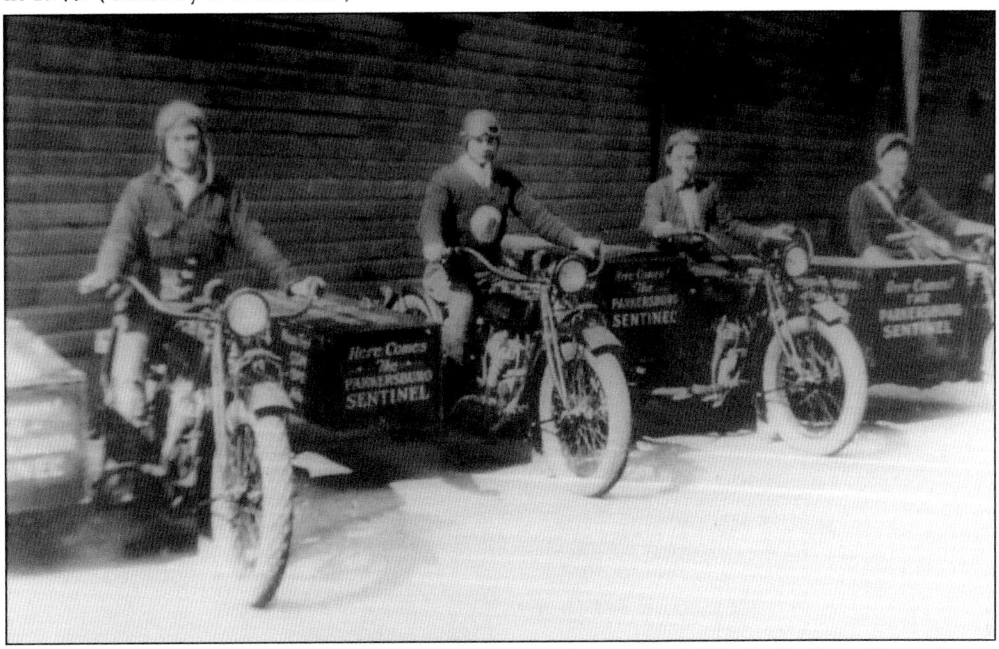

R.E. Hornor as proprietor and John W. Hornor as editor started *The Parkersburg Sentinel* as a weekly on July 17, 1875. Subscriptions were $2 a year "positively in advance." Editor Hornor stated, "politically our paper will be democratic." The paper's motto was "Cheap Meat, Cheap Bread, Cheap Transportation, and Cheap Money." The newspaper delivery boys pictured above promised speedy delivery on their motorcycles. (Courtesy of Paul A. Borrelli, Artcraft Studio.)

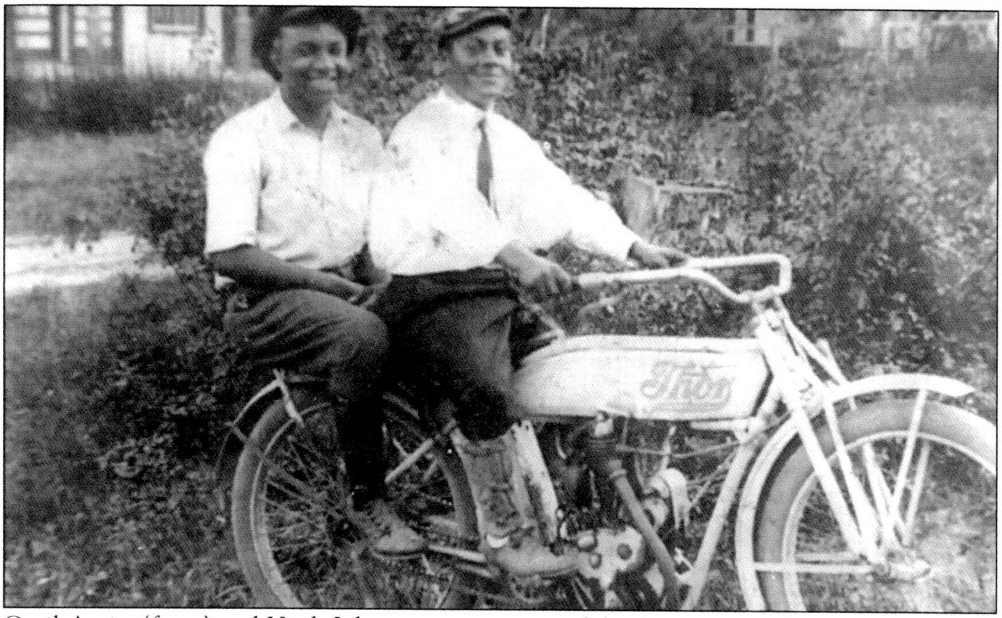

Cecil Amiss (front) and Hugh Johnson pose on one of the first motorcycles in Parkersburg in 1910. The Thor Moto Cycle and Bicycle Company was founded in 1903. At first the company sold component parts and the purchaser assembled the motorcycle. By 1908 dealerships were established around the country that sold assembled Thor Motorcycles. In 1920 the company ceased production. Today Thor motorcycles are collector's items. (Courtesy of Sumnerite Museum, Rae Brown, curator.)

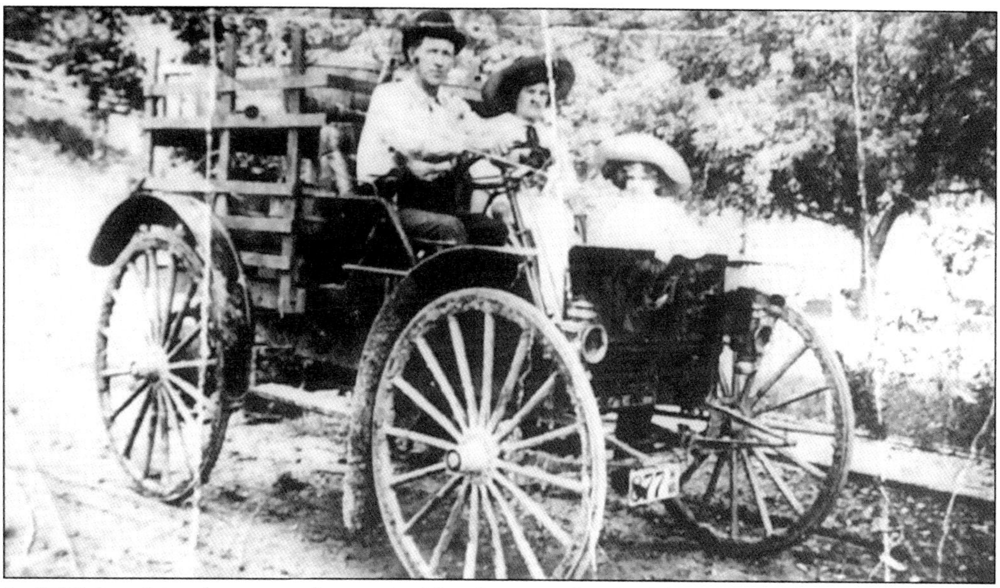

In 1908 Lou Murphy, a storekeeper in Murphytown, hitched his team of horses and went to Parkersburg for a load of groceries. He stopped at the International Harvester Dealer to look at new cars and told the salesman, "If you can get one of those through that axle deep mud to Murphytown, I'll buy it!" Shortly after he returned home and unloaded his groceries, the car, a 1906 International Harvester Motor Vehicle, pulled up in front of his store! (Courtesy of the family of Ruth Murphy Schoolcraft.)

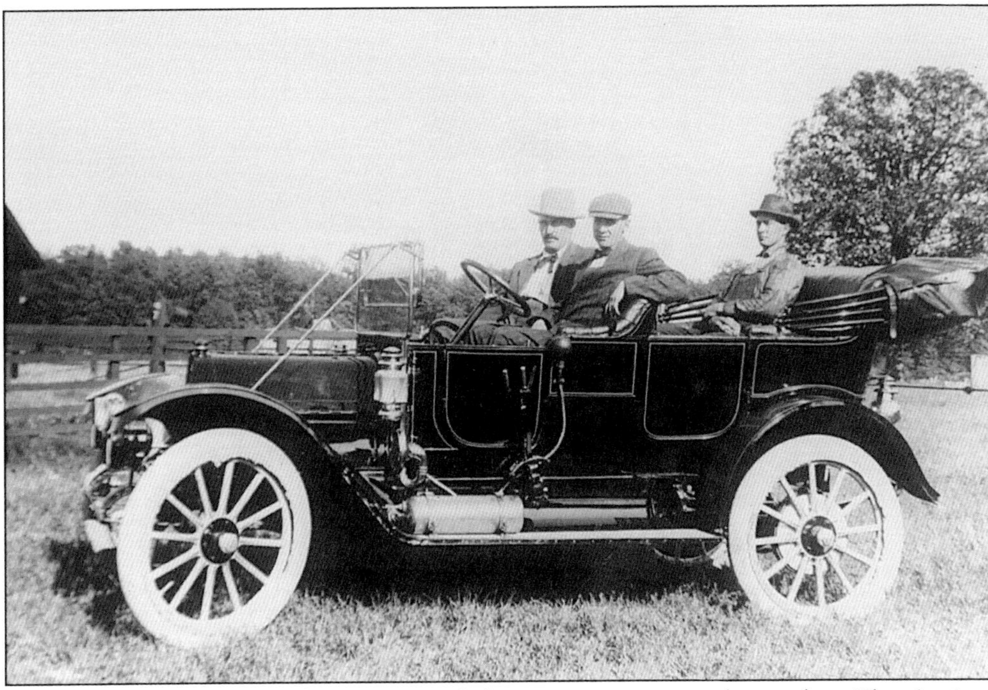

These three men enjoy a drive in one of the snazziest cars on the market. The Antique Automobile Club of America could not identify this car, other than to say that it was built around 1911. (Courtesy of the family of Mary Reece Dunlap.)

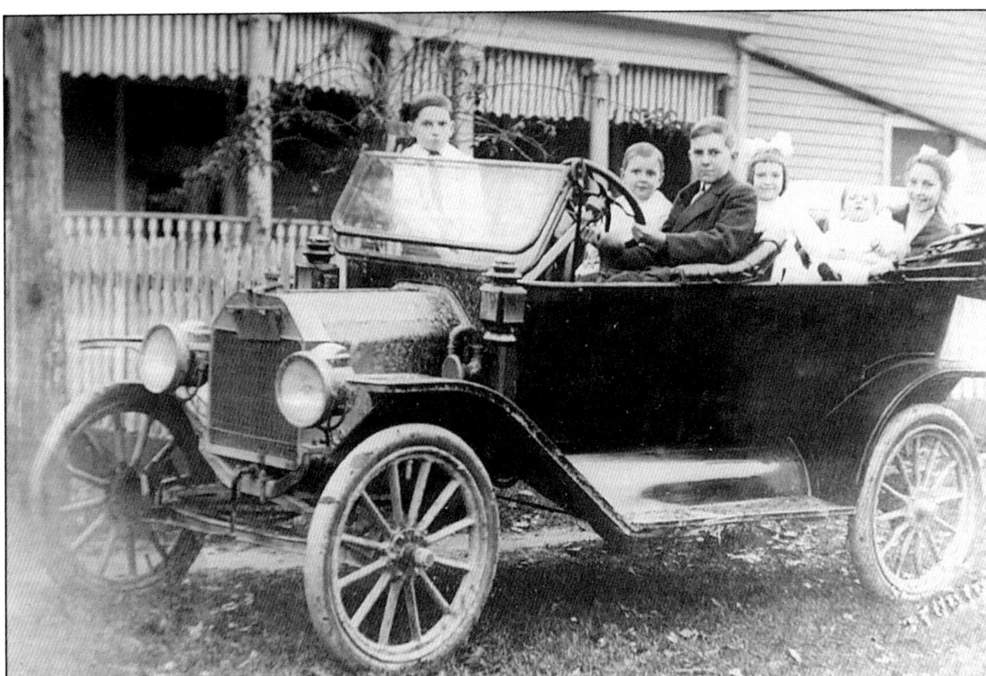

Going for a Sunday drive in a 1913 Model T Ford was a favorite family activity. (Courtesy of the family of Mary Reece Dunlap.)

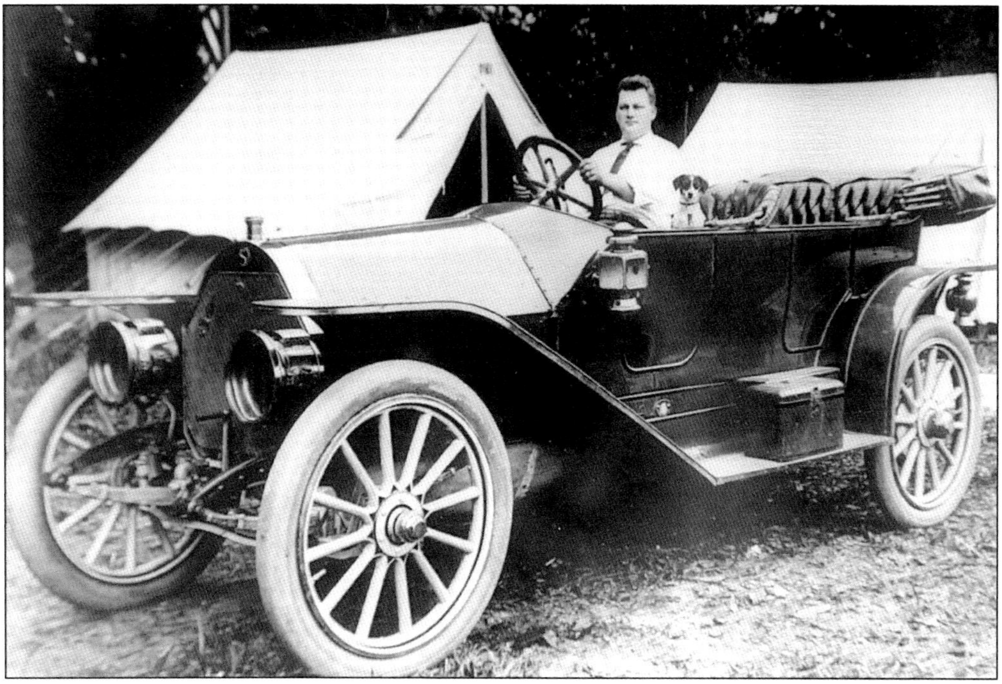

C.Z. Ruth, owner of Ruth's Furniture Store in Parkersburg, enjoyed driving out in the country in his *c.* 1911 Selden. (Courtesy of R.E. Enoch.)

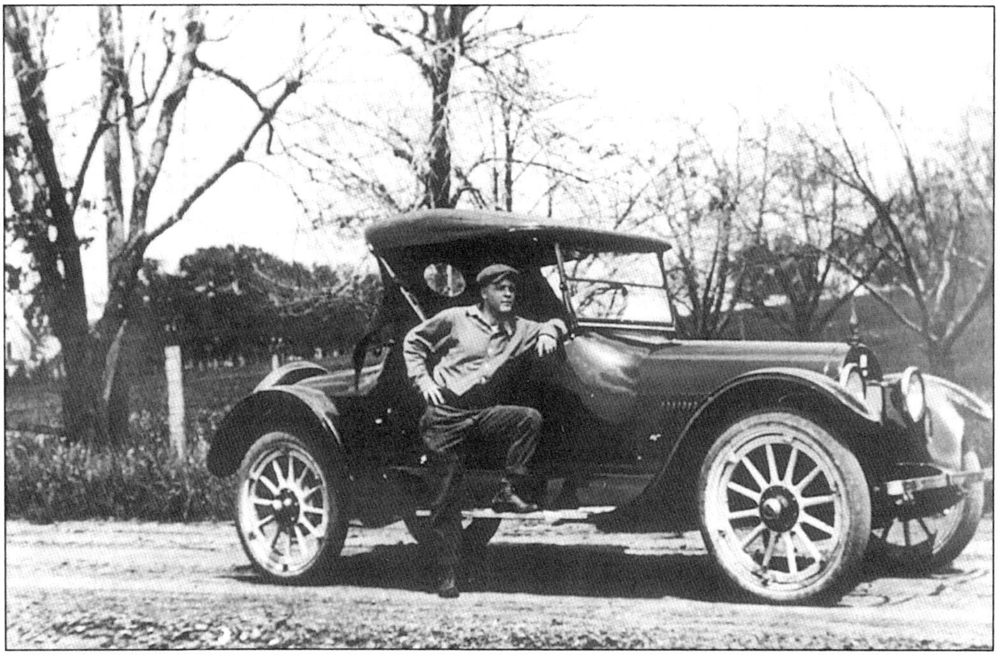

This young man is sure to impress the young ladies in his *c.* 1919 Buick Roadster. (Courtesy of Clarence Hackett.)

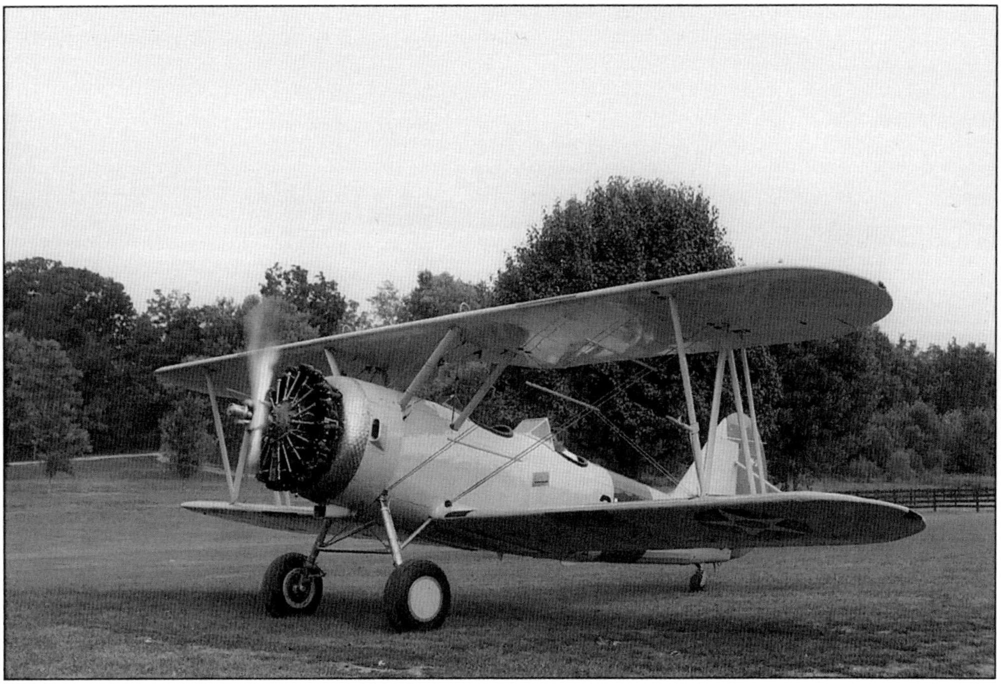

This bi-plane is an N3N-3, built at the Naval Aircraft Factory in Philadelphia in the late 1930s. Bi-planes such as this flew in and out of Stewart Air Park. The plane shown above is a restored N3N-3 owned by Mike Mundo of Marietta. (Courtesy of Mike Mundo, photograph by Fred Cornwell.)

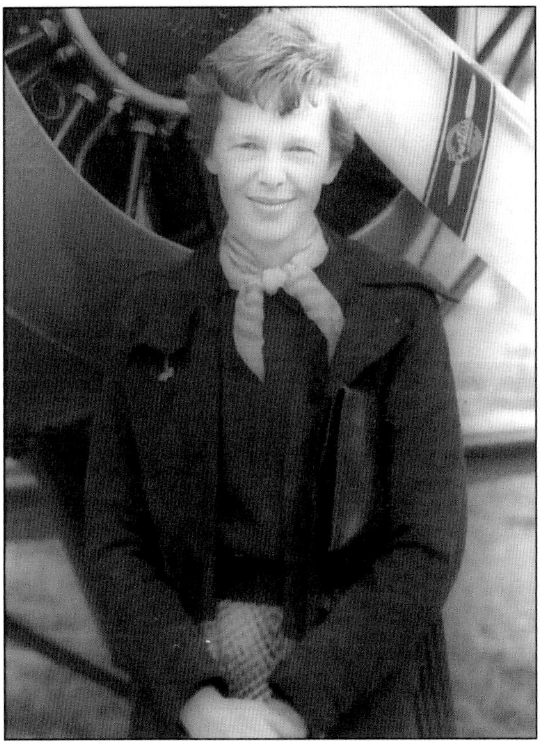

Stewart Air Park opened in 1935 on the field that is now the location of Grand Central Mall. The airport was owned by Wade Stewart, a promoter of flying in the Parkersburg area. Randy Ferrell of Kramer's Photo Supply remembers the Air park's promotion—"a penny a pound to fly around town." At the time, Ferrell weighed 75 pounds. "That was my first flight," he said. Amelia Earhart visited Stewart Air Park in 1936, four years after she became the first woman to cross the Atlantic Ocean alone. A year later she disappeared while attempting to circle the globe. (Courtesy of Paul A. Borrelli, Artcraft Studio.)

Three

Reading, Writing, and Arithmetic

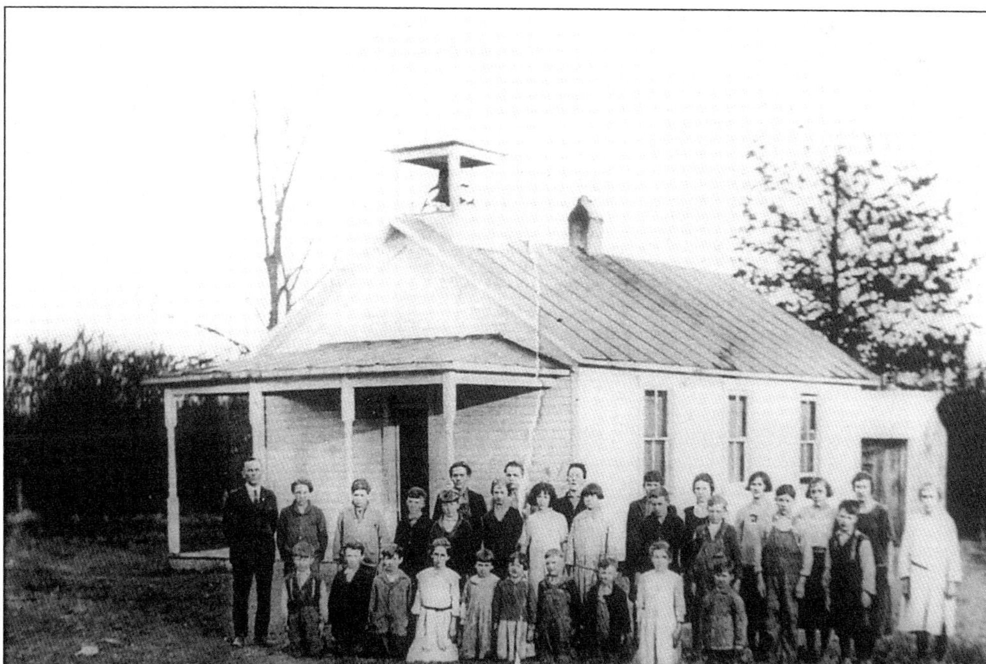

The Leafy Glen School was typical of one-room schools in Wood County. These schools were located in small communities around the county so that children could walk to school. Typically, each one had a slate blackboard across the front of the room and a pot-bellied stove in the center of the room. Restrooms were located down the path. (Courtesy of R.E. Enoch.)

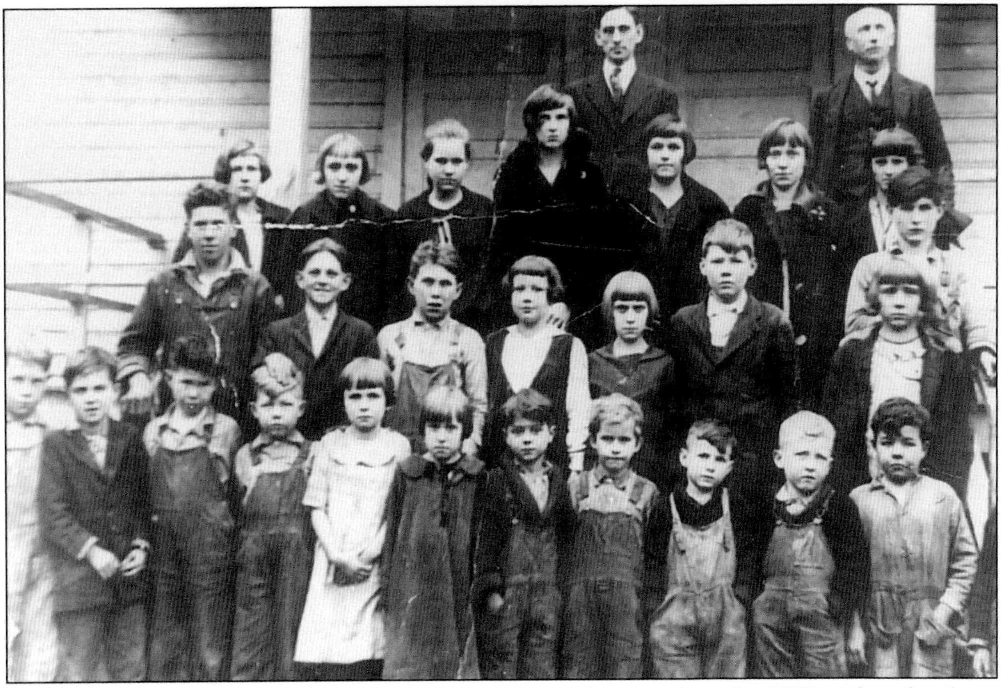

Winding School students and teachers pose for a group photograph in the 1920s. The school was located approximately seven miles east of Parkersburg off Route 50 near Red Hill on Winding Road. (Courtesy of Jacquelyn Goodman.)

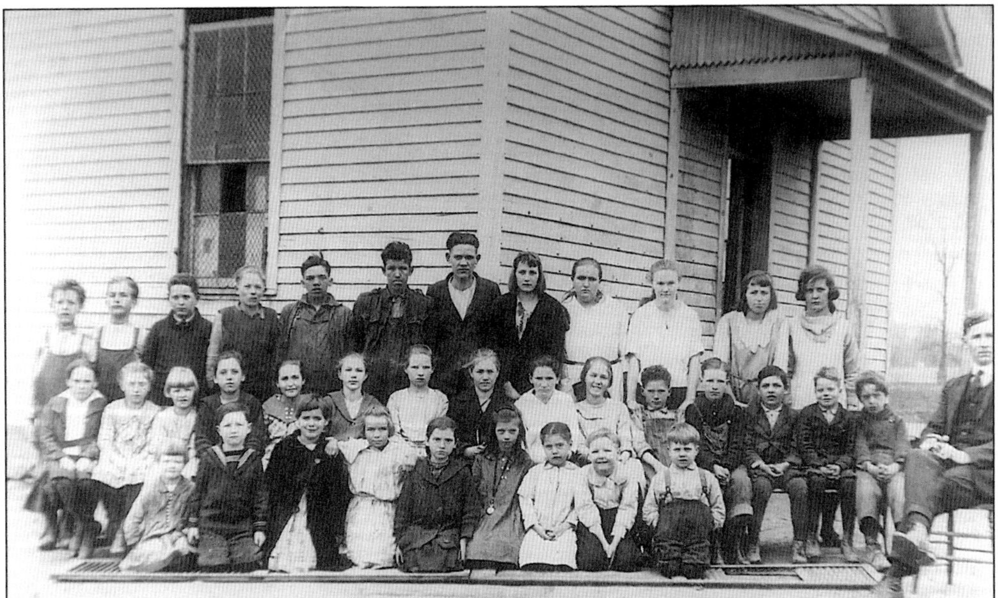

In 1848 J.J. Jackson of Parkersburg gave three men in Kanawha Station a small parcel of land with the stipulation that they build a school within two years. The men built both a school and a church on the land. The Kanawha Station school held classes until the late 1920s, and the building was later converted to a house, which still stands. (Courtesy of Sally Wyatt, researching Kanawha Station.)

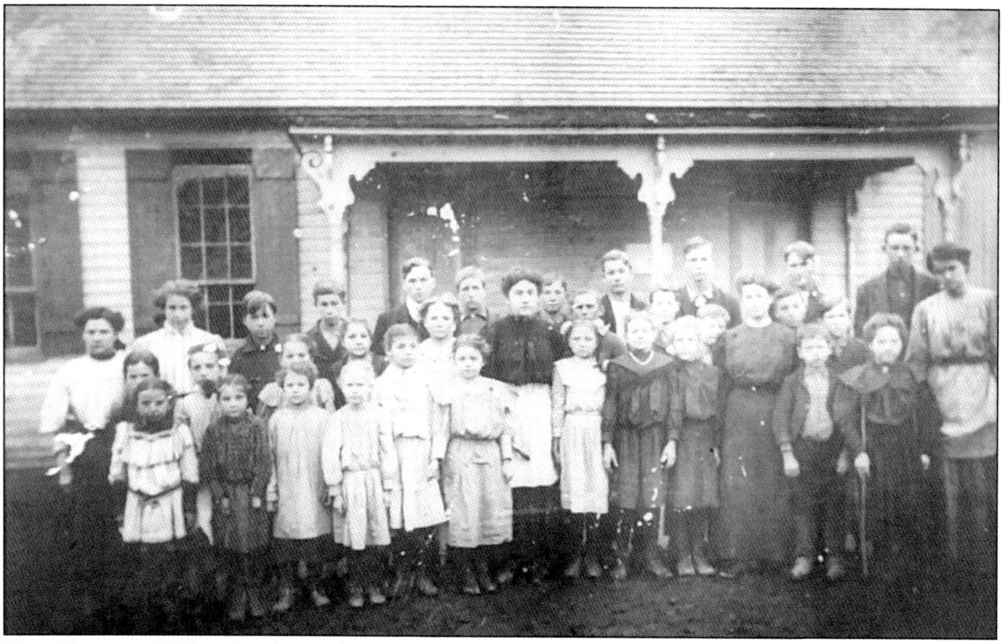

The Pleasant Hill School was located 15 miles east of Parkersburg on old Route 50. Jacob Schneider sold the land on which the school was built to the Wood County Board of Education in June of 1895 for $75. The two-room school opened in 1896. When the school closed in 1953, C.P. Jonas bought the building for $265, Ray Deem purchased two toilets for $5.25, Lewis Reese bought a toilet and coal house for $5, and Freda Smith purchased the land for $35. (Courtesy of Gladys Marshall.)

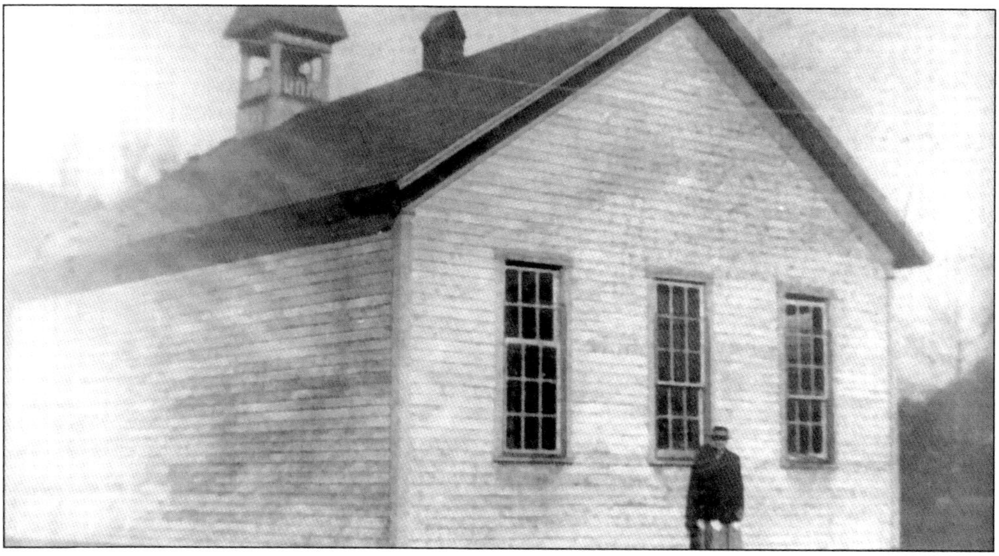

Harry and Ettie L. Barron sold land for the Pleasant Valley School to the Wood County Board of Education in 1914 for $75. The description of the property begins, "At a stick in the center of the N.W. Pike between mileposts 12 and 13 near the intersection of county road . . ." The one-room Pleasant Valley School was replaced with a four-room school built in 1950, which operated until the mid-1980s. Paul Reese purchased the school in June of 1994 and opened the Pleasant Valley Trading Company. (Courtesy of the family of Mary Reece Dunlap.)

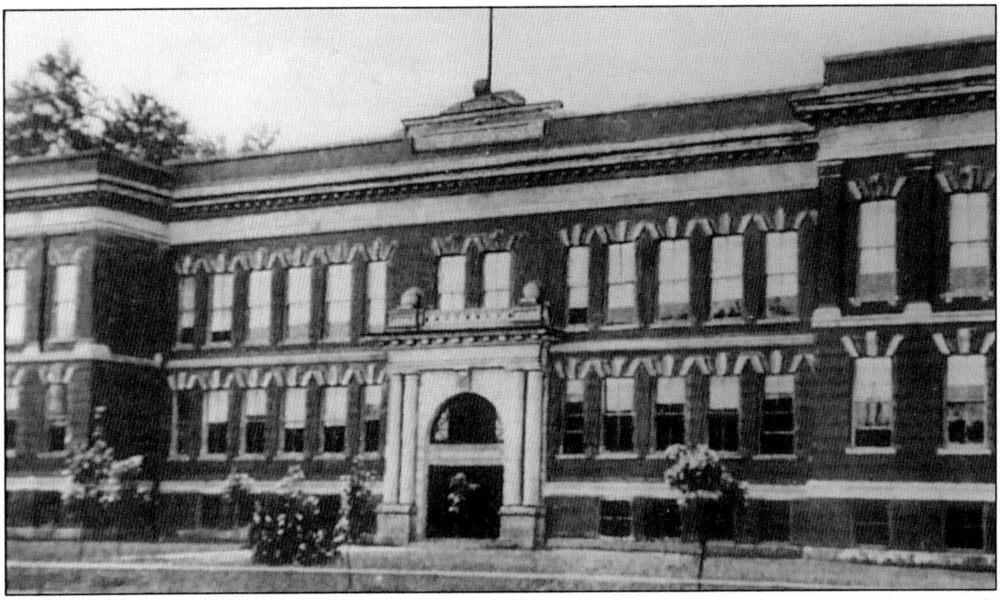

Built in 1904, McKinley Elementary School, at the corner of St. Mary's Avenue and Nineteenth Streets, honored assassinated President William McKinley. The school served elementary students from the rapidly growing area north of Thirteenth Street. It is the oldest elementary school still in use in Wood County. Current principal Fred Shreve is looking forward to celebrating the school's 100th anniversary. (Courtesy of McKinley Elementary School, Fred Shreve, principal.)

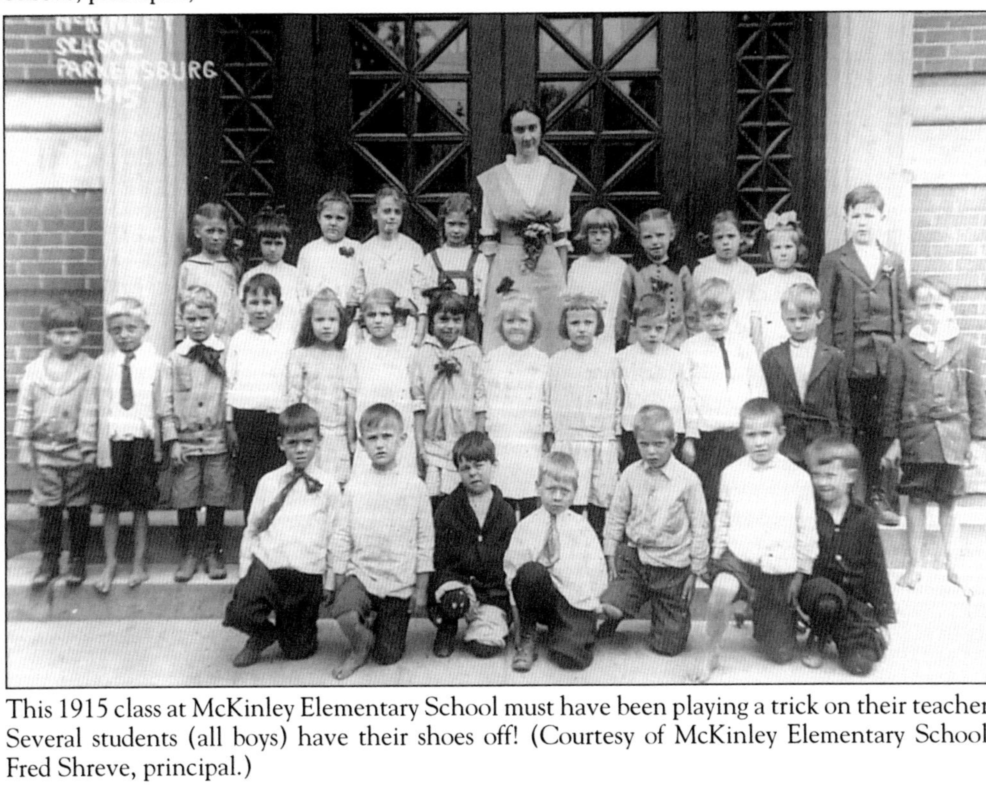

This 1915 class at McKinley Elementary School must have been playing a trick on their teacher. Several students (all boys) have their shoes off! (Courtesy of McKinley Elementary School, Fred Shreve, principal.)

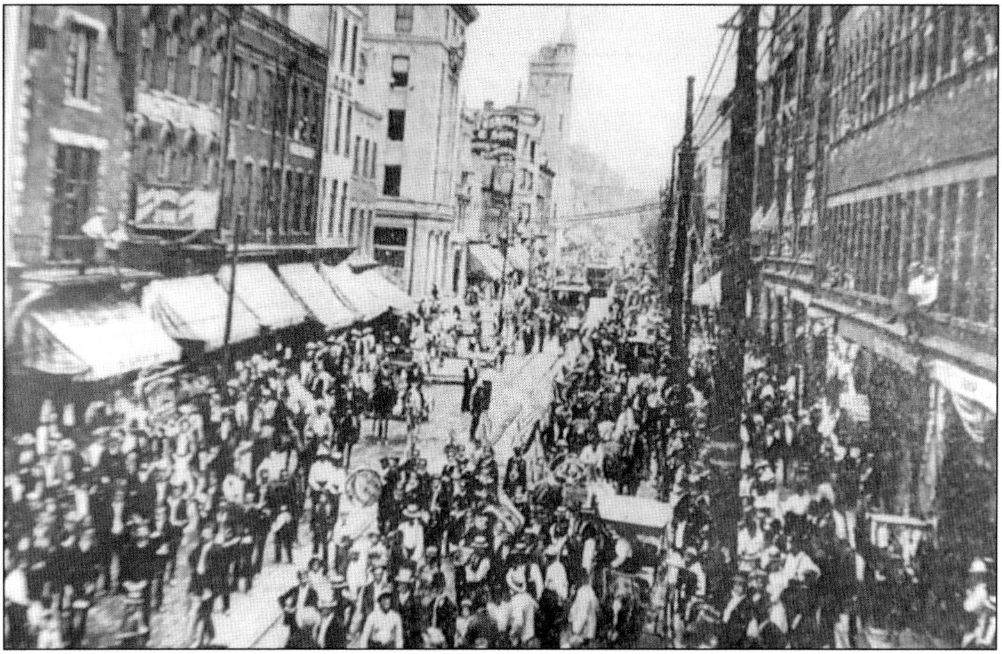

Mountain State Business College, founded in 1888 by Albert Grant Sine, is still in operation today. Out-of-town students boarded with local families for $10 to $12 a month. The school quickly outgrew its first location at 310 Market Street. Their next location at 705 Market Street was excellent for watching parades as in the picture above. Unfortunately, the building was destroyed in the November 30, 1929 fire that also destroyed the Camden Theater. Today Mountain State College is located at the corner of Sixteenth and Spring Streets. (Courtesy of Mountain State College.)

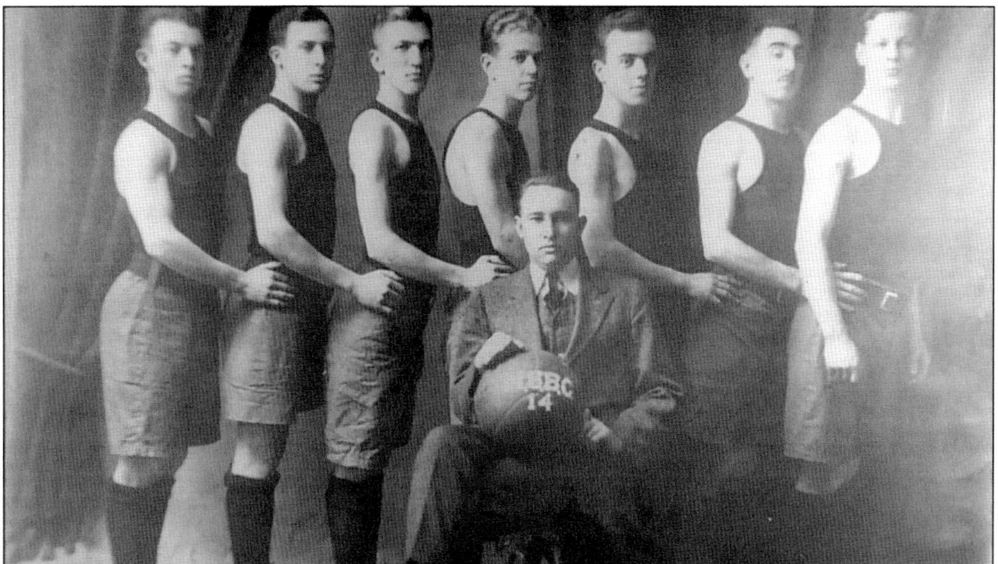

Pictured above is the Mountain State Business College basketball team of 1914. Although shorter and much differently dressed than today's teams, they played with just as much determination to win. (Courtesy of Mountain State College.)

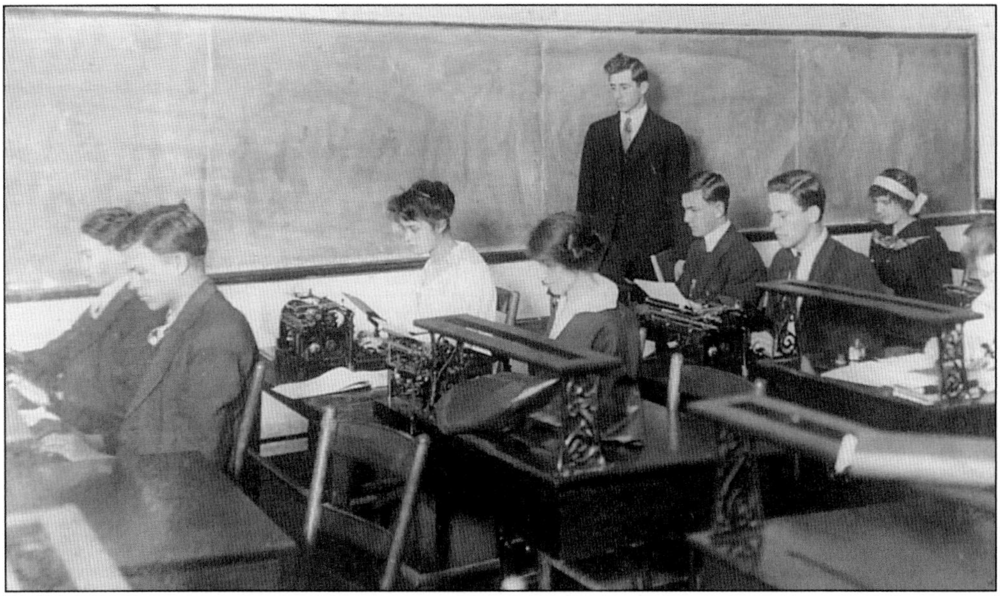

In the early 1900s students at Mountain State Business College took courses primarily in bookkeeping, penmanship, business arithmetic, shorthand, and typing. The curriculum has changed with the changing times. Today's students study medical transcription, travel, tourism, and computer skills. In the picture above, donated to Mountain State College by Mrs. John Bush, her father, John W. Everett is the typing instructor. (Courtesy of Mountain State College.)

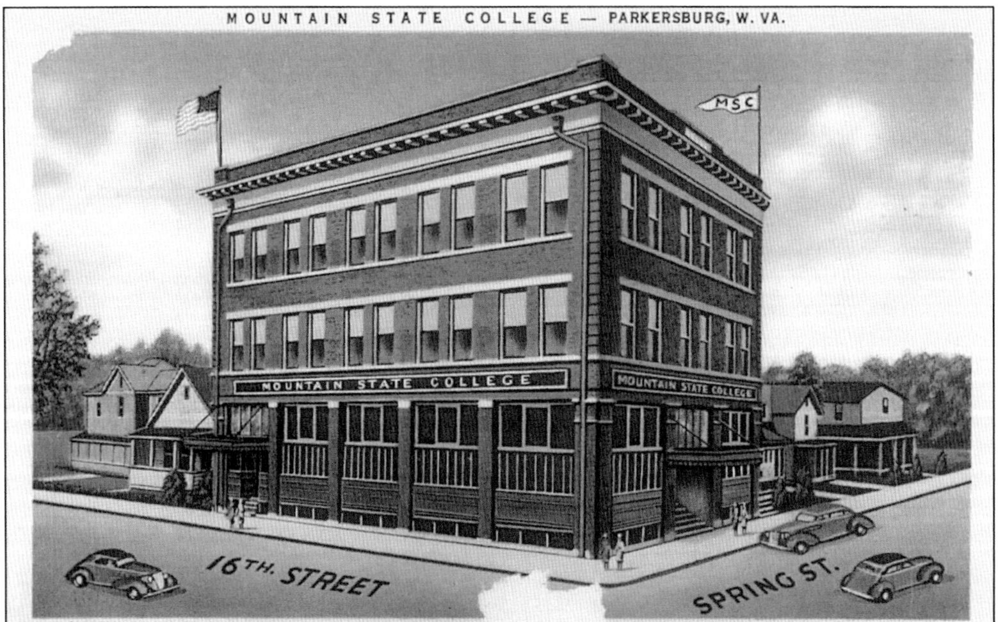

Mountain State College moved into this building in 1930. The building was constructed in 1910 and was originally a wholesale produce and grocery business. Classes are still conducted in this building. In 1967 the college constructed a technical center across the street from the main building. (Courtesy of Mountain State College.)

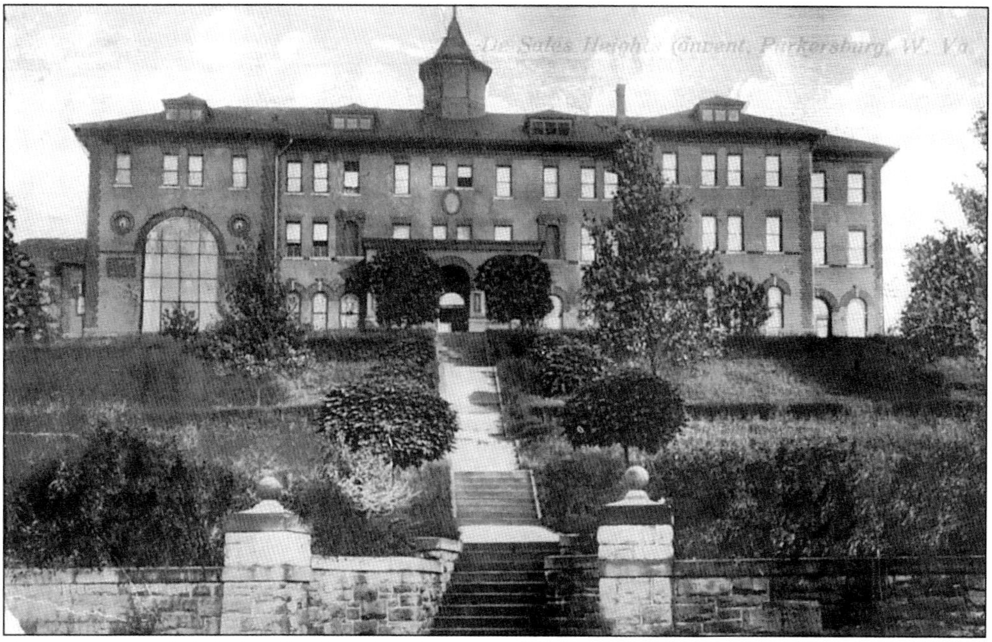

Construction of DeSales Heights Academy at 1600 Murdoch Avenue began in 1899. The academy had its first commencement in 1900, and it served as both a convent and school until 1992. The building was razed in 2002. (Courtesy of the West Virginia State Archives.)

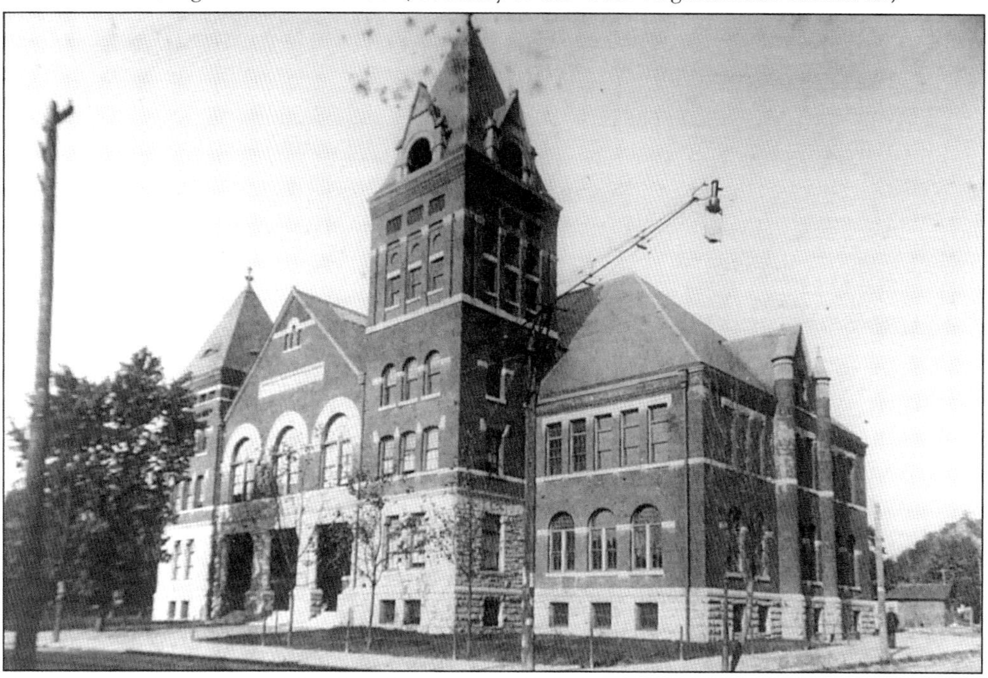

No photographs remain of the first Parkersburg High School. The second Parkersburg High School, located at the corner of Seventh and Green Streets, was dedicated in 1891 and cost $55,000 to build. Teachers received from $30 to $125 a month. Among the courses offered were Latin, German, physics, chemistry, algebra, English composition, and United States history. (Courtesy of *Mountain Trace*.)

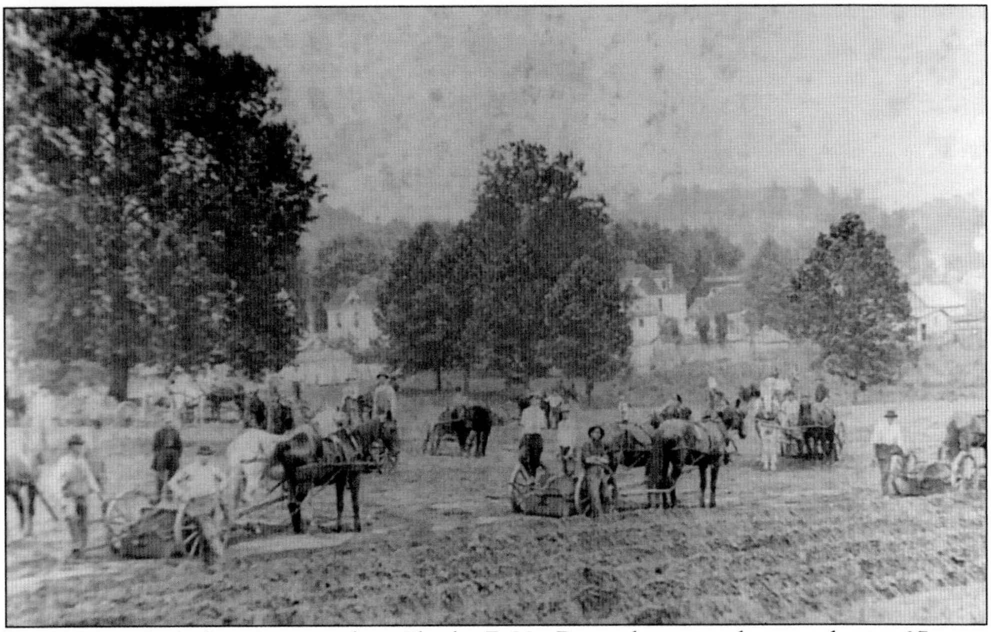

In 1916 board of education president Charles E. VanDevender insisted on purchasing 27 acres of land on Dudley Avenue to build a new high school, despite opponents' complaints that the site was a swamp filled with cattails, water snakes, and quicksand. The board of education, however, approved the purchase. Workmen using horse-drawn equipment prepared the field for construction. The building rests on a floating foundation to compensate for the quicksand. Therefore, very few cracks exist, even today. (Courtesy of *Mountain Trace*.)

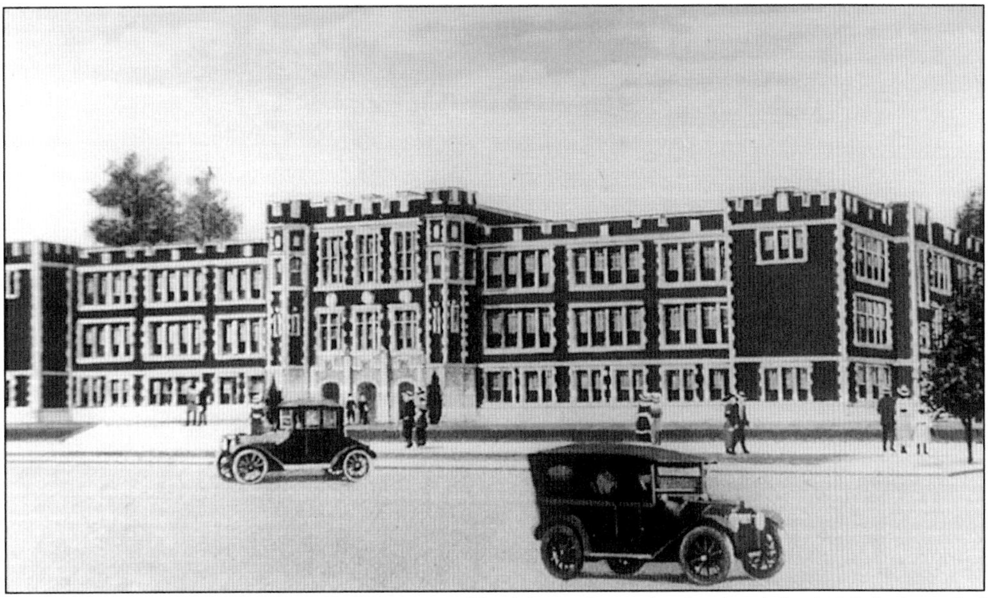

Parkersburg's growing population necessitated building a larger high school. In 1916 the board of education purchased 27 acres on Dudley Avenue to build a new school that would accommodate 1,200 students. The building pictured in the architect's drawing above cost nearly $500,000 including the grounds, building, and equipment. The first classes attended Parkersburg High School in the fall of 1917. (Courtesy of *Mountain Trace*.)

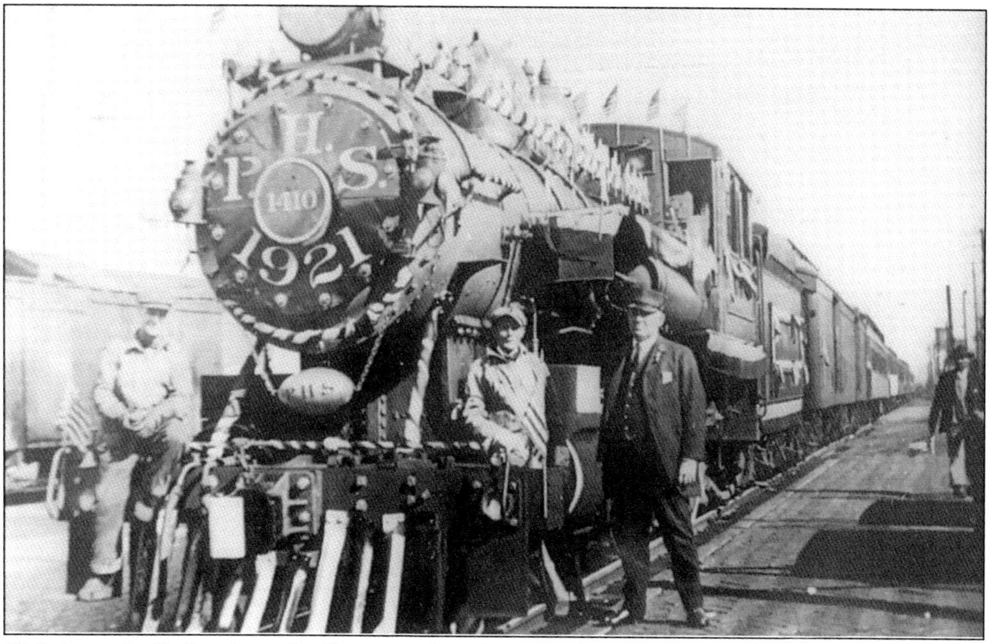

Old-timers in Parkersburg fondly remember the special trains to out-of-town football games. Sponsored by local businessmen, the first football train left Parkersburg to attend the Parkersburg-Huntington Championship in Huntington on November 5, 1921. The following year the Parkersburg Lions Club assumed sponsorship of the trains. The longest train to leave Parkersburg carried approximately 4,000 fans to Wheeling for the PHS-Wheeling game. Due to high costs, the trains were canceled in the late 1950s. (Courtesy of *Mountain Trace*.)

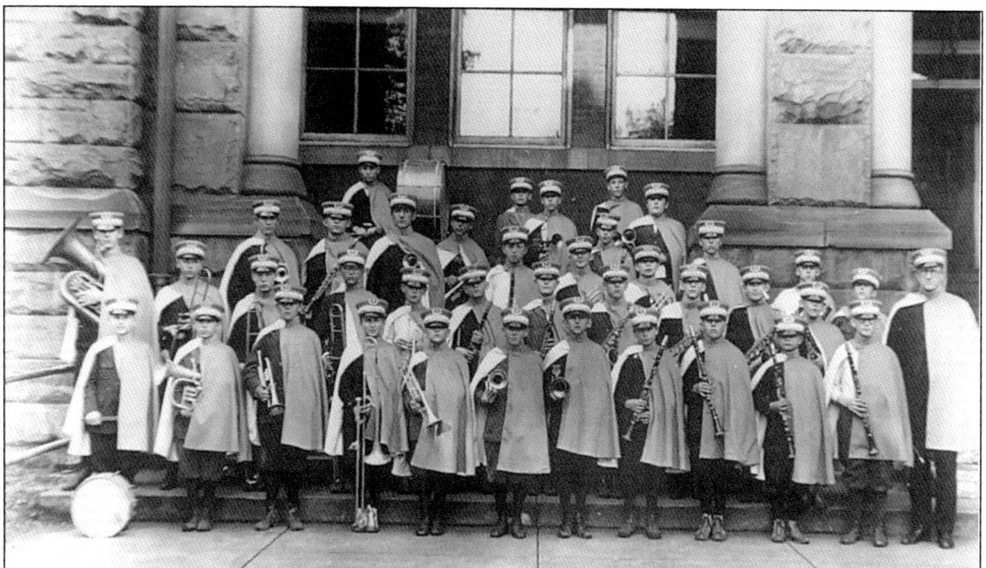

C.O. Chapman, a chemistry teacher, formed the first Parkersburg High School band in 1919. In 1924, under the leadership of Director George Dietz, the band became a uniformed marching band. The uniforms were red and white capes and caps with white trousers and shirts. Under Dietz, the band became an all-male military marching band. (Courtesy of Blennerhassett Island Historical State Park.)

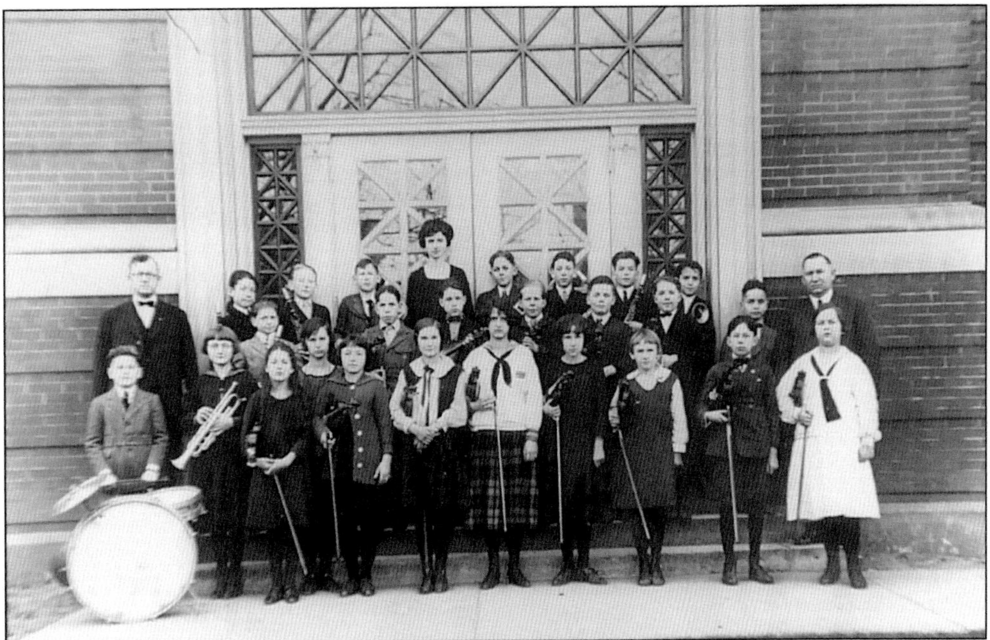

According to the 1924 *Quill*, "Since last September pupils and teachers alike have been disturbed by the racket issuing from the auditorium." However, the *Quill*, continued, "Them days is gone forever." Apparently, the Parkersburg High School Orchestra, pictured above, had improved. According to the *Quill*, "Everybody loves to peep in the door of the auditorium on Tuesday evening. The orchestra has played many times this year and has received many compliments on its work." (Courtesy of Blennerhassett Island Historical Park.)

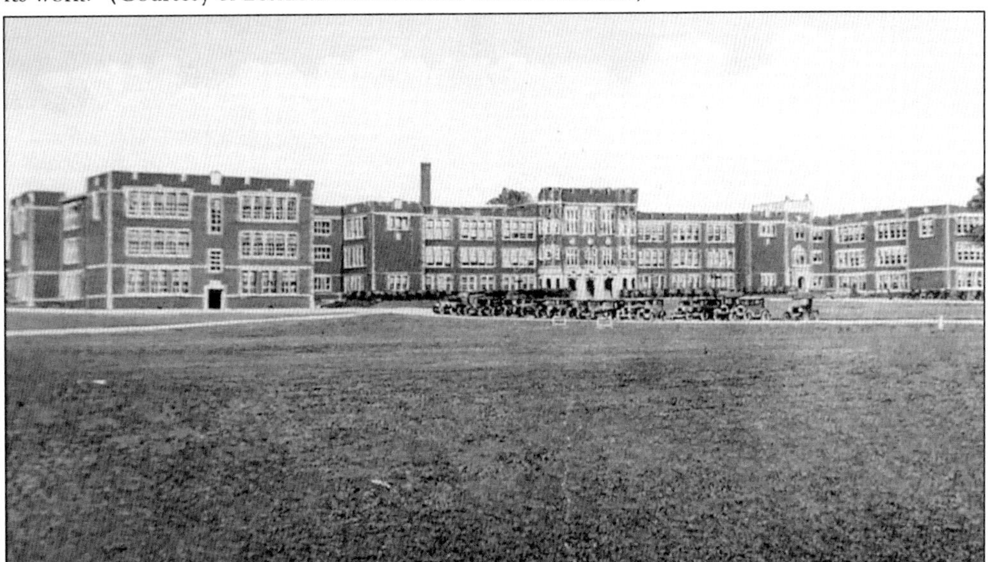

Construction of the wings, necessitated by the need for additional classroom space at Parkersburg High School, was approved in 1928. Two wings were added that nearly doubled the capacity of the school. Seventh and eighth grade classes met in the south wing until 1956 when two junior highs were completed. Only sophomores, juniors, and seniors have attended the high school since 1960. (Courtesy of *Mountain Trace*.)

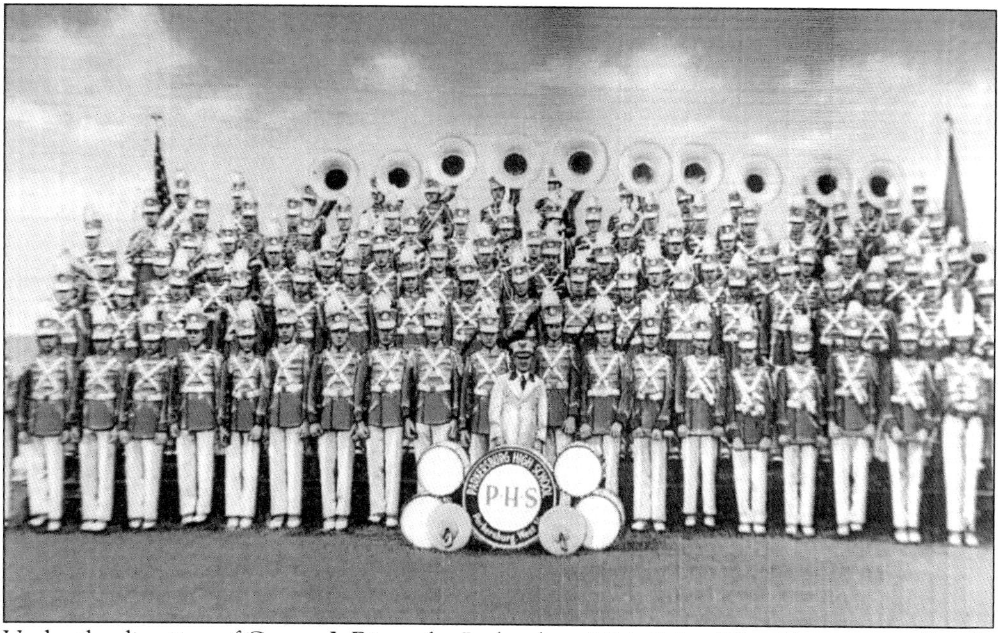

Under the direction of George J. Dietz, the Parkersburg High School Band became an all-male military marching band. Pictured above c. 1941, the band was recognized as one of the best high school musical organizations in the United States. The band traveled extensively and won the first four International Lion's Club band contests in Rhode Island, Illinois, Pennsylvania, and New Orleans. (Collection of B. Leavengood.)

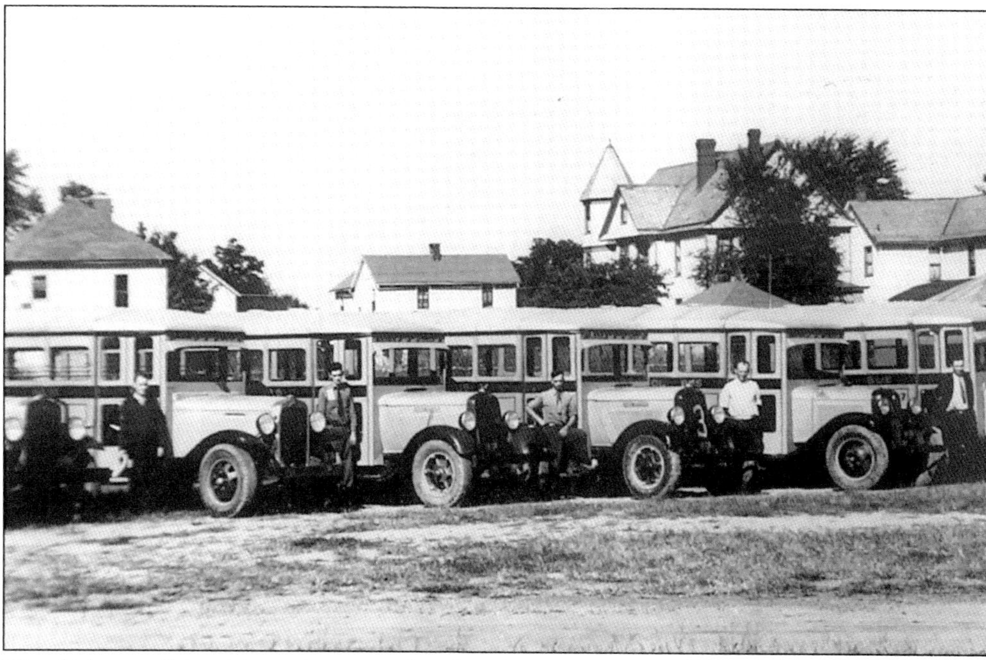

Wood County Schools' new buses are lined up for inspection at the bus garage on Nineteenth Street in 1942. Many students, including myself, remember the days on the bus. I rode Bus Number Nine from Deerwalk to Parkersburg High School every day for four years. This meant leaving home before 7 a.m. and not returning until 5 p.m. (Courtesy of Darrell Deem.)

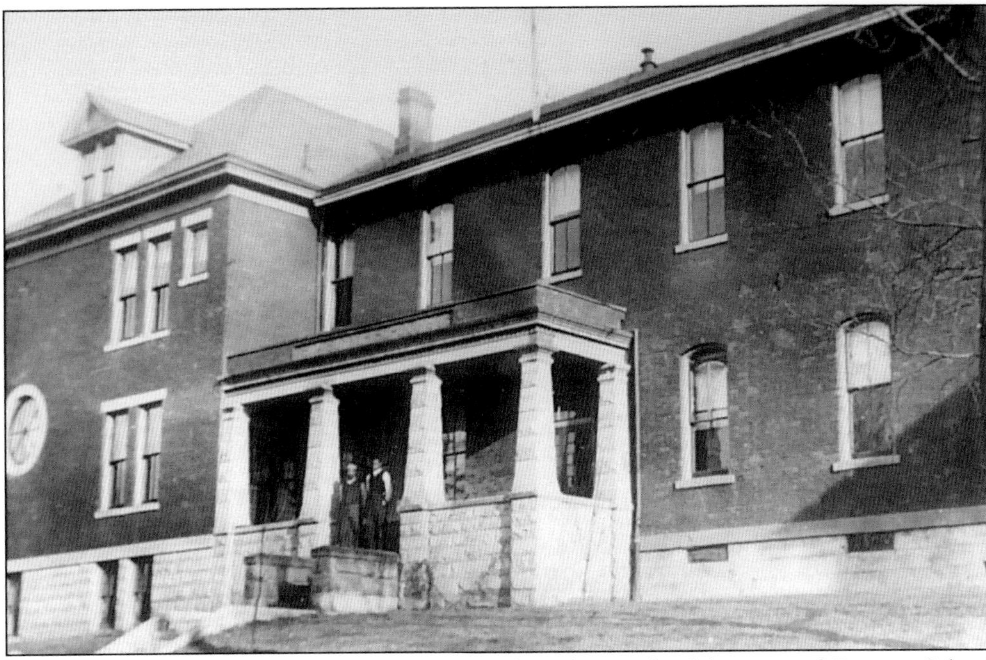

Classmates Jimmy Harris and James Sprigg stand on the porch of the original Sumner School at Fifth and Avery Streets. The school was named for United States Senator Charles Sumner of Massachusetts, an outspoken champion of rights for blacks from 1848 to 1877. During the Civil War, Sumner pushed for the emancipation of slaves and introduced the Thirteenth Amendment to the Senate in 1864. (Courtesy of Sumnerite Museum, Rae Brown, curator.)

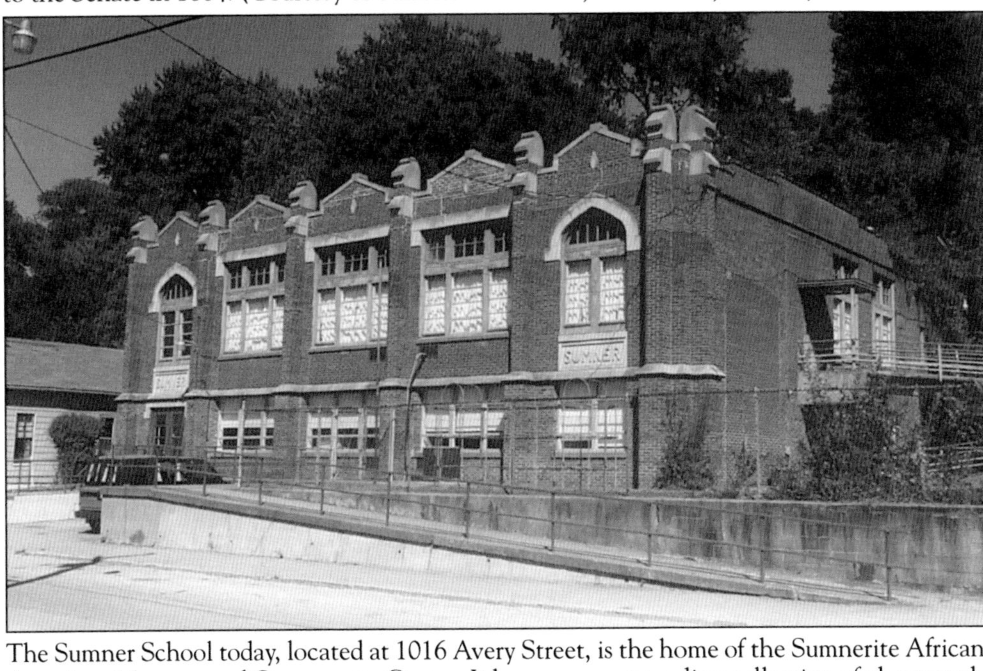

The Sumner School today, located at 1016 Avery Street, is the home of the Sumnerite African-American Museum and Community Center. It houses an outstanding collection of photographs and memorabilia of the African-American community in Parkersburg. Rae Brown, curator, organized the museum. (Photograph by Fred Cornwell.)

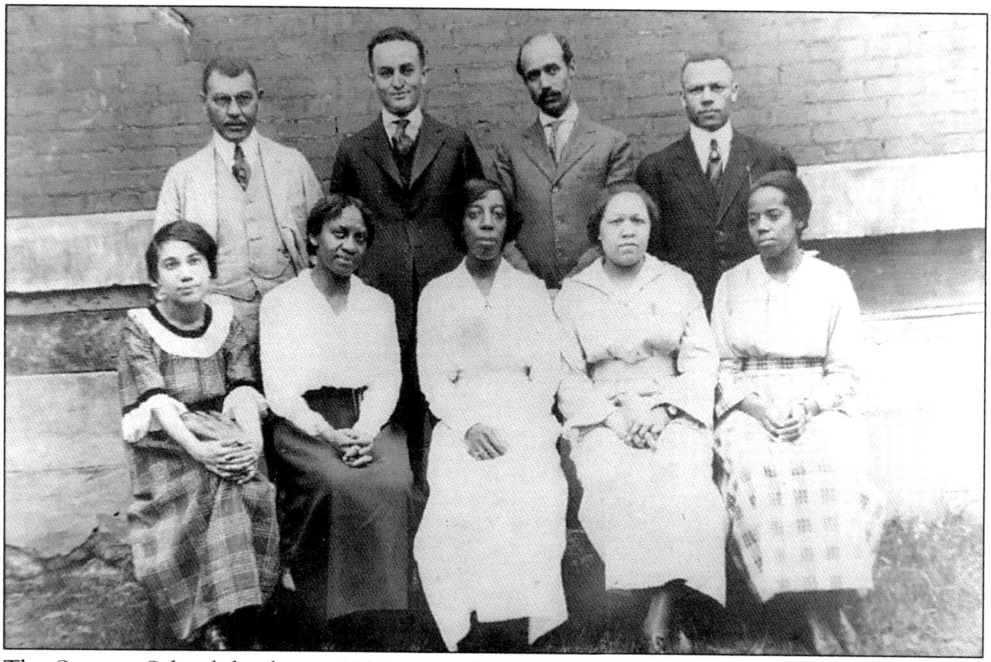

The Sumner School faculty, c. 1930, poses for a group photograph. (Courtesy of Sumnerite Museum, Rae Brown, curator.)

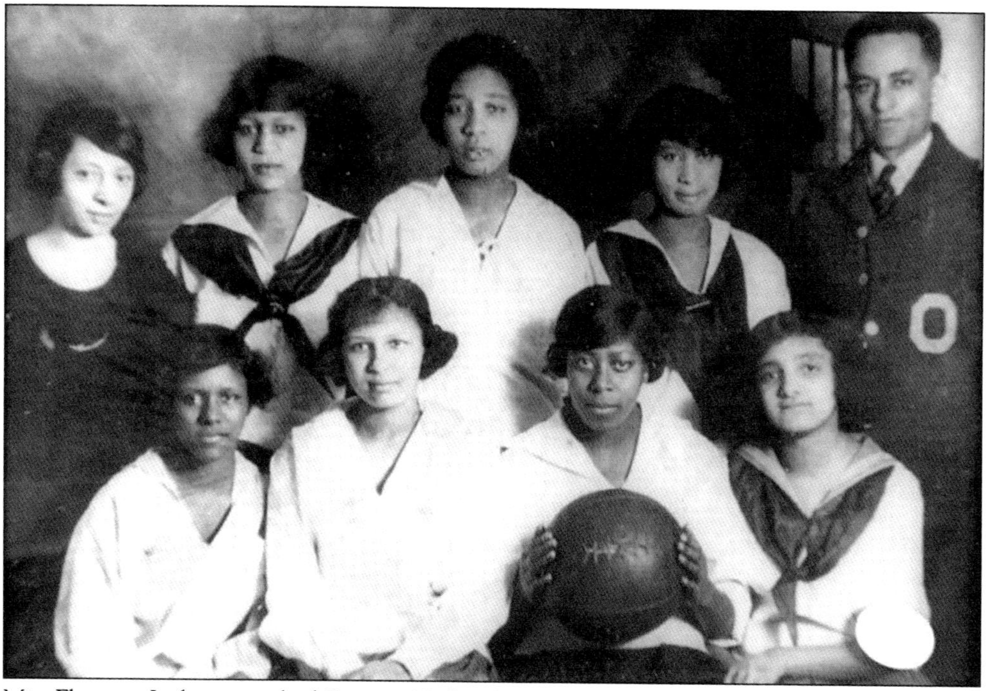

Miss Florence Jackson coached Sumner High School's girls basketball team. Rae Brown, curator of the Sumnerite Museum, remembers most of the girls' names. From left to right, they are (front row) Viola Brass, Zelda Robinson, Nellie Comdey, and Grace Brown; (back row) Miss Florence Jackson, unidentified, Minnie Fleming, Naomi Tibbs, and Principal J.R. Jefferson. (Courtesy of Sumnerite Museum, Rae Brown, curator.)

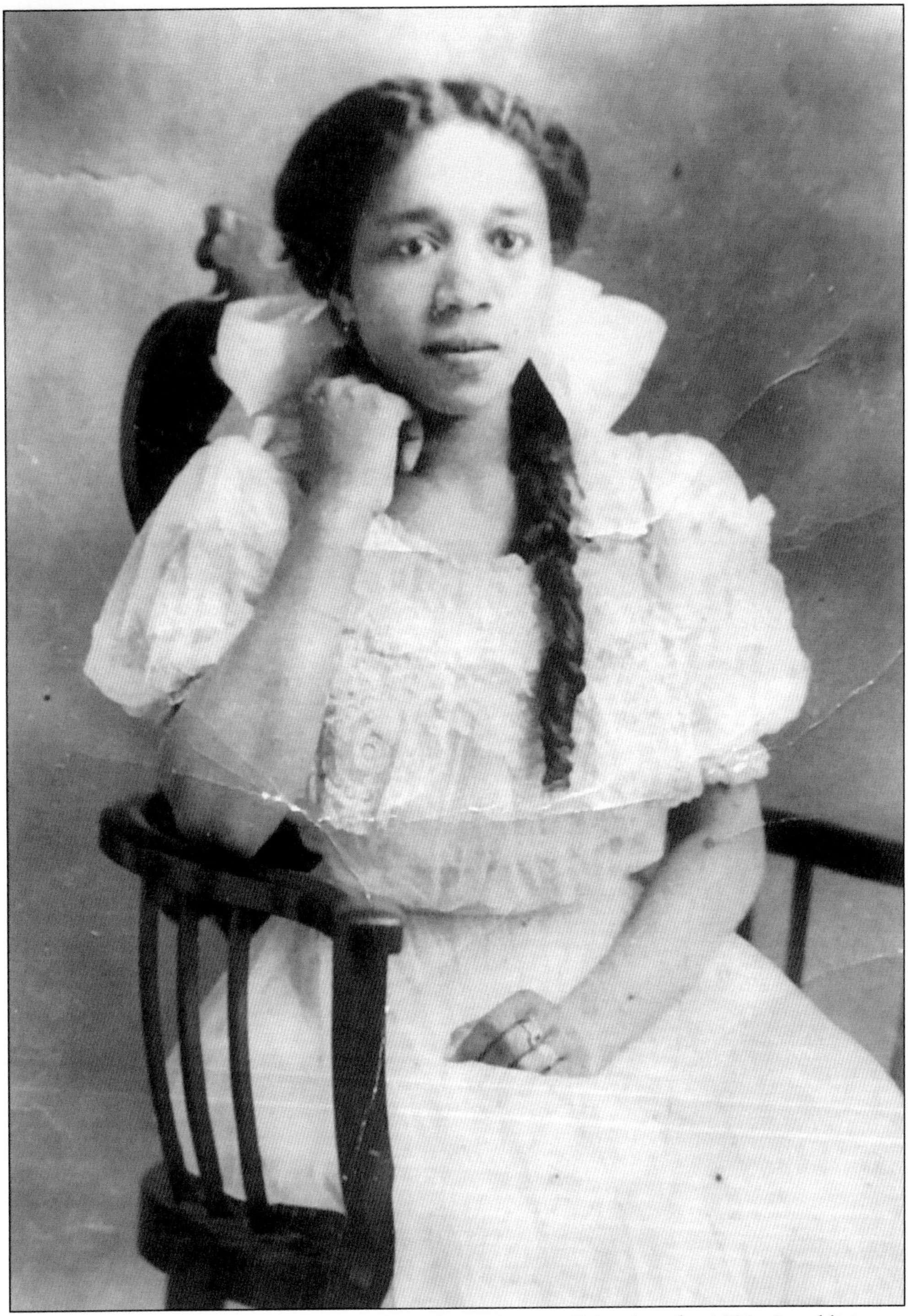

Ethel Carr Watson taught fifth and sixth grades at Sumner School in the 1930s. In addition to her regular classroom instruction, she taught acrobatics, classical ballet, and, according to Rae Brown, "every kind of dance." Ms. Watson and her students presented a musical revue at the Smoot Theater in 1935. (Courtesy of Sumnerite Museum, Rae Brown, curator.)

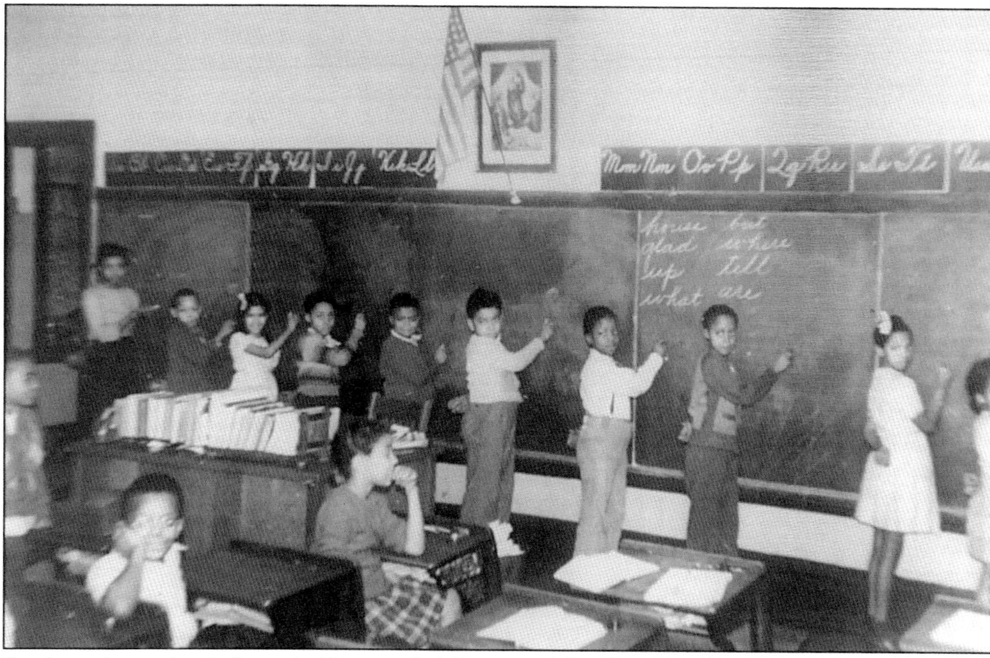

Students in grades 1 through 12 attended Sumner School. Miss Almeda Brown's fourth grade class at Sumner School poses for the camera. At the blackboard, from left to right are Hazel Bateman, Lewis Jones, Barbara Davis, Melanie Brown, Clifford Martin Jr., Emory Carr, Roger Fitzgerald, Tom Donaway, Lois Jones, and Virginia Lee Hatcher. Seated, from left to right, are Sonny Jones, Caroletha Ballard, and Billy Seymour. Clifford Martin Jr. later became principal of Sumner School. (Courtesy of Sumnerite Museum, Rae Brown, curator.)

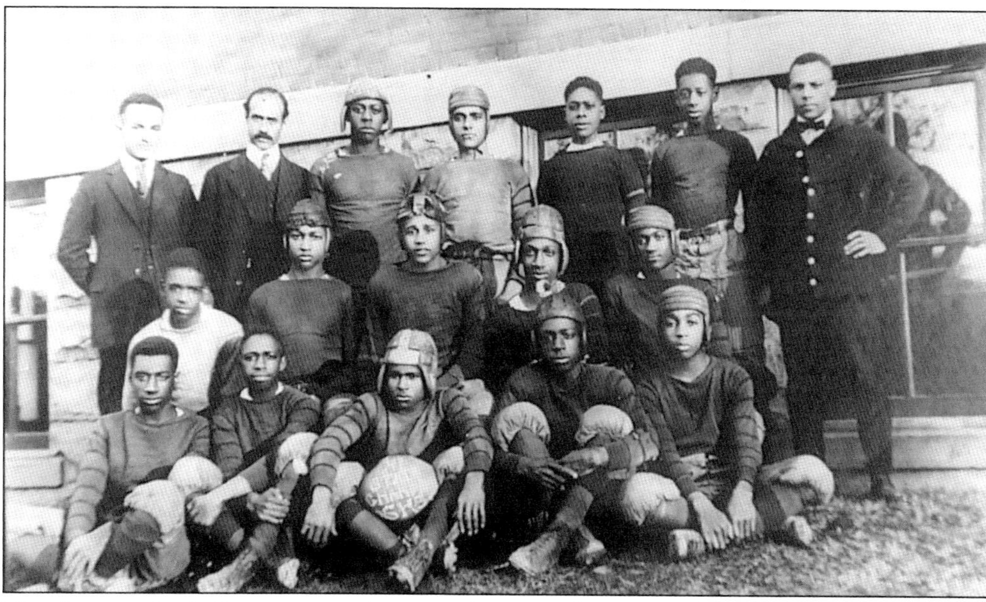

The Sumner football team won the state championship in 1917. The team played schools in Clarksburg, Fairmont, Wheeling, and Morgantown. The team, unable to afford their own equipment, used castoff uniforms and helmets from Parkersburg High School's football program. (Courtesy of Sumnerite Museum, Rae Brown, curator.)

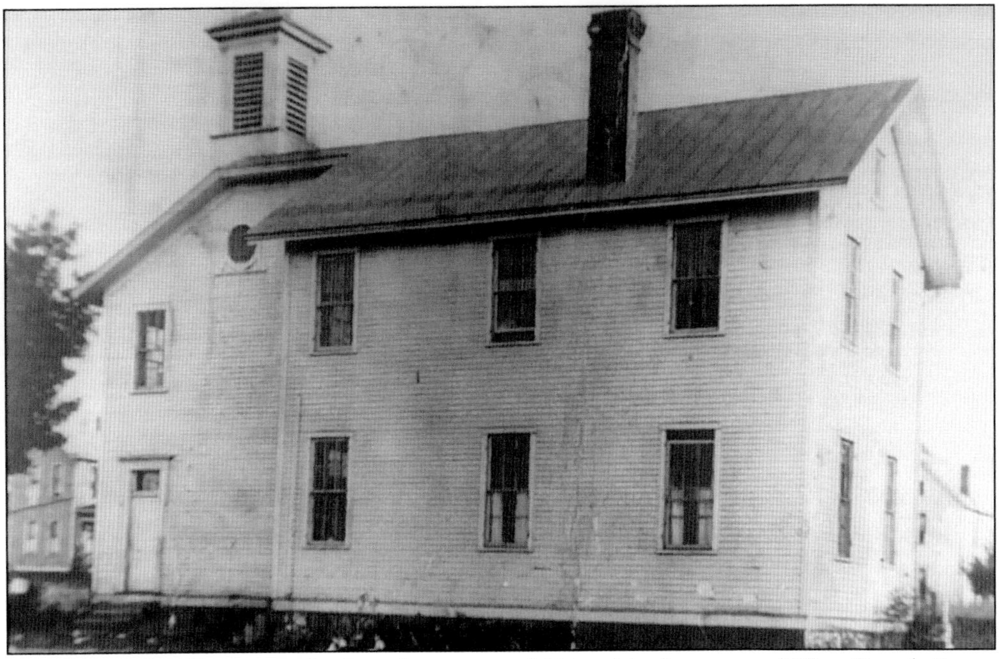

This frame schoolhouse was built at the corner of Columbia Avenue and West Fourth Street in Williamstown in 1870. At first a two-room school, the building had two additional rooms added in 1890 at the cost of $2000. Williamstown elementary and high school students attended this school until 1908 when a larger school was constructed on Williams Avenue. (Courtesy of Pat Peters.)

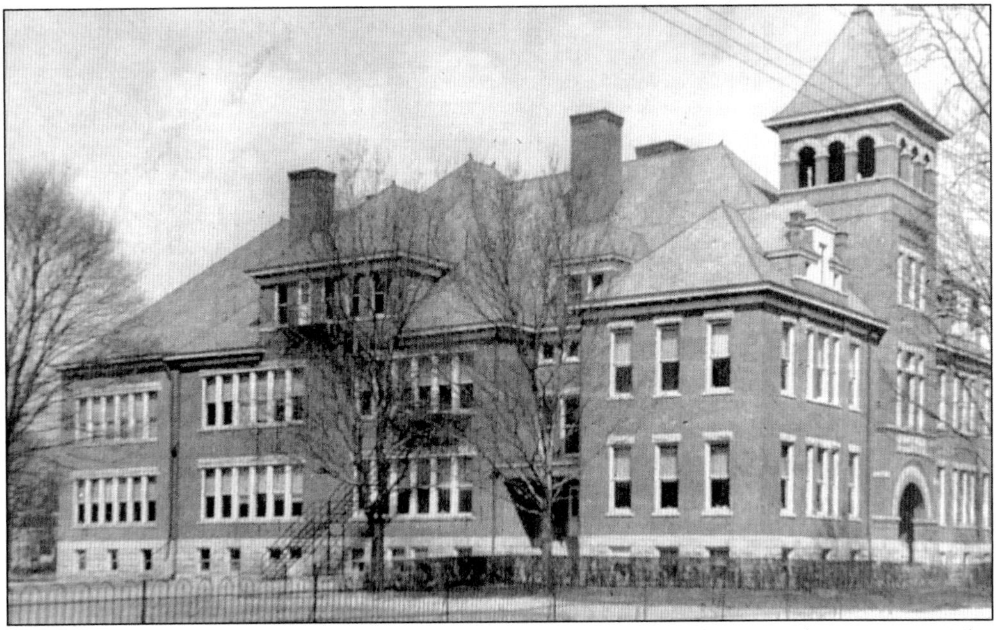

The cornerstone for the new, larger Williamstown school was laid on October 28, 1907. The building, which cost $32,993 to construct, housed grades kindergarten through twelve from the fall of 1908 until the present high school opened in September 1956. Today the building, minus the third floor, serves as the Williamstown Elementary School. (Courtesy of Pat Peters.)

Four

Expanding Our Horizons

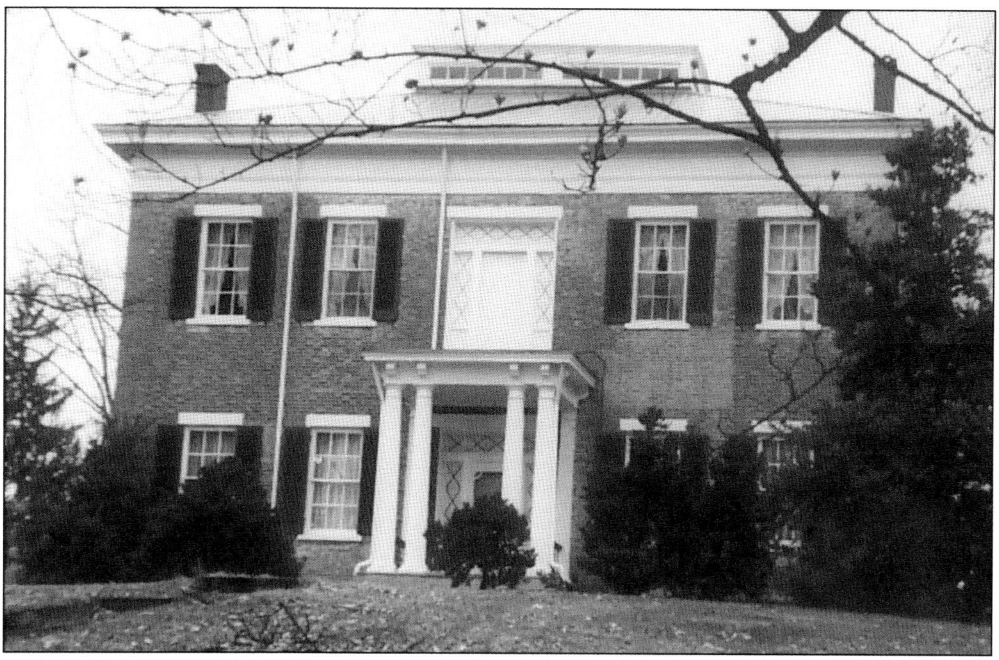

Built by James McNeil Stephenson around 1834, "Oakland," as he called the house, still stands today. Oakland was the center of a 1,000-acre plantation. The Union Army camped on the grounds during the Civil War. One of Parkersburg's leading citizens, Stephenson owned a tanning yard at the corner of Market and Harriet (later Fourth) Streets in Parkersburg. He served as president of the Northwestern Bank and as a delegate to the Virginia assembly from Wood County in 1847. (Courtesy of James Miracle.)

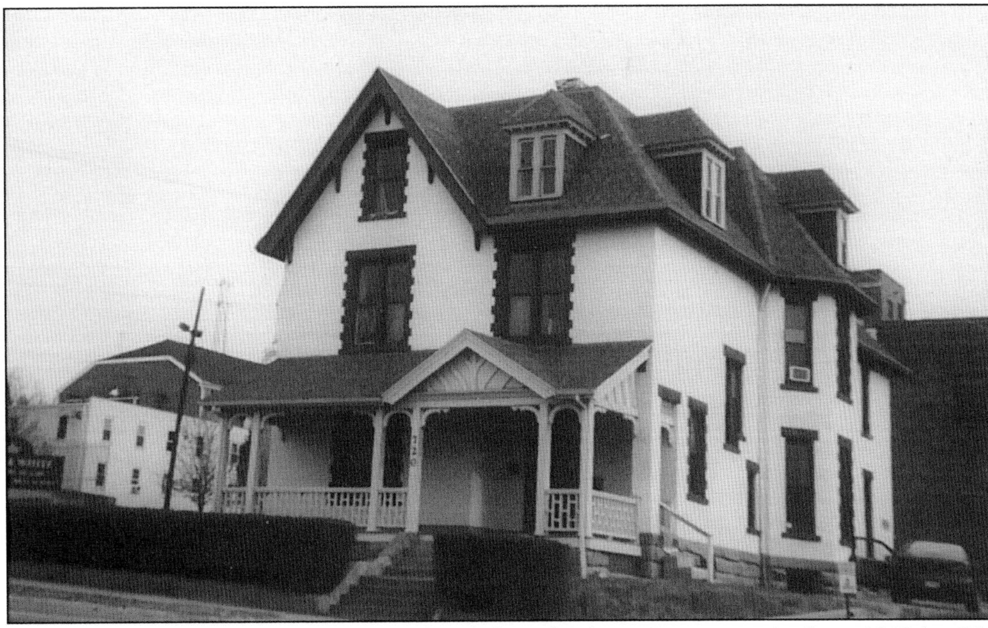

This magnificent home at the corner of Eighth and Juliana Streets was built in 1888 by S.L. Gould, owner of the Parkersburg Mill. Today the home serves as the office of Rusen and White, Attorneys at Law. (Courtesy of the West Virginia State Archives.)

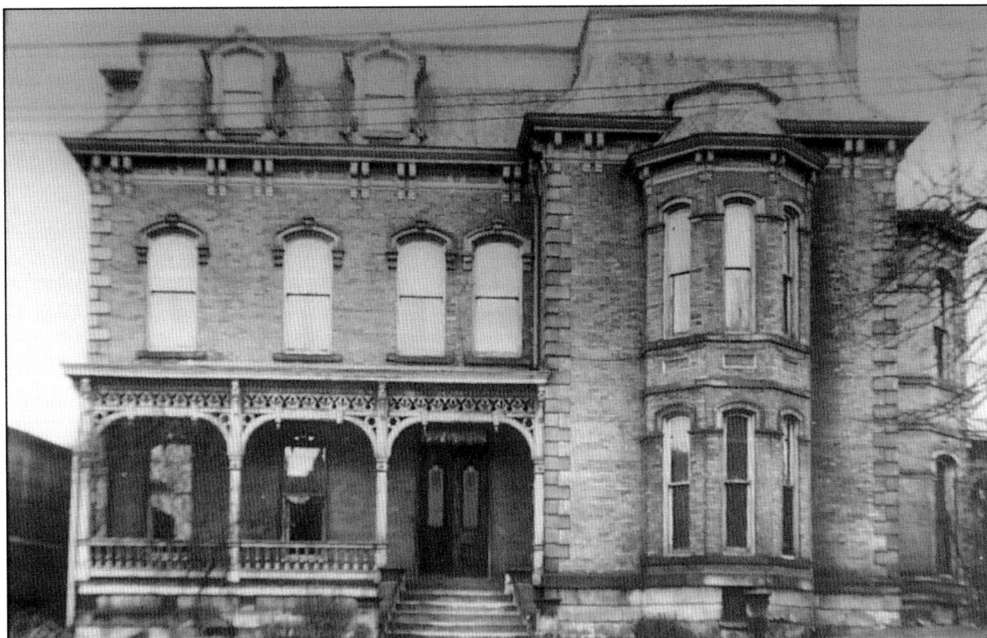

Gen. John Jay Jackson built this three-story, twelve-room mansion at Third and Market between 1838 and 1840. He called the home "Corrinda." Jackson held many important political positions between 1856 and 1901, including prosecuting attorney of Wood County, judge of the West Virginia Fifth Judicial District, member of the United States House of Representatives, and judge of Wood County's criminal court. The house later became a nightclub and was destroyed by fire. (Courtesy of Paul A. Borrelli, Artcraft Studio.)

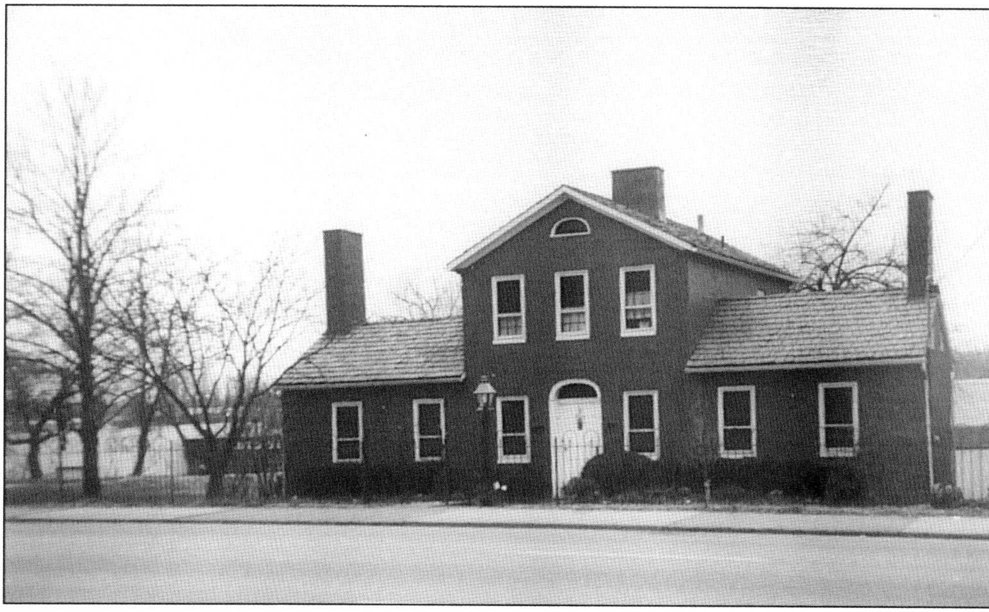

Tillinghast A. Cook built this brick house in 1825. Cook fought in the War of 1812 under William Henry Harrison. He served as Wood County sheriff between 1853 and 1857. He is perhaps best remembered for his leadership of the temperance campaign in Parkersburg during the 1830s. In 1833 the Parkersburg Temperance Society was formed. All members signed a pledge "to each other and the world, our sacred honors, that we will not use them (ardent spirits)." The house still stands amid the businesses on Murdoch Avenue and is home to the Junior League of Parkersburg. (Courtesy of James Miracle.)

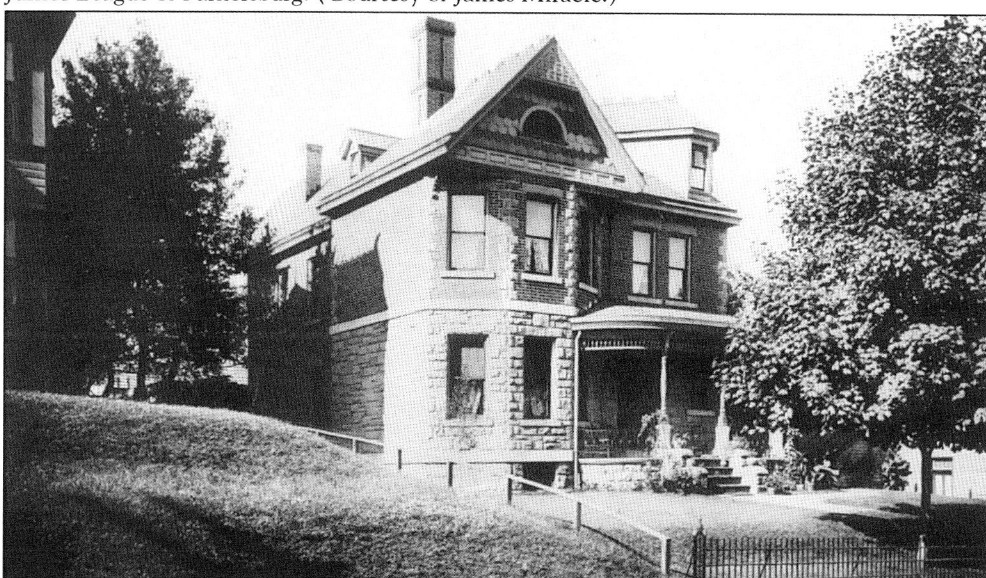

This elegant home at 420 Thirteenth Street belonged to Thomas A. Savage. Savage operated a dry goods and grocery store at 1227 Avery Street. He was also general manager of the Springdale Ice Company and owner of Savage Flats, an apartment building at Thirteenth and Avery. Today the home is the Avery-Savage House Bed and Breakfast. (Courtesy of the West Virginia State Archives.)

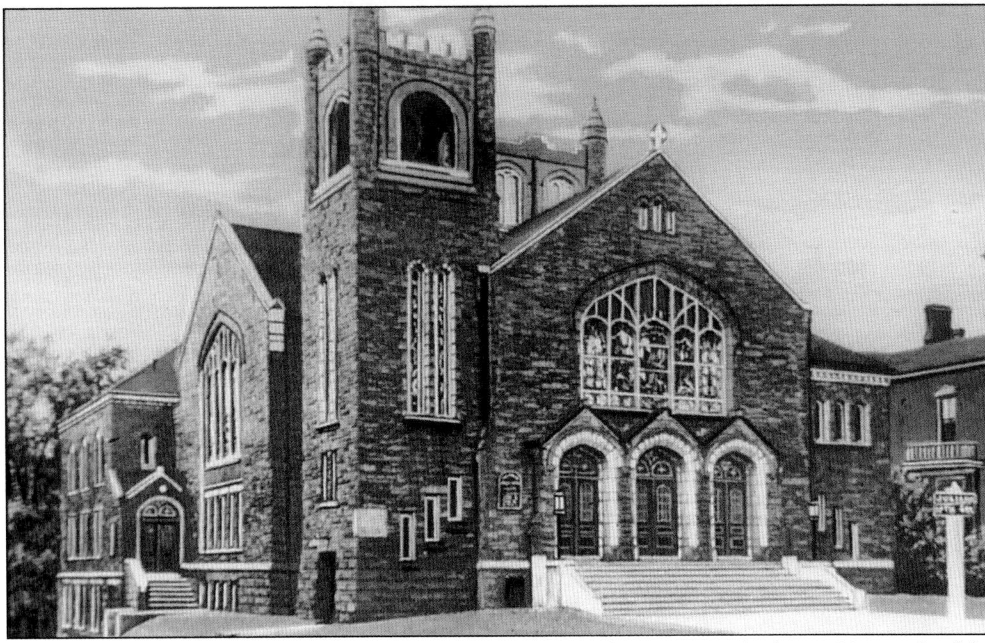

The first Methodist church building in Wood County was a log structure built in 1804 south of the Little Kanawha River. By 1811 a Methodist society had been organized in Parkersburg. The First Methodist Church, pictured above, was dedicated on January 11, 1911 and is still in use today. Both the exterior and interior architectural styles are Gothic. (Collection of B. Leavengood.)

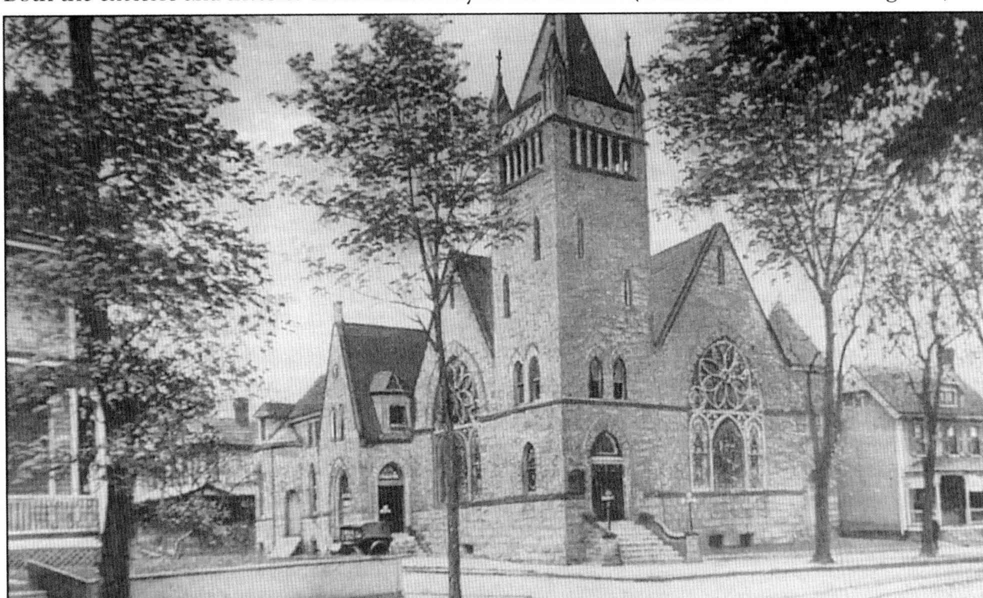

Rev. James McAboy, founder of the First Baptist Church, embraced Presbyterianism while living in Athens, Ohio. When he returned to Parkersburg, McAboy organized the First Presbyterian Church at the Wood County Courthouse on February 23, 1833. The newly organized church held their first religious services the next day. Twenty-six persons attended, including several slaves. Today Calvary Temple Evangelistic Church worships in the former Presbyterian Church at Tenth and Market Streets. (Collection of B. Leavengood.)

Construction began on the first Trinity Episcopal Church, pictured above, on July 11, 1846, on property donated by John Fryatt Snodgrass. The first rector, Rev. Thomas Smith, did not live to see the church completed. He died on April 4, 1847, and, at his request, was buried under the doorstep of the church. Smith said he was a "poor sinner and wanted to be trampled under the feet of all who entered." The church opened for services in May 1850. (Courtesy of Trinity Episcopal Church.)

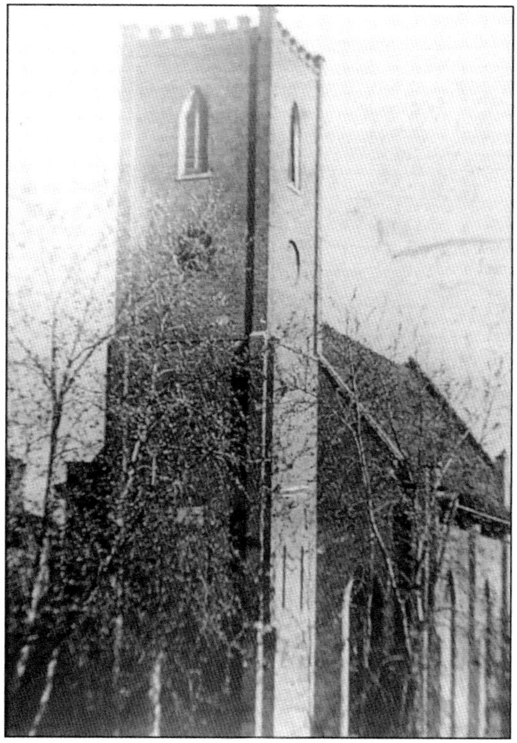

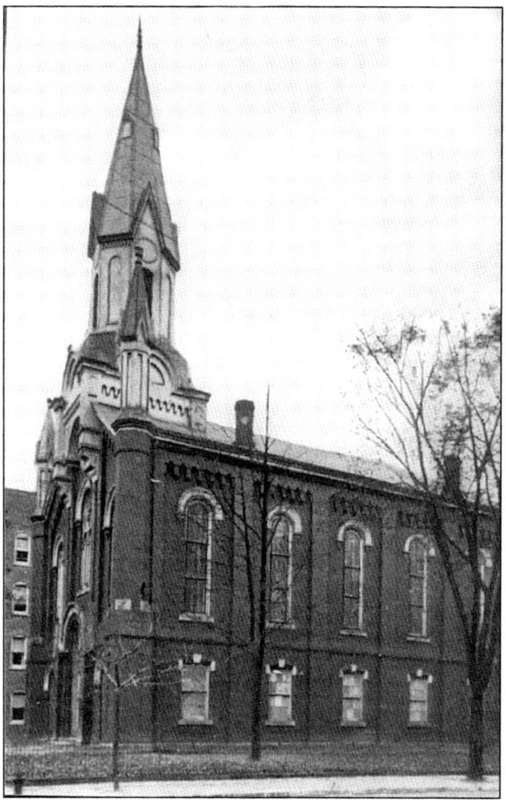

The first Baptist church in Wood County was the Mount Zion Church at Mineral Wells, established in 1815. Two years later a group of 24 persons met at the home of Rev. James McAboy on Avery Street to form an association, which became the predecessor of the First Baptist Church of Parkersburg, pictured on the left. Deacon Lysander Dudley presented the congregation with plans from his hometown church in Wallingford, Connecticut. The plans were well-received, and the congregation agreed to build a similar church, asking Dudley to oversee its construction. The church was completed in 1877 at 813 Market Street and is still in use today. The First Baptist Church is on the National Register of Historic Places. (Collection of B. Leavengood.)

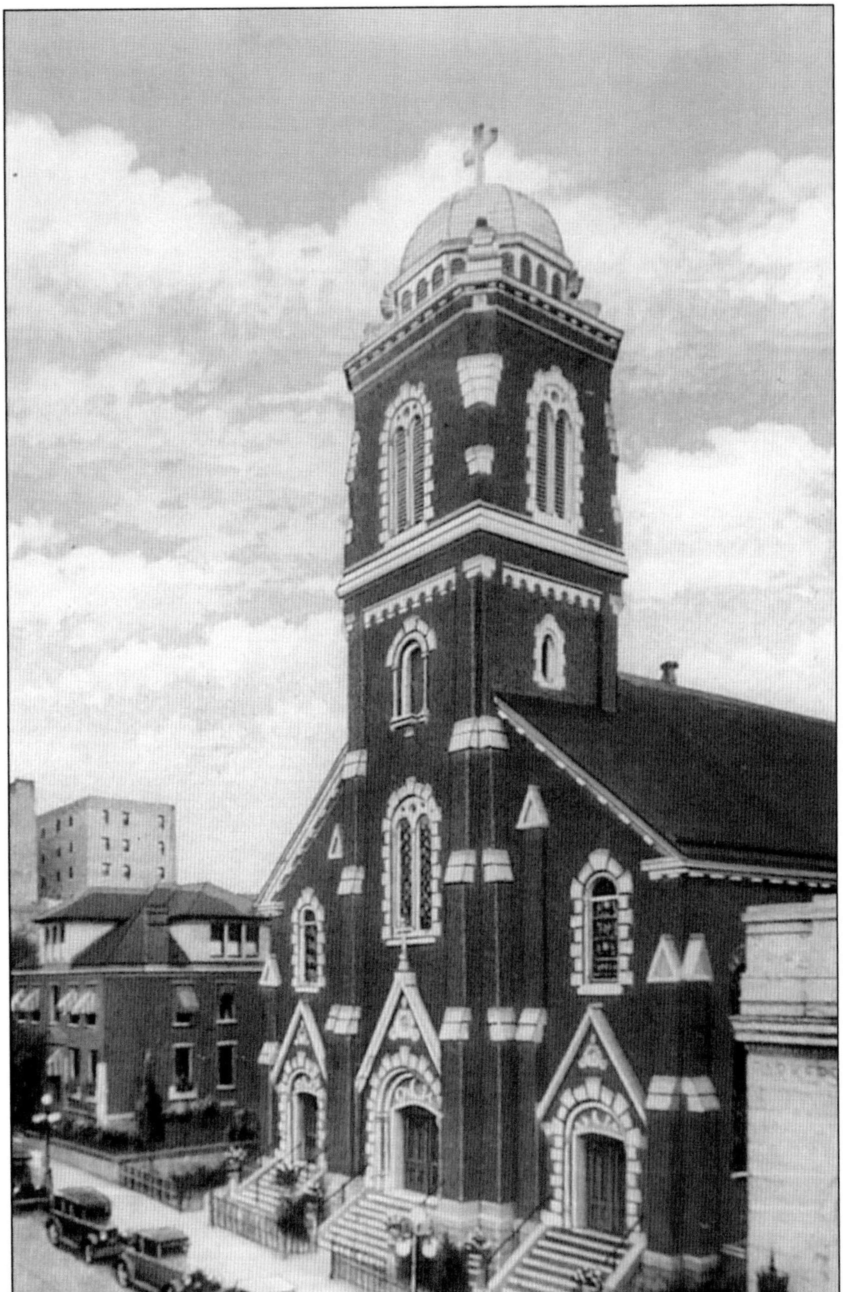

Although Catholic families had settled in Wood County as early as 1800, it was not until 1845 that a priest was assigned to serve the Catholic population of the county. In April of 1850 the cornerstone was laid for the predecessor of today's St. Francis Xavier Church. The present church on Market Street was completed in October of 1870 at a cost of $85,000. By 1895, the parish's membership totaled 303 persons. (Collection of B. Leavengood.)

Anne Gaither Thompson married Johnson Newlon Camden on June 22, 1858. Camden amassed a fortune as John D. Rockefeller's right hand man in West Virginia. Anne made their home at 717 Ann Street the social center of Parkersburg. She died August 6, 1918, at the age of 83. Camden heirs offered the Camden mansion to the City of Parkersburg for use as a city hospital with the stipulation that the name of the hospital be Anne Camden Memorial Hospital. (Courtesy of Camden-Clark Memorial Hospital.)

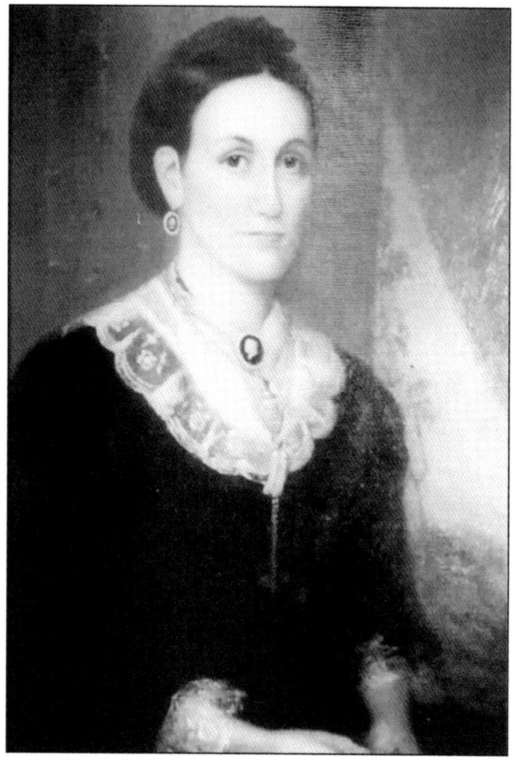

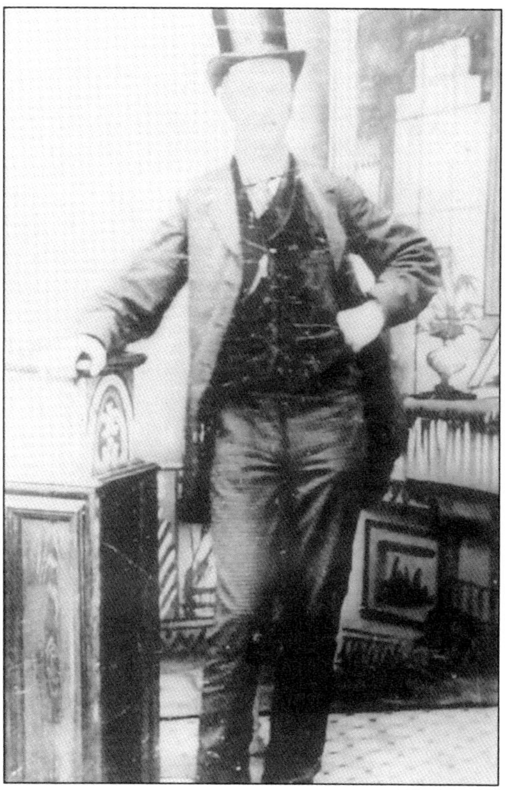

In 1831, 22-year-old Andrew Gibson Clark rode horseback from Winchester, Virginia, to Parkersburg. He studied medicine under Parkersburg doctors McGuire and Stafford before going to Lexington, Kentucky, to further his studies at Transylvania University. In 1843 the now Dr. Clark returned to Parkersburg to establish his practice. After a long and distinguished career, Dr. Clark died in 1902 at the age of 93. He bequeathed $10,000 to the City of Parkersburg to be used in founding a hospital for the poor. (Courtesy of Camden-Clark Memorial Hospital.)

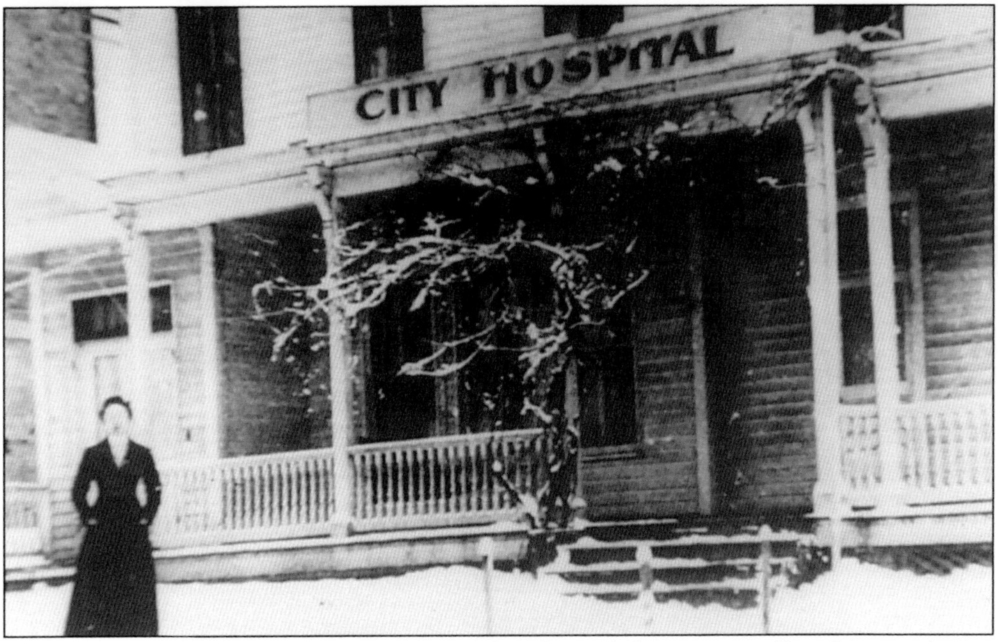

On July 14, 1897, the Parkersburg City Council authorized the issuance of bonds to purchase a site for a city hospital. The city bought a home at 514-516 Wells Street (now Thirteenth Street) for $6,500 to use as a hospital later that year. Dr. William Johnson Davidson, superintendent of the new hospital, reported to the city council that from February 1 to September 1, 1898, 70 patients received care. Of that 70, three died—one from a stab wound, another from typhoid, and the last from an unspecified disease. (Courtesy of Camden-Clark Memorial Hospital.)

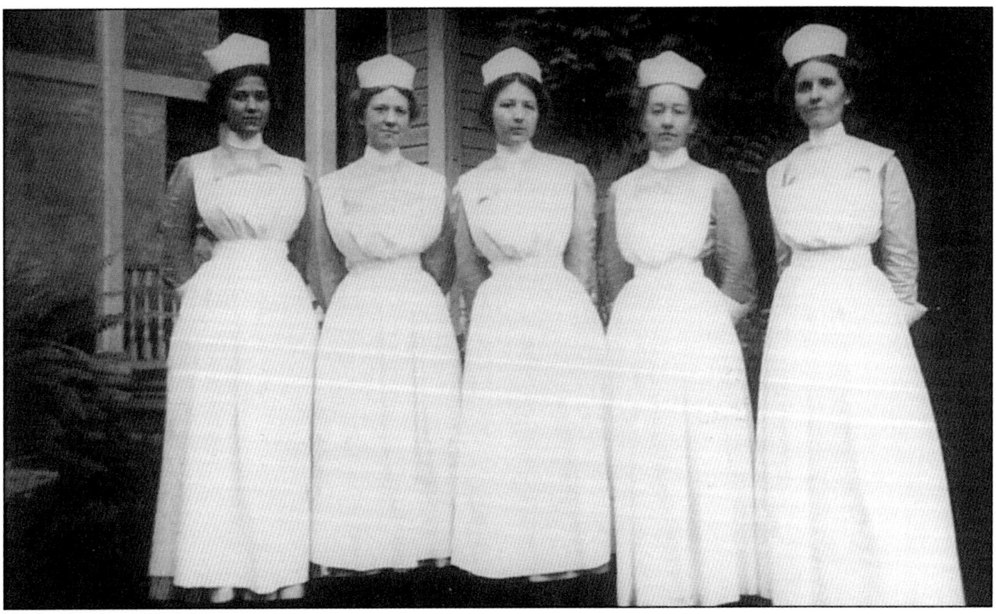

The first hospital nursing school program in West Virginia began at City Hospital on March 15, 1898. Fifteen young women enrolled in the program, which included classes in obstetrics, anatomy, and general nursing. Pictured above are five members of the first class. Nine of the original 15 enrollees graduated in 1903. (Courtesy of Camden-Clark Memorial Hospital.)

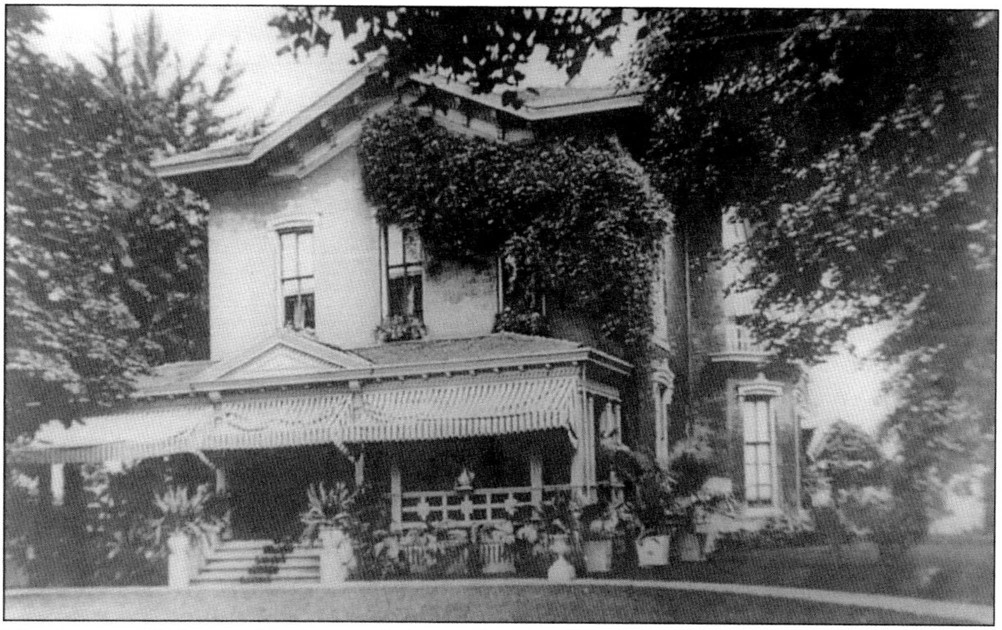

The home of Johnson Newlon and Anne Gaither Camden at 717 Ann Street was one of Parkersburg's finest homes. Their heirs donated the house to the City of Parkersburg for use as a hospital. By combining funds donated by Dr. Andrew Clark, the Camden heirs, and charitable donations with City of Parkersburg monies, the city remodeled the mansion and added an annex for use as a hospital. The Camden-Clark Memorial Hospital was dedicated on April 16, 1920. (Courtesy of Camden-Clark Memorial Hospital.)

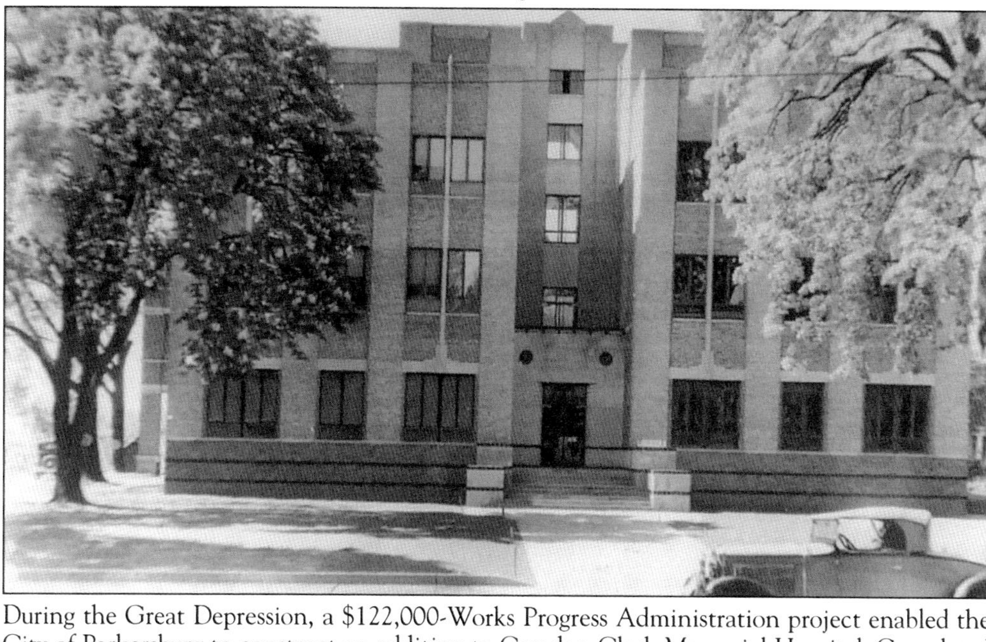

During the Great Depression, a $122,000-Works Progress Administration project enabled the City of Parkersburg to construct an addition to Camden-Clark Memorial Hospital. Completed in 1940, the new wing added 61 beds, bringing the total number of beds to 165. The new addition substantially expanded the isolation ward and the obstetrical department. (Courtesy of Camden-Clark Memorial Hospital.)

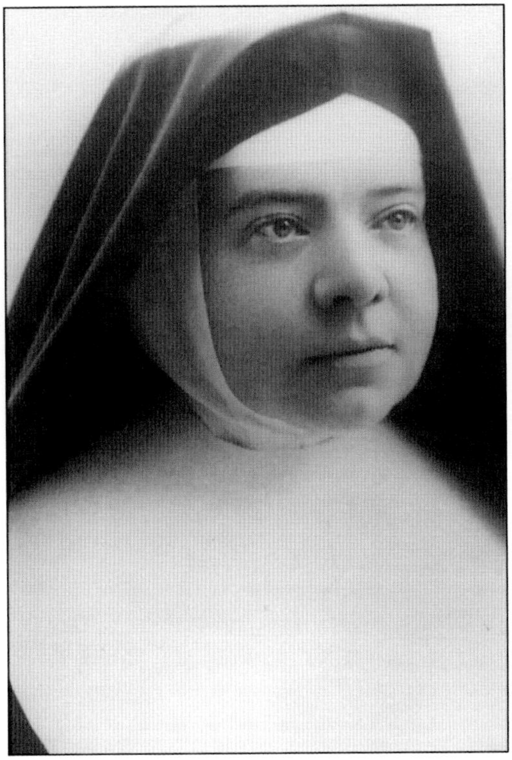

Mother Liguori Pittman received the habit of the Sisters of Saint Joseph in 1867 at the age of 18. She became Assistant Superior in 1883. In 1898 Mother Pittman became General Superior of the Sisters of St. Joseph in Wheeling, a position she held for 15 years. One of the most important acts of her administration was the construction of a new St. Joseph's Academy in Wheeling. In addition, she established St. Mary's Hospital in Clarksburg and St. Joseph's Hospital in Parkersburg. She organized a school of nursing in each hospital. Mother Pittman died at Wheeling Hospital on Saturday October 16, 1920 at the age of 72. (Courtesy of St. Joseph's Hospital.)

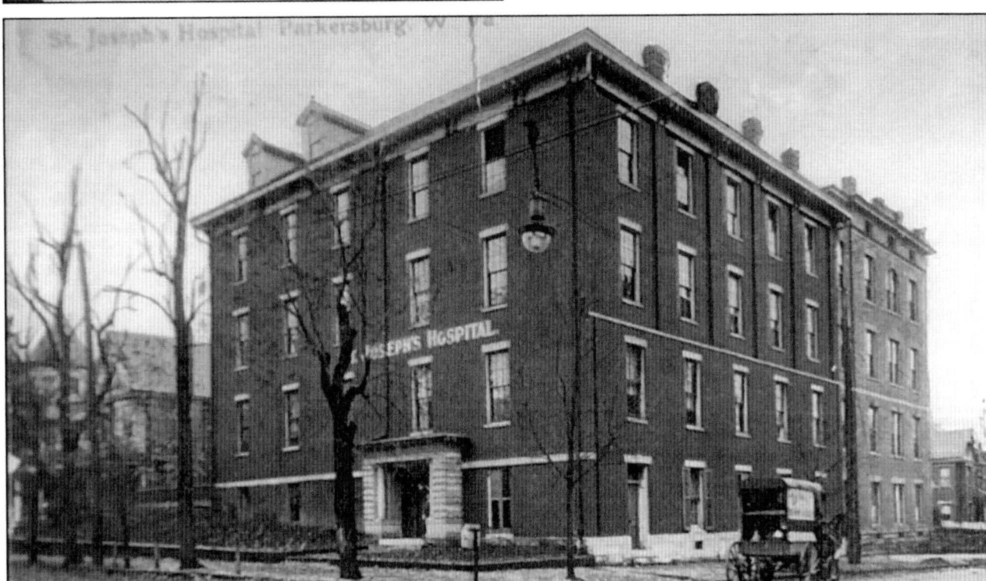

At the end of the 19th century, Parkersburg newspapers called for a new hospital that would serve all the people, especially the poor who could not afford medical care. In 1900 Mother Liguori Pittman, Superior of the Sisters of St. Joseph in Wheeling, sent three sisters to Parkersburg to establish St. Joseph's Hospital. The sisters rented and later purchased a former convent and school from the Sisters of Visitation at the corner of Fifth and Avery Streets to use as a hospital. St. Joseph's Hospital was chartered in 1902. (Courtesy of St. Joseph's Hospital.)

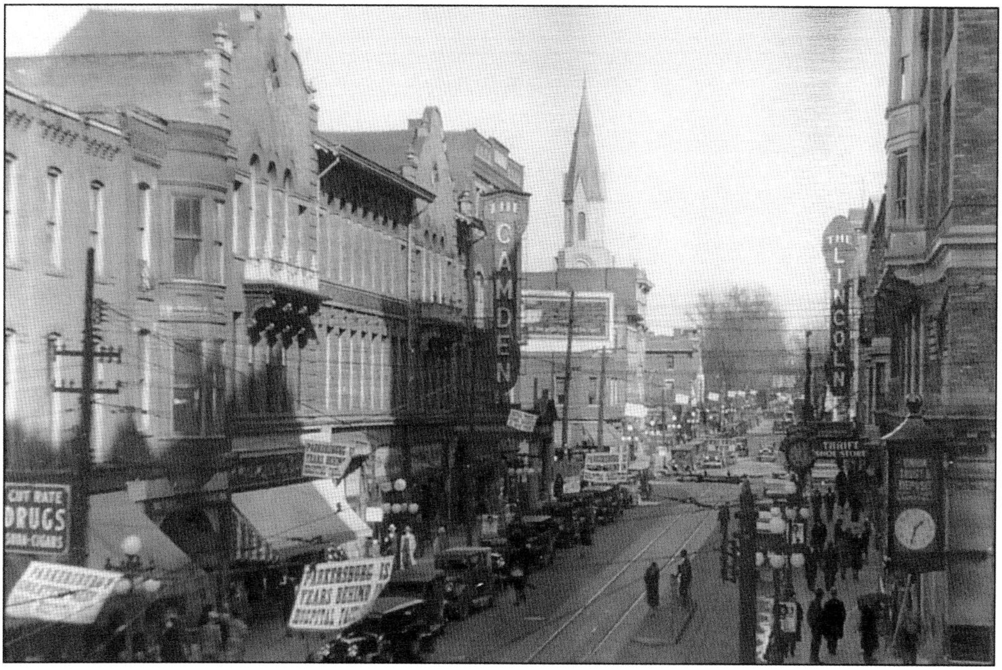

By 1929 it was evident that a larger, more modern hospital was needed to meet the needs of the growing population of Parkersburg and surrounding communities. Despite the crash of the stock market in October of 1929, the Sisters sent out an SOS (Save Our Sick) appeal. Banners on downtown streets promoted the campaign, which raised $332,180 from November 1 through November 11. (Courtesy of St. Joseph's Hospital.)

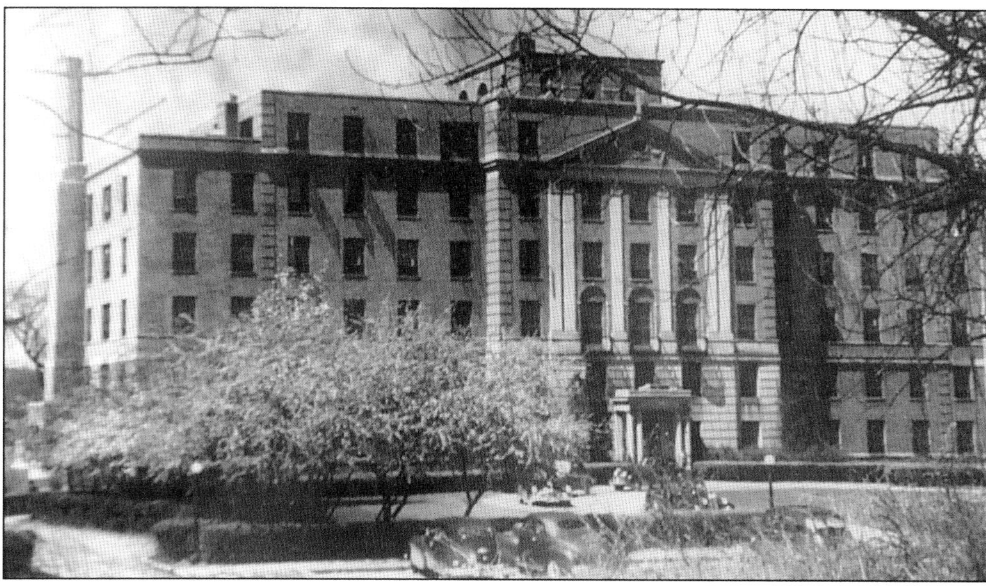

The new 192 bed St. Joseph's Hospital opened on October 13, 1931, at its present site, the corner of Nineteenth Street and Murdoch Avenue. The modern hospital had built-in sterilizers for its seven operating rooms, a central food service, and a sophisticated boiler room for heating the hospital. Built with room for expansion in mind, today St. Joseph's Hospital has 343 beds and over 1,000 employees and physicians. (Courtesy of St. Joseph's Hospital.)

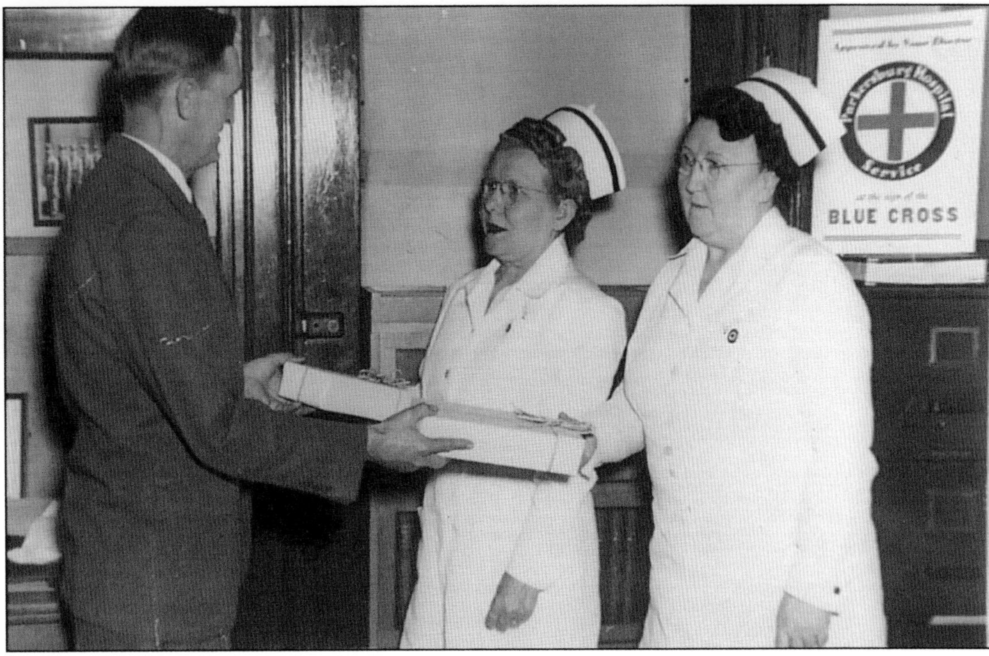

Personnel at both Parkersburg hospitals assumed additional duties during World War II. In recognition of their efforts Parkersburg mayor Earl S. Stephens presented war service emblems to Mrs. Grace M. Short, RN, and Camden-Clark Memorial Hospital Superintendent, and Nelle Cleary, RN, of St. Joseph's Hospital to give their employees and volunteers in appreciation of their war efforts. (Courtesy of Camden-Clark Memorial Hospital.)

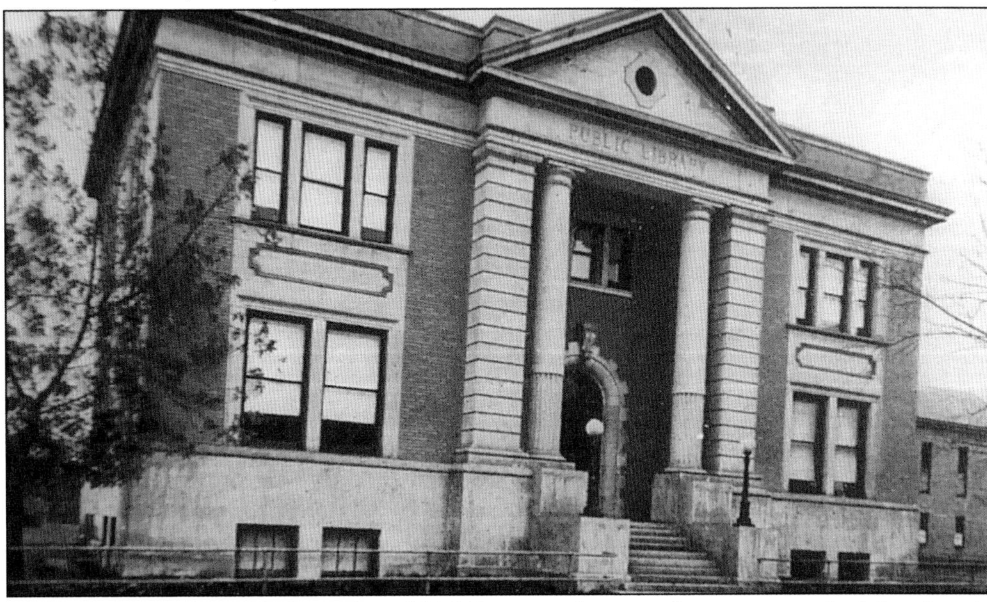

The Carnegie Library, built with a $34,000 grant from steel magnate and philanthropist Andrew Carnegie, opened in 1905 at the corner of Eighth and Green Streets. The four-story structure intrigued patrons with its glass block flooring and spiral staircase. The library served Wood Countians for 69 years, closing in 1974. Today the Transallegheny Bookstore occupies the building. (Collection of B. Leavengood.)

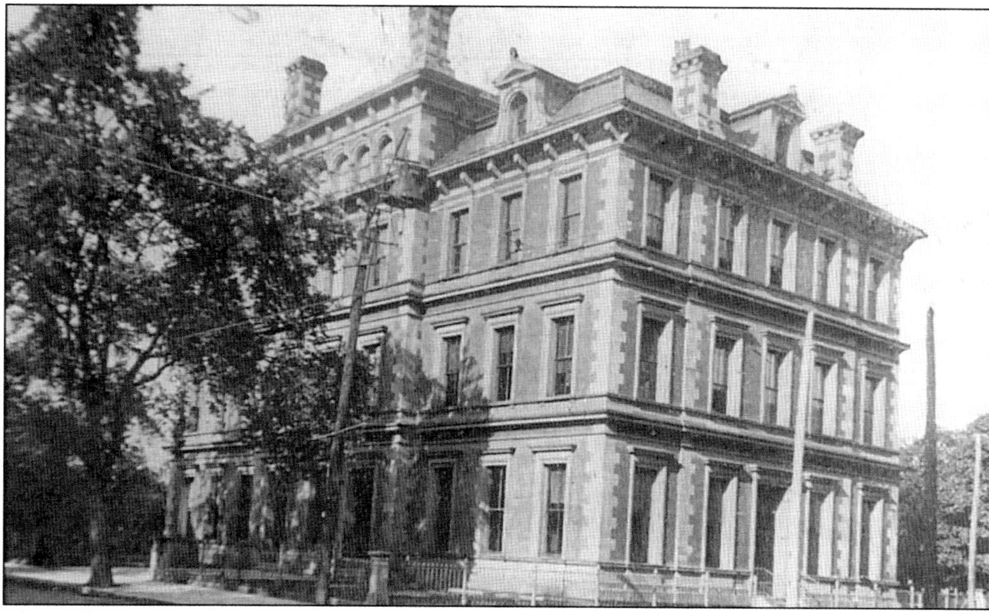

The Federal Building at the corner of Fifth and Juliana Streets served at various times as a customs house, federal weather bureau, and home of the Fourth Federal Judicial District, as well as a post office. The building was completed in 1878 at a cost of $378,000. It served as Parkersburg's post office until 1931 when a new building was constructed next door exclusively for the use of the post office. The Federal Building was demolished a few years later. (Collection of B. Leavengood.)

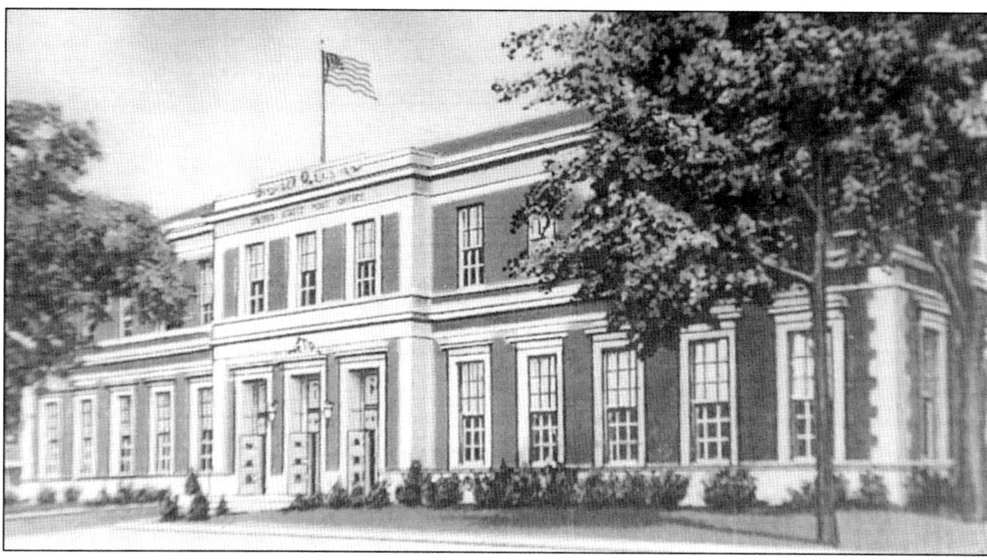

Parkersburg's new post office at Fourth and Juliana opened on November 13, 1931 with pomp and ceremony. West Virginia congressman Robert Hogg, Parkersburg mayor Allen Murdoch, and U.S. postmaster J. Walter Bee spoke. Each lauded the new building as evidence of the growth of Parkersburg. The Parkersburg High School Band and the American Legion Drum and Bugle Corps provided music for the occasion. Following the ceremonies workers began moving equipment from the postal department in the old federal building to the new post office. The building is still in use today. (Collection of B. Leavengood.)

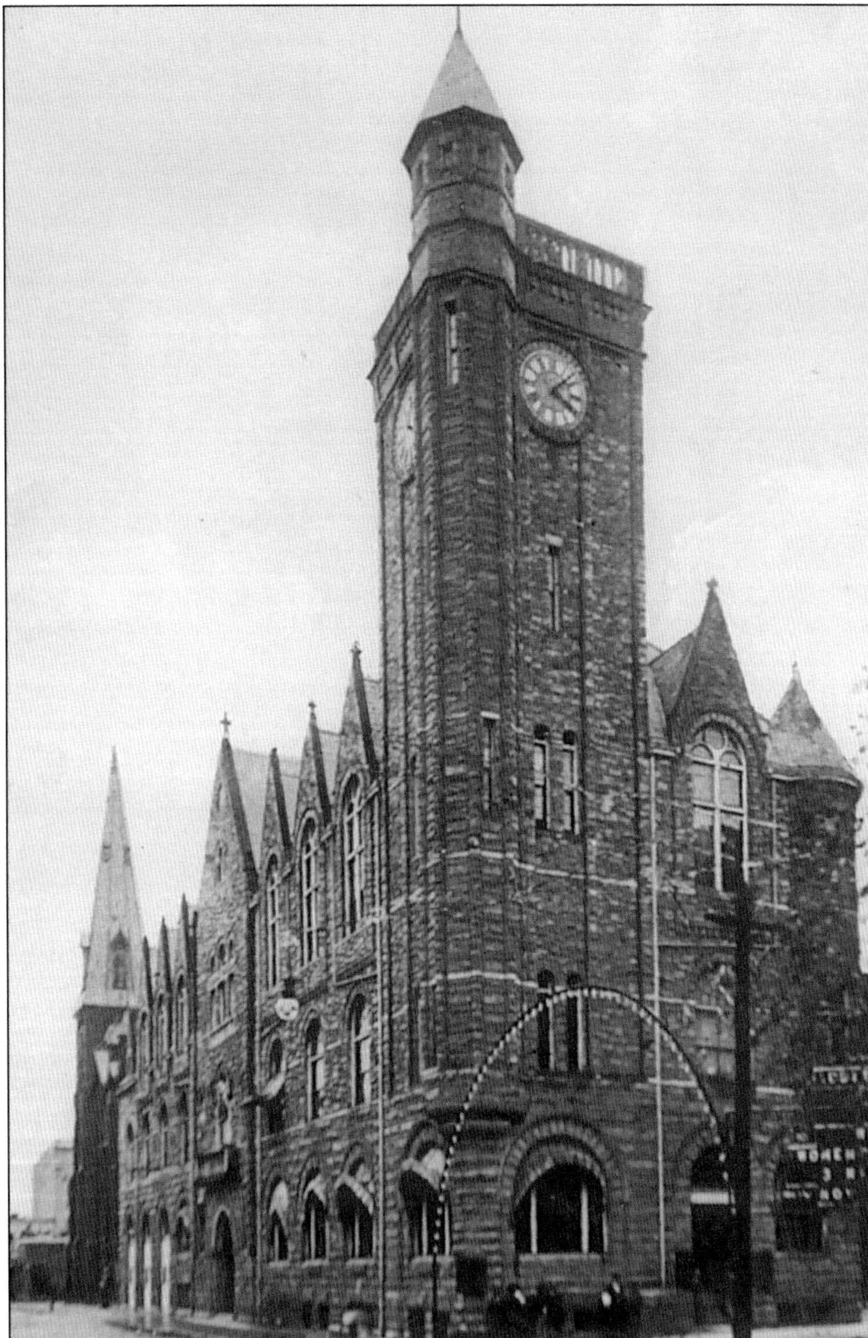

Parkersburg's new city hall, located at the corner of Fifth and Market Streets, opened on October 1, 1897. According to the October 2 *Parkersburg Sentinel*, the formal opening was "a dazzling success." The largest crowds arrived at 7:00 p.m. when the building was brilliantly illuminated. The halls and stairways were so crowded and hot that several ladies fainted. An estimated 5,000 people attended the opening. The building was demolished in 1981. (Collection of B. Leavengood.)

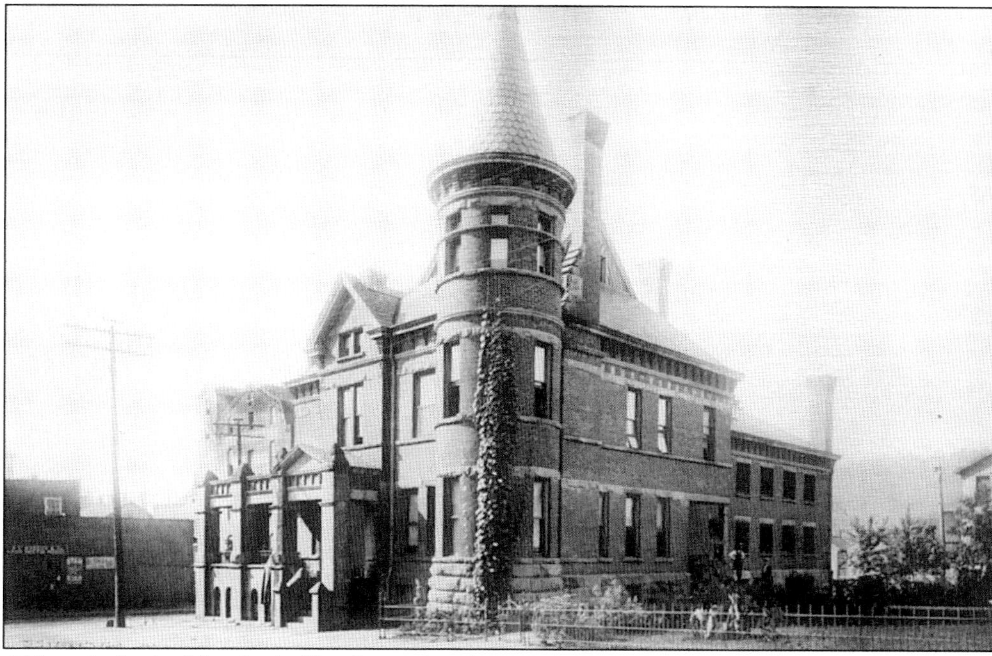

Although this building looks like the set for a horror movie, it was actually the Wood County Jail. Built in 1889, the jail housed prisoners until it was demolished in the 1970s. During the 1913 and 1937 floods prisoners were evacuated from the building by boat. The Salvation Army Band played for prisoners on Sunday afternoons. (Courtesy of the West Virginia State Archives.)

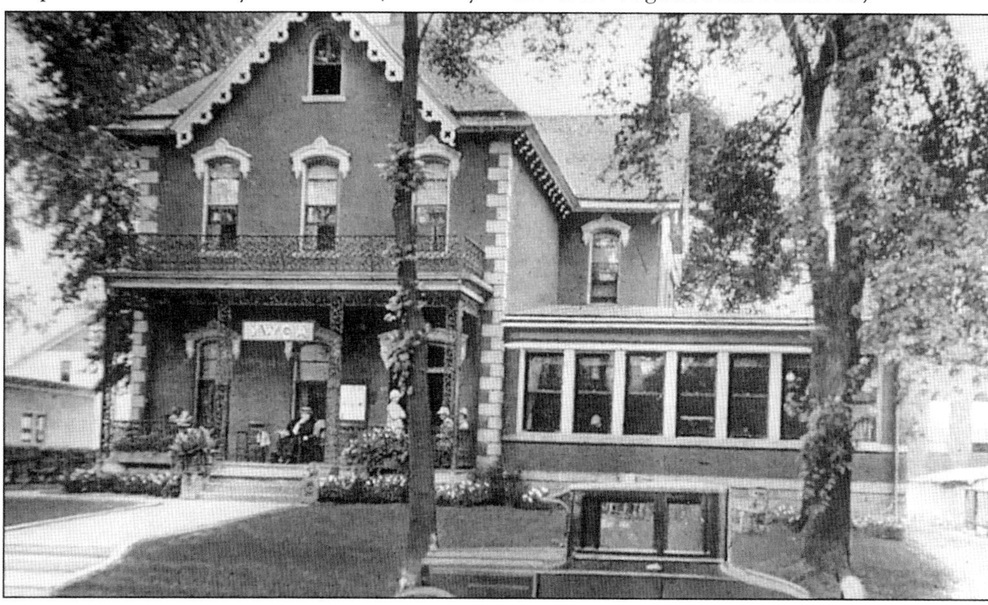

The Young Women's Christian Association (YWCA) was incorporated on February 14, 1914. However, it was not until after World War I ended in 1917 that the YWCA began a fund-raising campaign to build a permanent headquarters for their activities. The new building completed in 1920 and located at 411 Seventh Street served as YWCA headquarters until 1975. Today the YWCA is located on Dudley Avenue and provides a wide range of activities and services, including an excellent day care center. (Collection of B. Leavengood.)

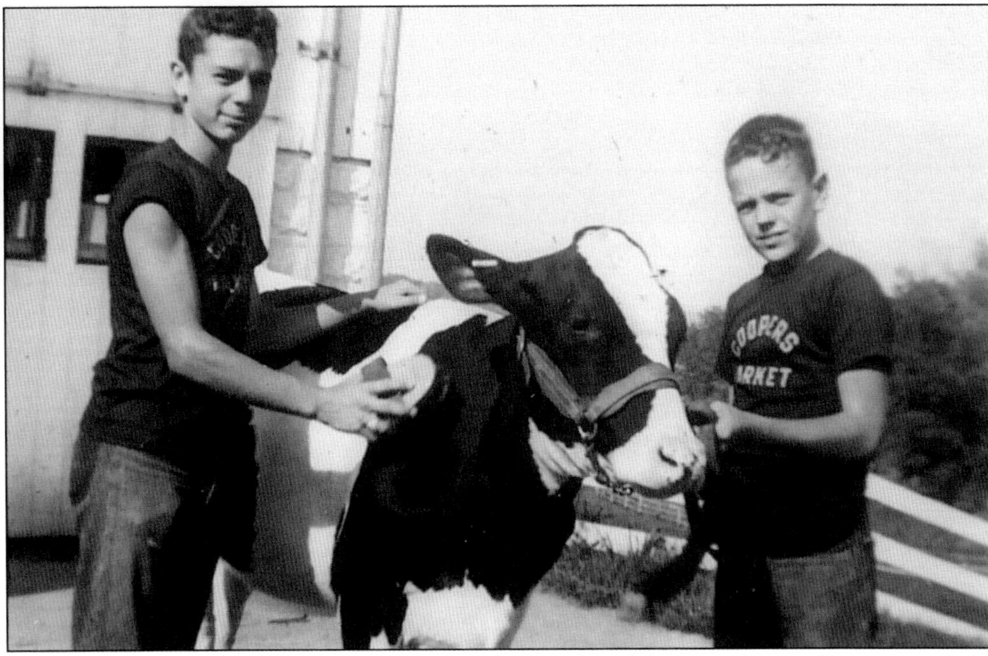

Four-H Club members completed projects during the club year. Originally many of the projects were directed to rural areas. Farm boys often raised a cow, as in the above picture of the Florence boys, *c.* 1948, and competed for ribbons at the county fair. Girls learned to cook and sew. Today's projects are more diverse and include such topics as "Making Your Money Make Sense," "Rockets Away," and "Teens Take the Lead." (Courtesy of the West Virginia Extension Service.)

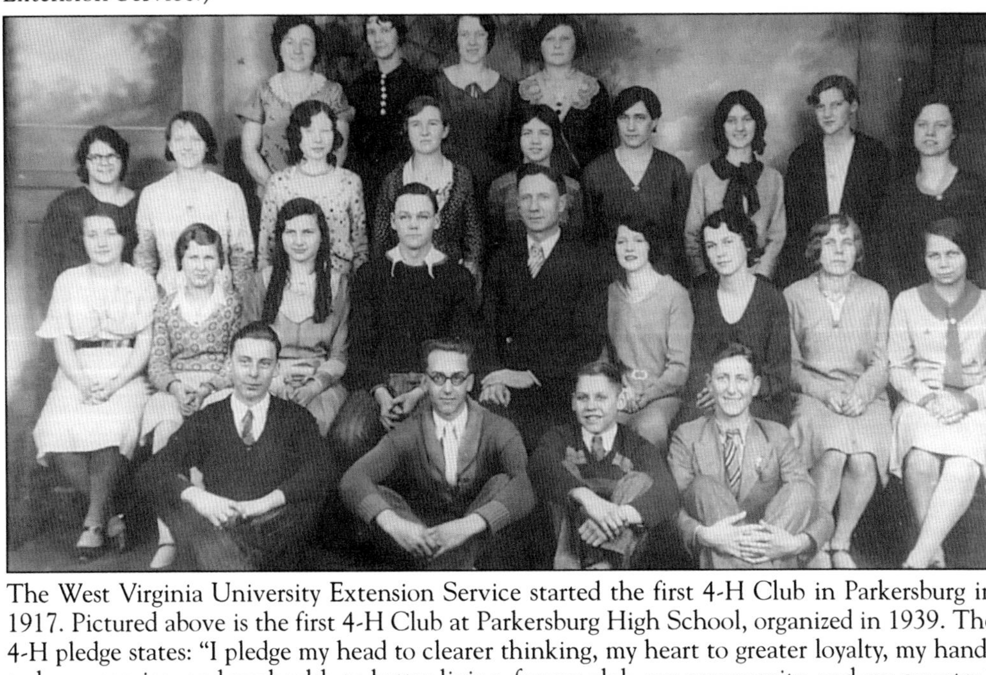

The West Virginia University Extension Service started the first 4-H Club in Parkersburg in 1917. Pictured above is the first 4-H Club at Parkersburg High School, organized in 1939. The 4-H pledge states: "I pledge my head to clearer thinking, my heart to greater loyalty, my hands to larger service, and my health to better living, for my club, my community, and my country." (Courtesy of the West Virginia Extension Service.)

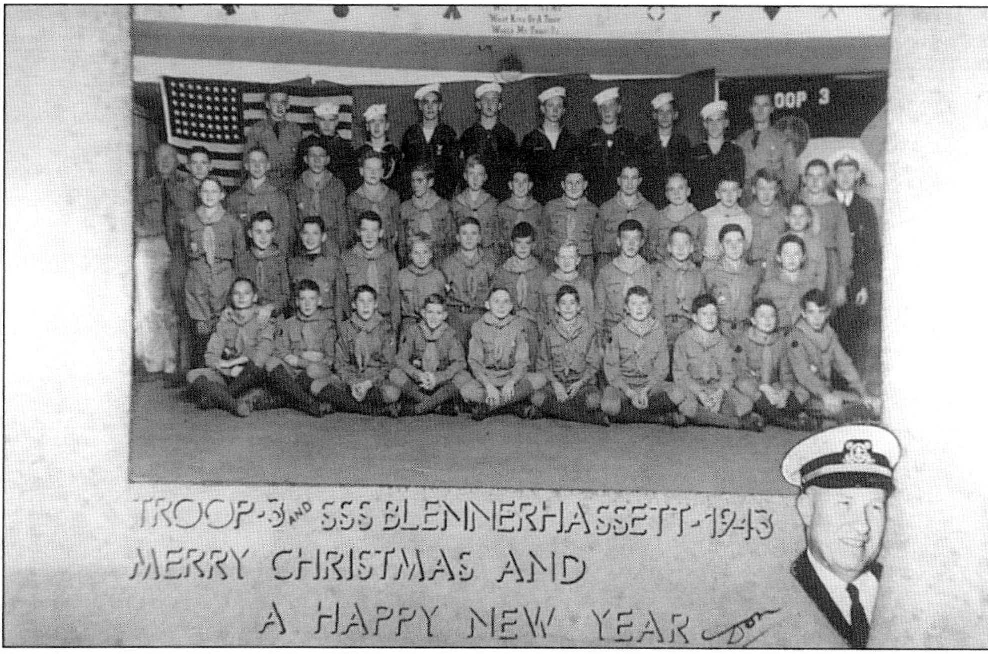

Boy Scout Troop Three is the oldest scout troop with continuous service in Parkersburg. Don "Skipper" Lowe started the troop in 1917 and was Scoutmaster until 1975 when, on the first day of camp, he had a stroke and died at camp. His last request was that camp proceed as scheduled, which it did. Each year Scoutmaster Lowe made a Christmas card using a group photo of Troop Three. (Courtesy of Boy Scout Troop Three.)

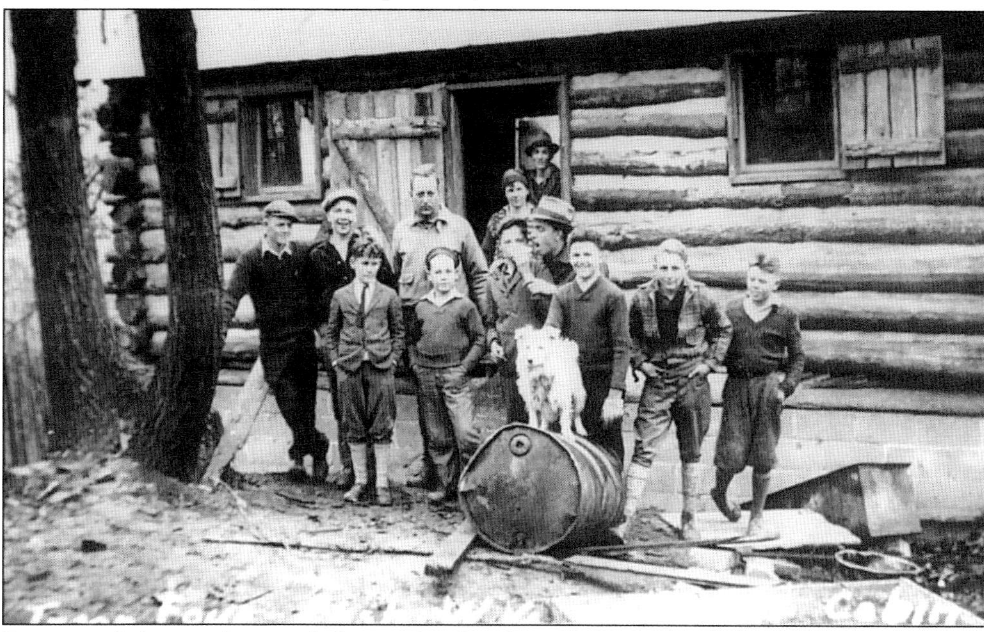

Because of the condition of the roads, the distance to Camp Kootaga, and the lack of automobiles in the 1920s, several Wood County scout troops built cabins just outside the city limits to use as a base for scouting activities. The unidentified troop pictured above stands in front of their cabin. (Courtesy of Boy Scout Troop Three.)

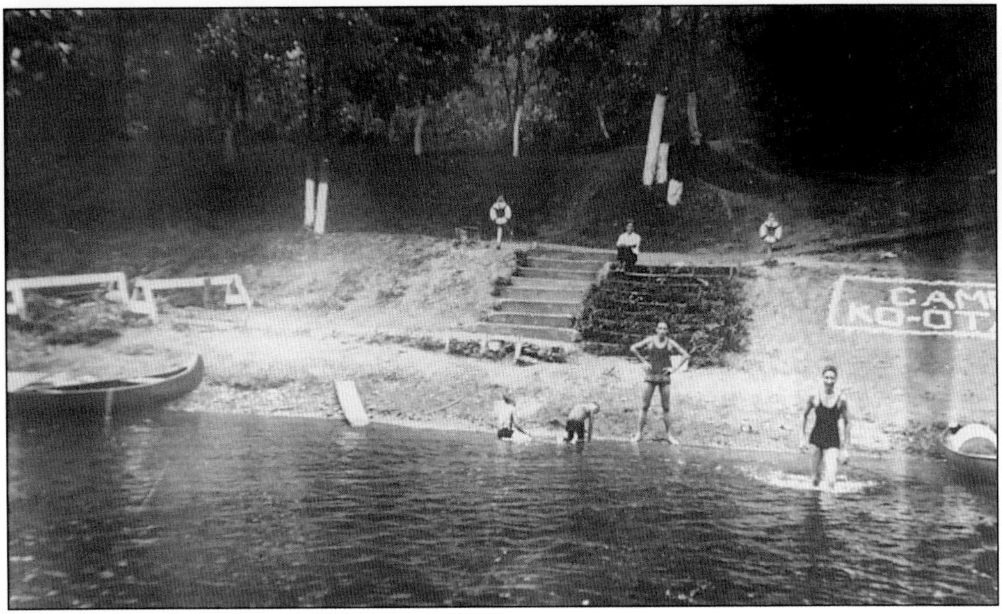

Swim trunk styles have changed since August of 1930 when this group of scouts cooled off with an afternoon swim in the Hughes River at Camp Kootaga. "Kootaga" is an American Indian word meaning "good friend." The name was given to the Wood County Boy Scout Council and to the camp in honor of Monroe Jackson Rathbone, a "good friend" and supporter of the early scout movement in Wood County. (Courtesy of Boy Scout Troop Three.)

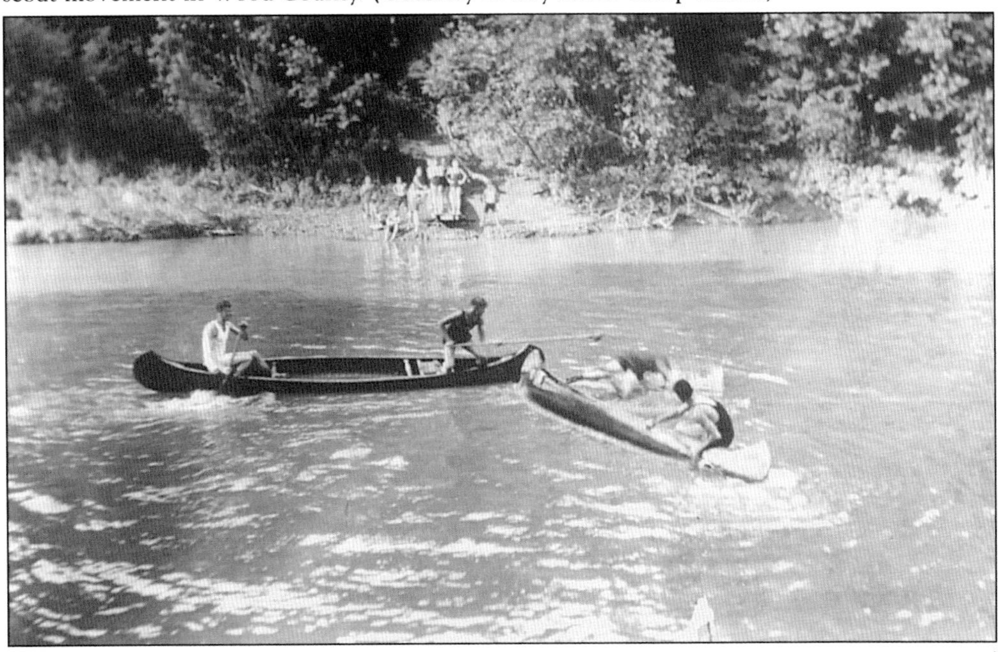

In 1927 knocking a fellow scout out of his canoe with an oar was called "jousting." Teams competed each year at Camp Kootaga to see who could remain in the canoe the longest. The scout with the lance in the canoe to the left is Smith D. Turner, who became a senior vice-president of Standard Oil. Turner donated to Troop 3 land for camping that is now called "Smitty's Camp". (Courtesy of Boy Scout Troop Three.)

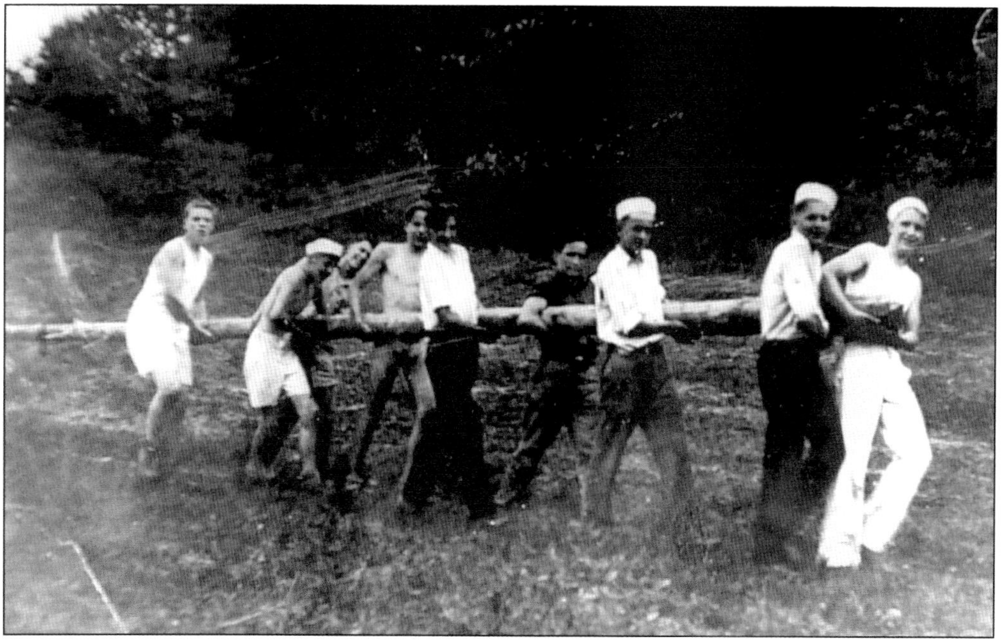

One of the first responsibilities at Troop Three camp was bringing in the flagpole. A team of scouts went into the woods searching for a suitable tree—preferably a standing dead tree—to cut down and carry back to camp. After the United States and scout troop flags were hoisted, camp was officially underway. Pictured above is a group of sea scouts at Camp Kootaga in the 1930s. (Courtesy of Boy Scout Troop 3.)

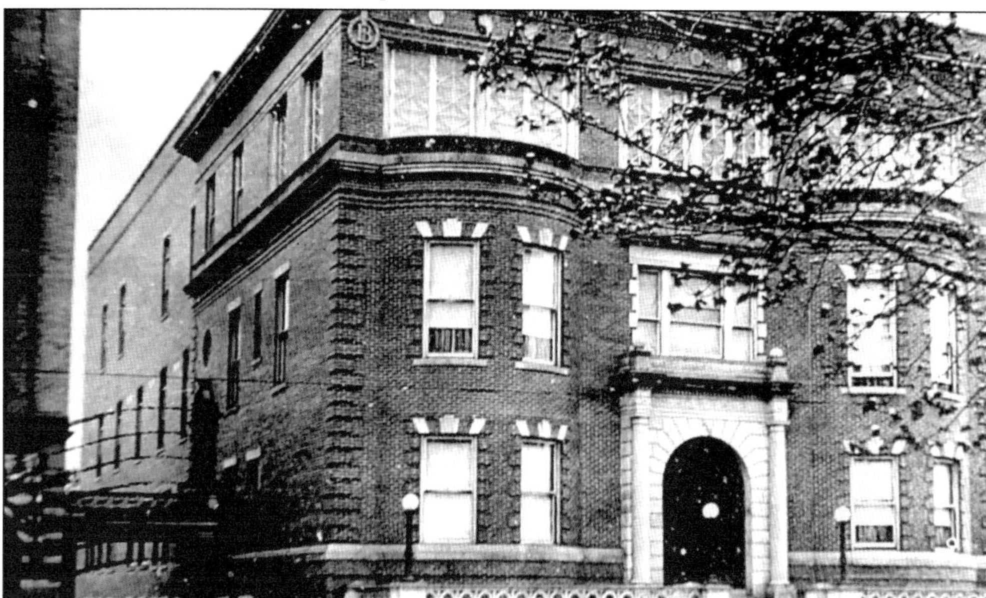

The Benevolent and Protective Order of Elks was organized in 1891. In 1904 the Parkersburg Elks dedicated their lodge, number 198, at 515 Juliana Street. Still in use today, the Elks Lodge is on the National Register of Historic Sites. A civic-minded and patriotic organization, the Elks supported many community activities as well as providing dancing and fine dining for their members. (Collection of B. Leavengood.)

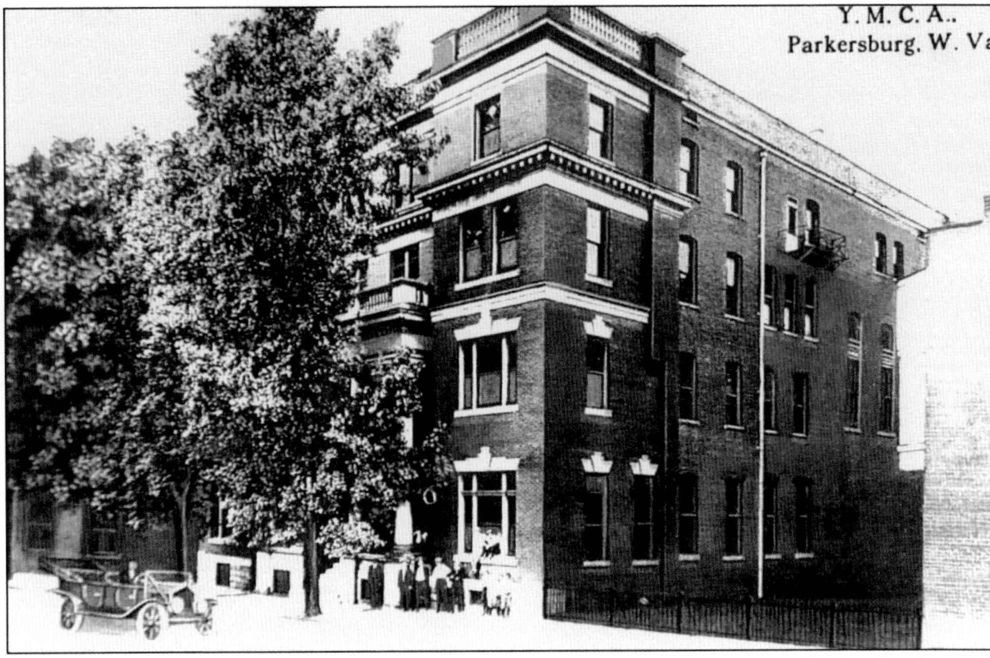

Chartered in 1902, the Young Men's Christian Association (YMCA) launched a fund-raising campaign to build permanent headquarters. Dedicated on October 5, 1905, and completed in 1907, the four-story YMCA building on Eighth Street between Juliana and Market Streets cost $200,000 to build. The basement had a gymnasium with bathrooms, a bowling alley, swimming pool, showers, and lockers. Shortly after opening, the YMCA had 1,000 members. (Collection of B. Leavengood.)

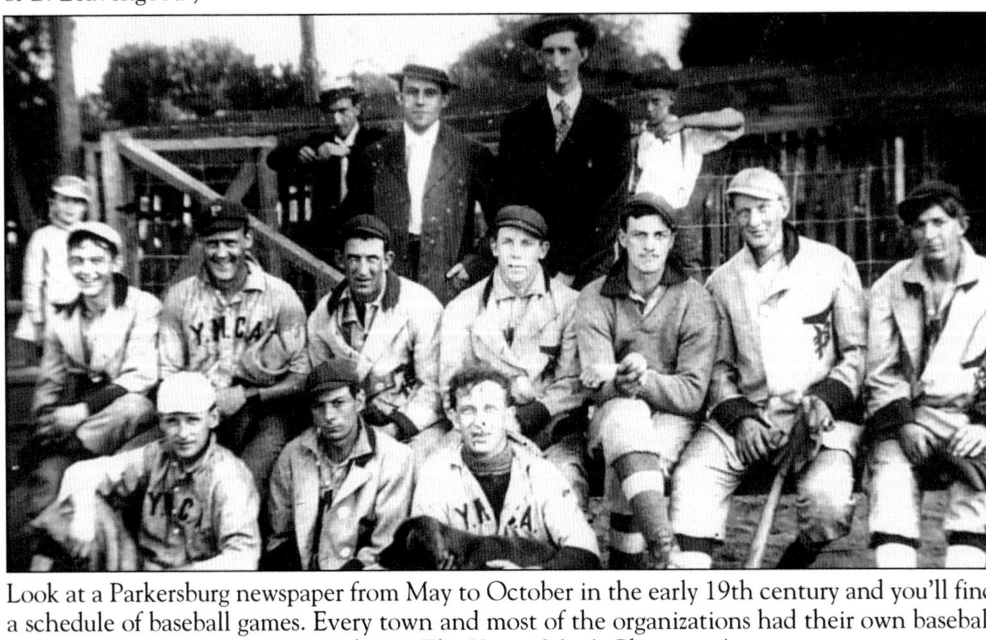

Look at a Parkersburg newspaper from May to October in the early 19th century and you'll find a schedule of baseball games. Every town and most of the organizations had their own baseball team and field. Competition was fierce. The Young Men's Christian Association team, pictured above, played at the YMCA park at 1341 Juliana Street, site of the Calvary Temple Evangelistic Church (formerly the First Presbyterian Church). (Courtesy of R.E. Enoch.)

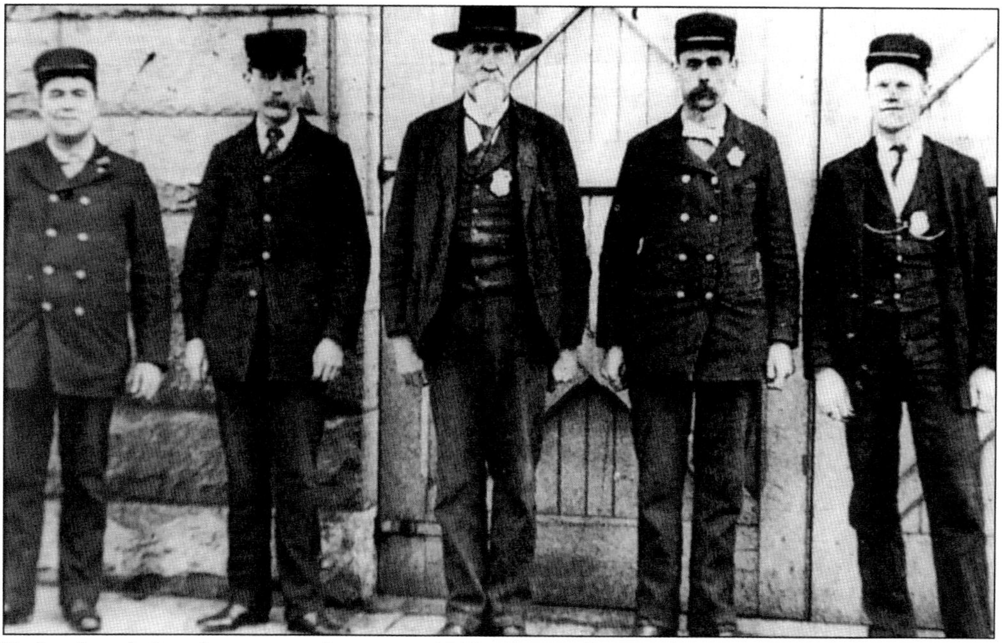

Parkersburg's fire department began in 1887 when a fire warden was appointed to examine the "stovepipes, fireplaces, flues, and chimneys in each and every house within the limits of the city." It was not until 1897 that a paid fire department was established. Pictured above are the original paid firemen, identified, from left to right, as Bill Hydenruch, Walter Pilcher, Capt. John Montgomery, Ed Chaddock, and Charles Goosman. (Courtesy of the Parkersburg Fire Department.)

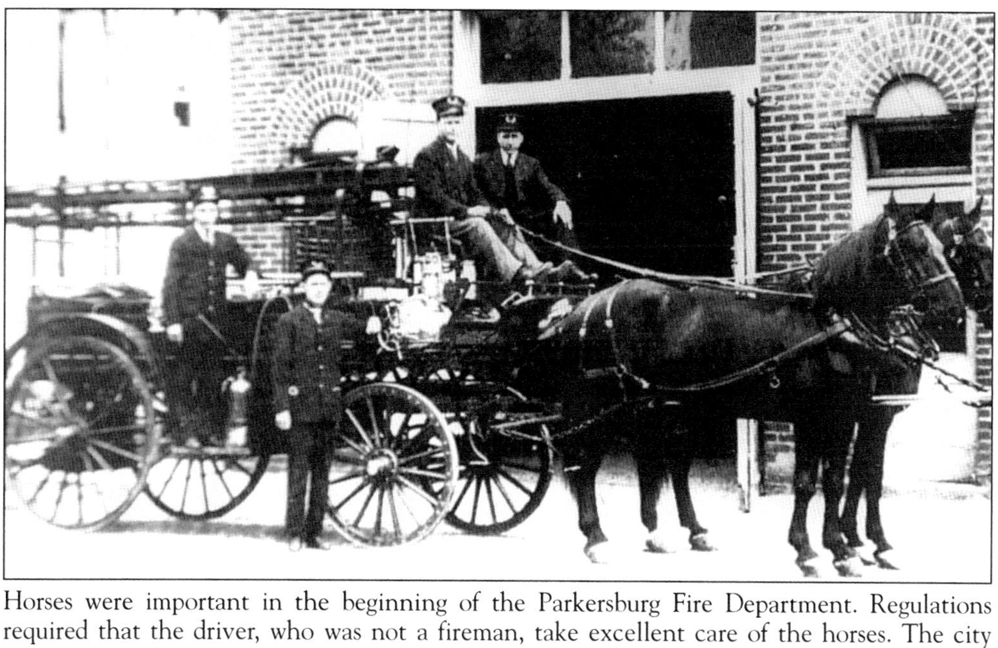

Horses were important in the beginning of the Parkersburg Fire Department. Regulations required that the driver, who was not a fireman, take excellent care of the horses. The city ordinance read, "On arriving at a fire in cold or wet weather, the horses must be blanketed, and shall also, if practicable, be housed in the nearest company's quarters." (Courtesy of the Parkersburg Fire Department.)

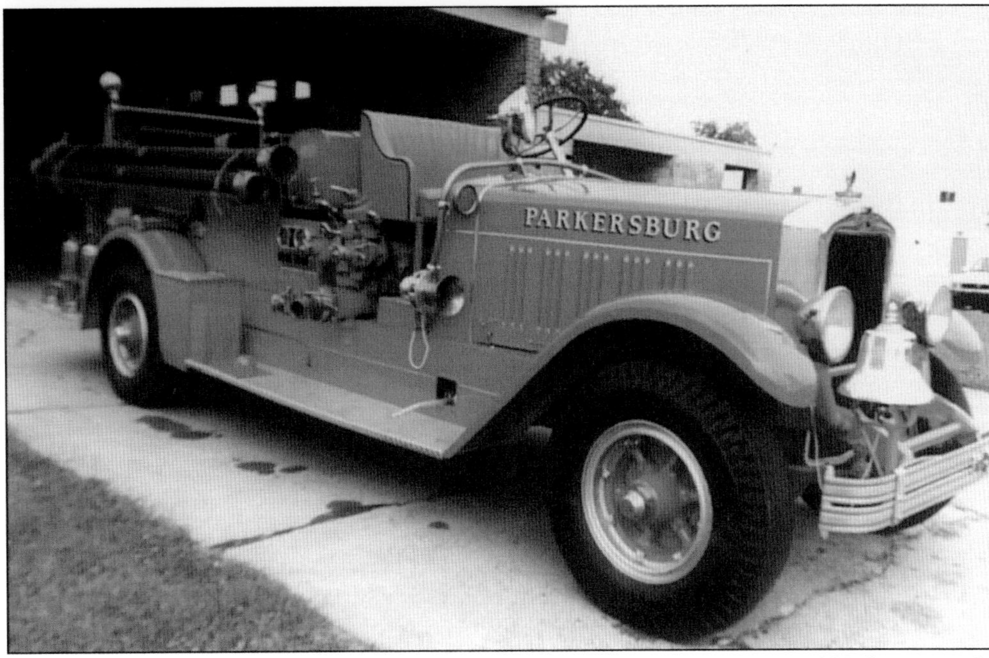

This antique fire engine belongs to the Parkersburg Fire Department. It is a 1932 American La France. The truck has a V-12HP engine, which was one of the most important developments for American La France because of its power and durability. The 1932 model also had a rear end chain drive. The truck is stored at Station Six and is used in parades. (Courtesy of the Parkersburg Fire Department, Station Six.)

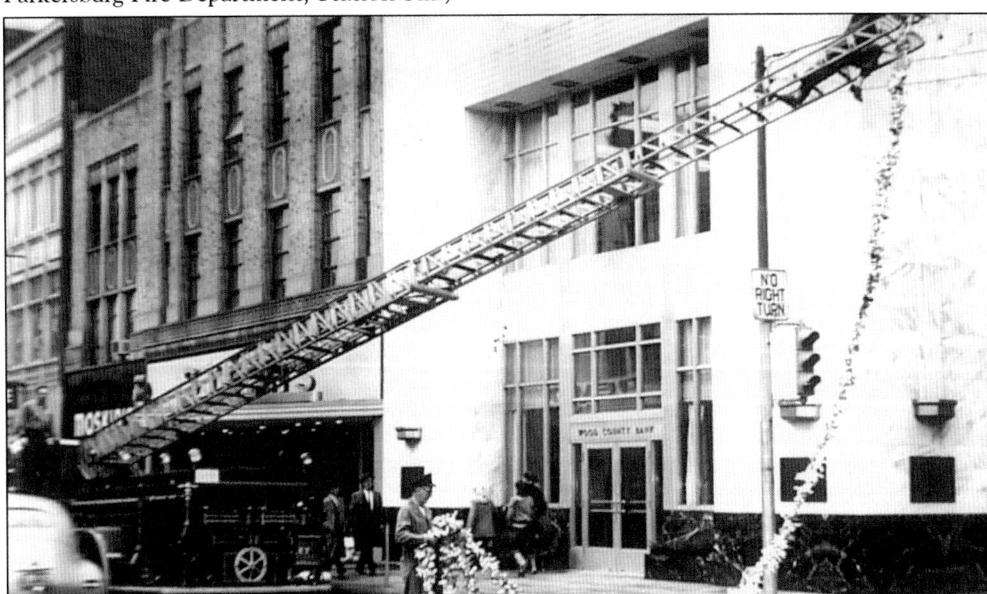

Firemen do more for their community than fight fires. They are called upon every year to use their long ladders to put up Christmas decorations. Pictured above are members of the Parkersburg Fire Department decorating Market Street in the early 1940s. (Courtesy of the Parkersburg Fire Department.)

Five

Earning A Buck

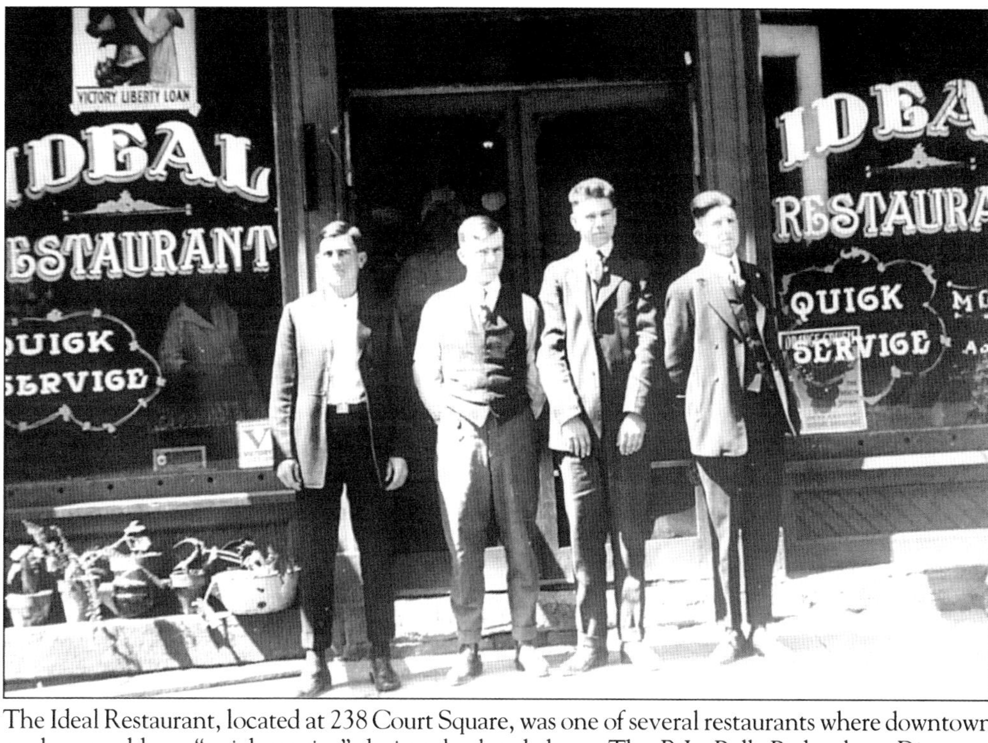

The Ideal Restaurant, located at 238 Court Square, was one of several restaurants where downtown workers could get "quick service" during the lunch hour. The R.L. Polk Parkersburg Directory shows that the restaurant was open in 1915 and 1916. The ad for Liberty Bonds indicated that the Ideal Restaurant remained open through World War I. (Courtesy of Mike Naylor.)

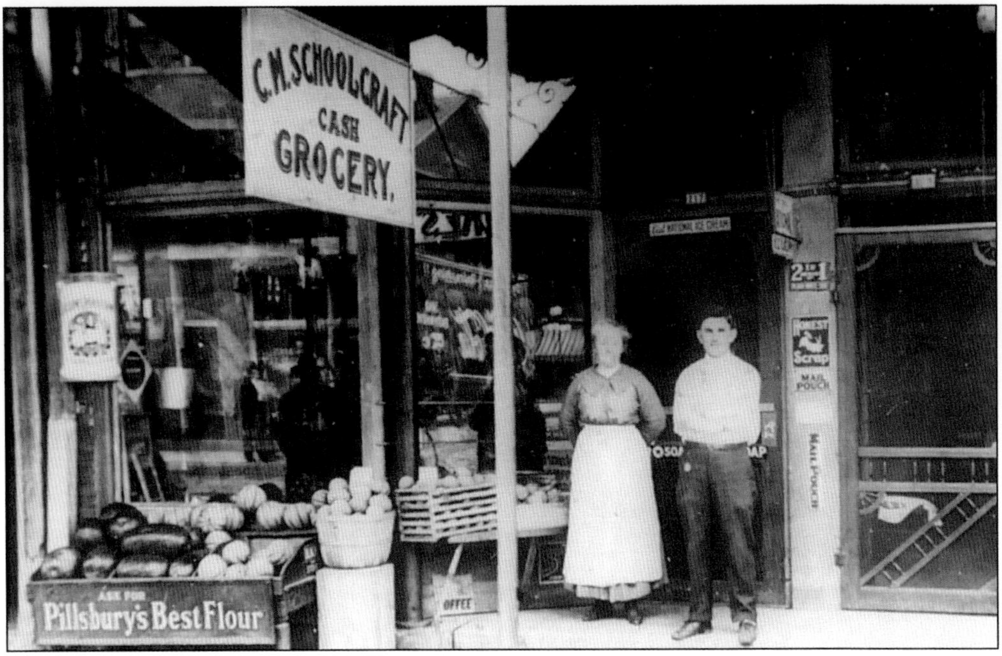

The Schoolcraft Grocery, located at Second and Juliana Streets where the Bureau of Public Debt is today, was one of several small grocery stores in Parkersburg. Clarence Milton Schoolcraft owned the store in the 1920s. Small groceries may not have had the variety of products that supermarkets do today, but they offered personal service. (Courtesy of the family of Ruth Murphy Schoolcraft.)

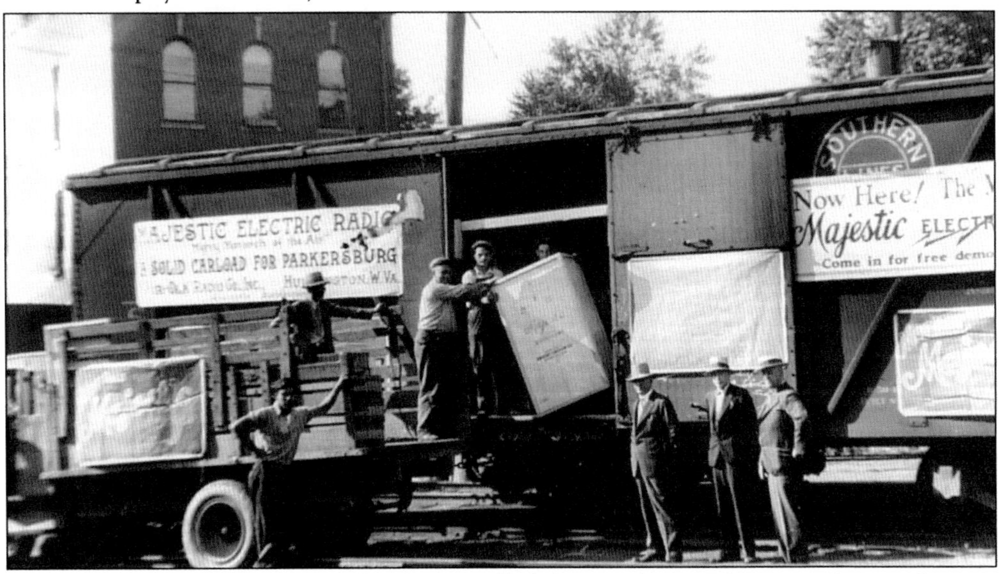

The Majestic Radio comes to Parkersburg! Called the "tombstone" because of its tombstone-like shape, the Majestic was first made by the Grigsby-Grunow Company in Chicago, and later by the Majestic Radio and Television Corporation. During the Depression many families sat around their Majestic radio listening to Jack Benny go down into his vault to check on his money or the saga of Helen Trent, a woman looking for love over the age of 35. (Courtesy of Blennerhassett Island Historical State Park.)

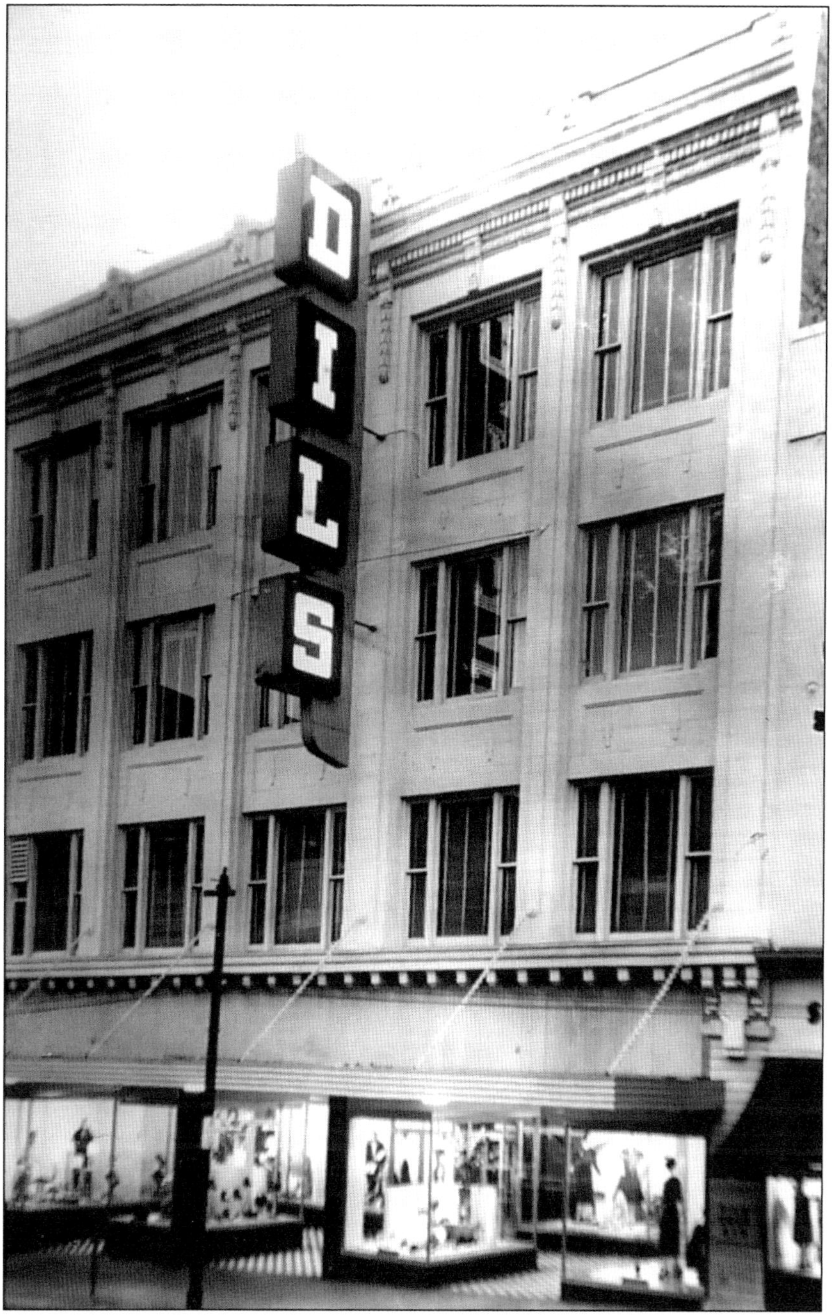

The Dils sign on Market Street welcomed shoppers for 88 years. The Dils tradition of excellence began in 1890 when Henry H. Dils III and Jacob McKinney opened a dry goods store on the east side of Market Street, just above Fourth. The store prospered until Henry H. Dils's untimely death due to typhoid fever in 1895. Five years later, Henry's wife Sarah and her two sons, Henry III and Sam, opened a store in the 400 block of Market Street. The store was an immediate success. In 1905, needing room to expand, Henry and Sam purchased the three-story Beehive Store at 521-523 Market Street. Dils Brothers and Company Department Store did business at this location until it closed on January 16, 1988. (Courtesy of Edwin L.D. Dils.)

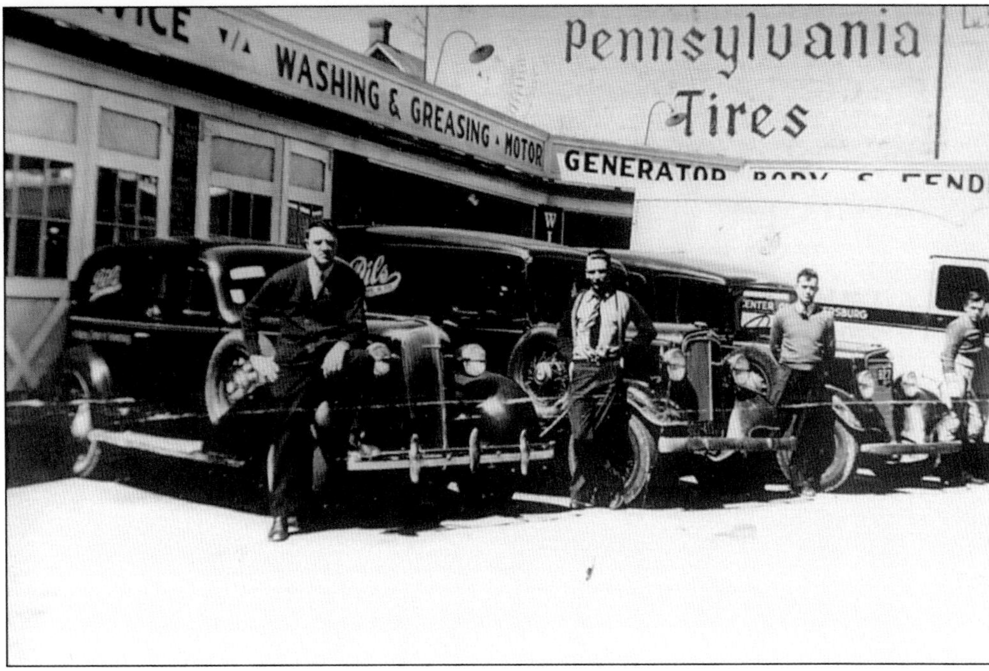

Dils Brothers and Company offered free delivery of all purchases in a ten-county area. Pictured above is their fleet of delivery vehicles in the mid-1930s. (Courtesy of Edwin L.D. Dils.)

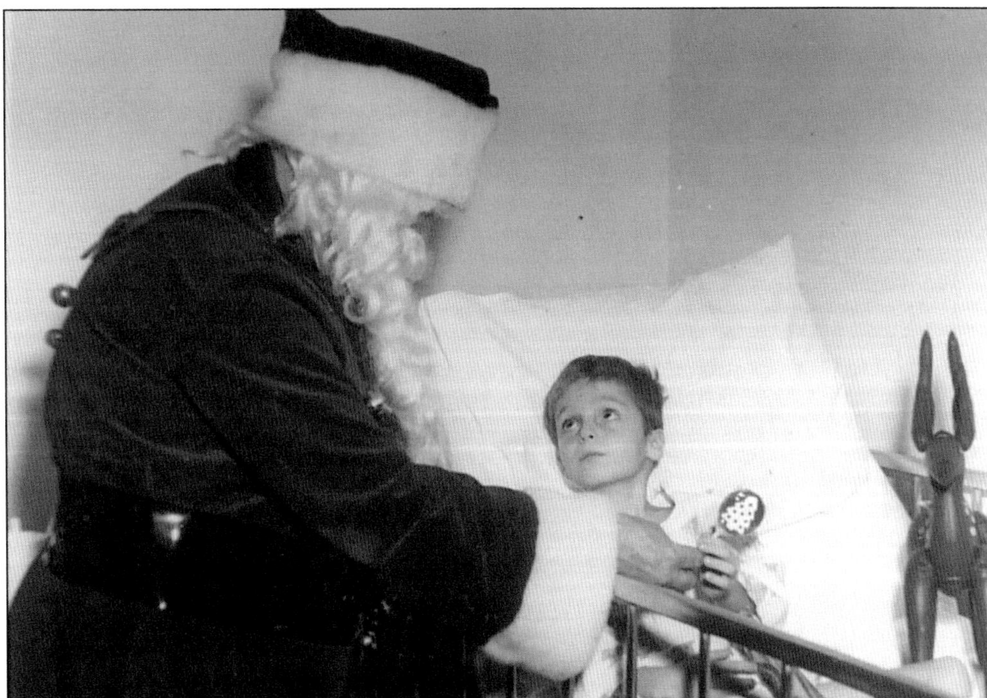
Every year Dils Brothers and Company helped Santa deliver gifts to every child in local hospitals during the Christmas season. Judging from the look on this young man's face, Santa's visit was much appreciated. (Courtesy of Edwin L.D. Dils.)

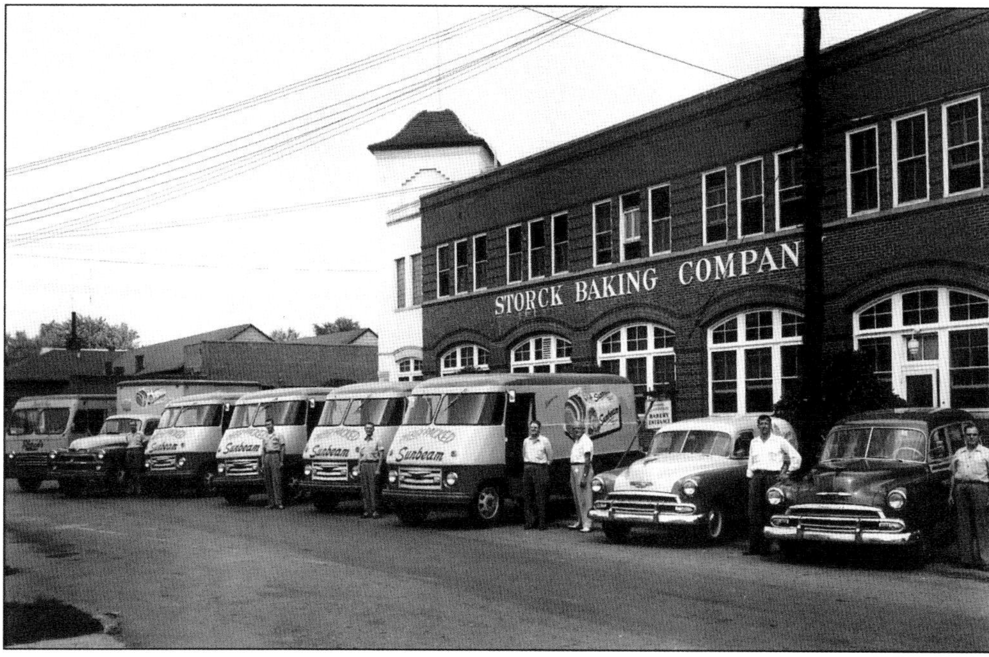

Louis Storck started the Storck Bakery in 1919 at Nineteenth and Latrobe Streets. Pictured above is Storck's delivery fleet during the 1940s. For many years Storks was Parkersburg's leading bakery until it closed in 1975. The empty building still stands. (Courtesy of Paul A. Borrelli, Artcraft Studio.)

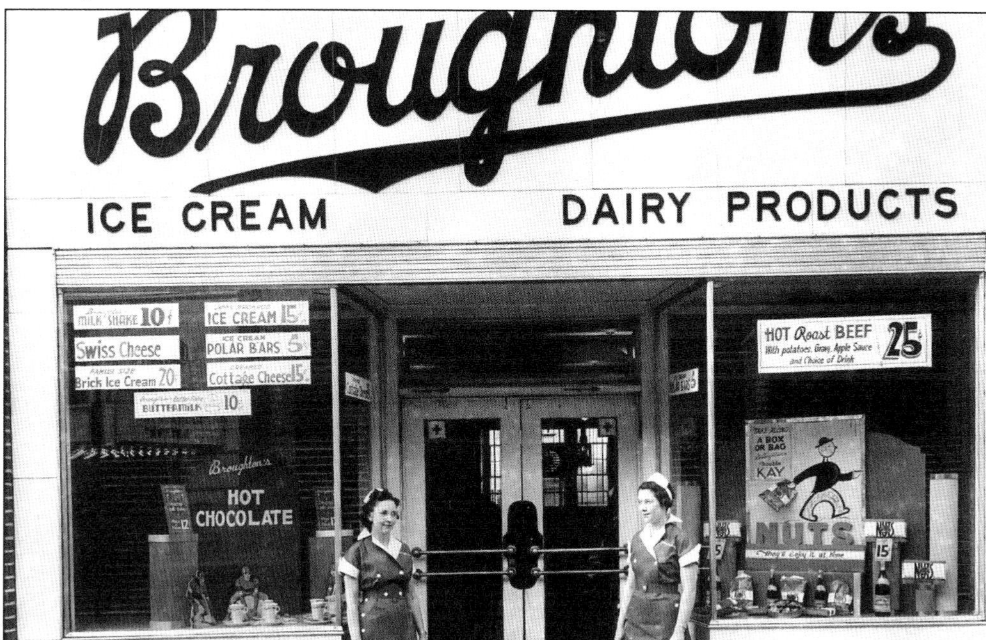

Although Broughton's dairy and ice cream manufacturing facilities were in Marietta, Broughton's was very much a part of the Parkersburg scene. This store, located at 717 Market Street next door to Montgomery Ward, was a favorite stopping place for downtown workers and shoppers in the 1930s and 1940s. (Courtesy of Paul A. Borrelli, Artcraft Studio.)

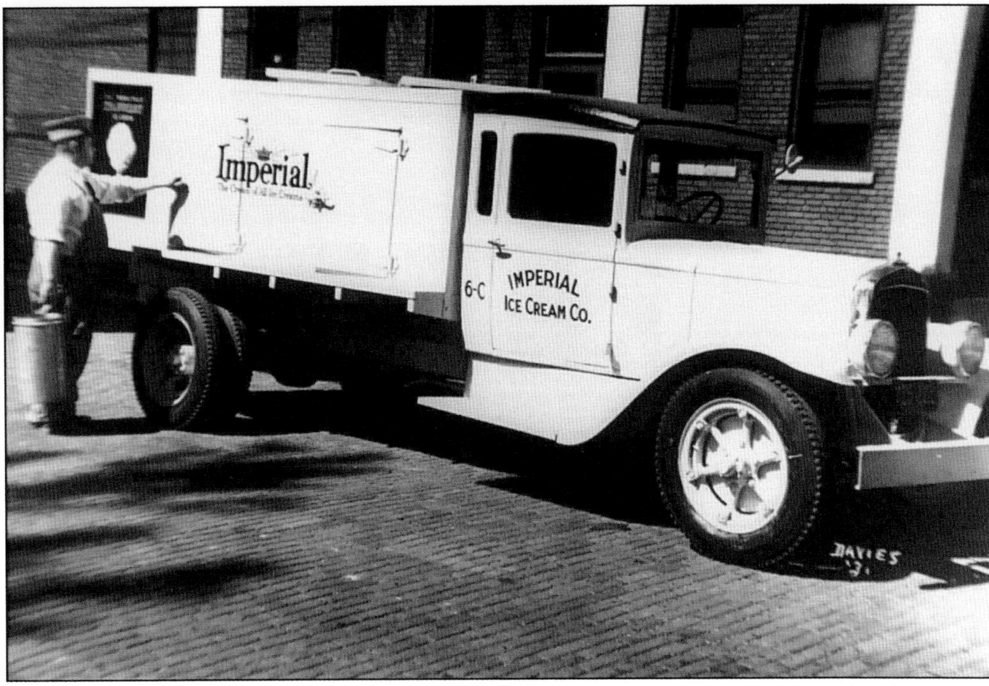

On March 18, 1920, the Imperial Ice Cream Company announced that its Parkersburg plant was nearing completion. The company had plants in Fairmont, Wheeling, Grafton, and Clarksburg. By mid-April the Imperial Ice Cream Company claimed in local newspaper ads, "Imperial—the cream of all ice cream will be good tonight, tomorrow, and every night." The ice cream was delivered in the white truck pictured above, which was owned by Mullen Motors. (Courtesy of Mullen Motors.)

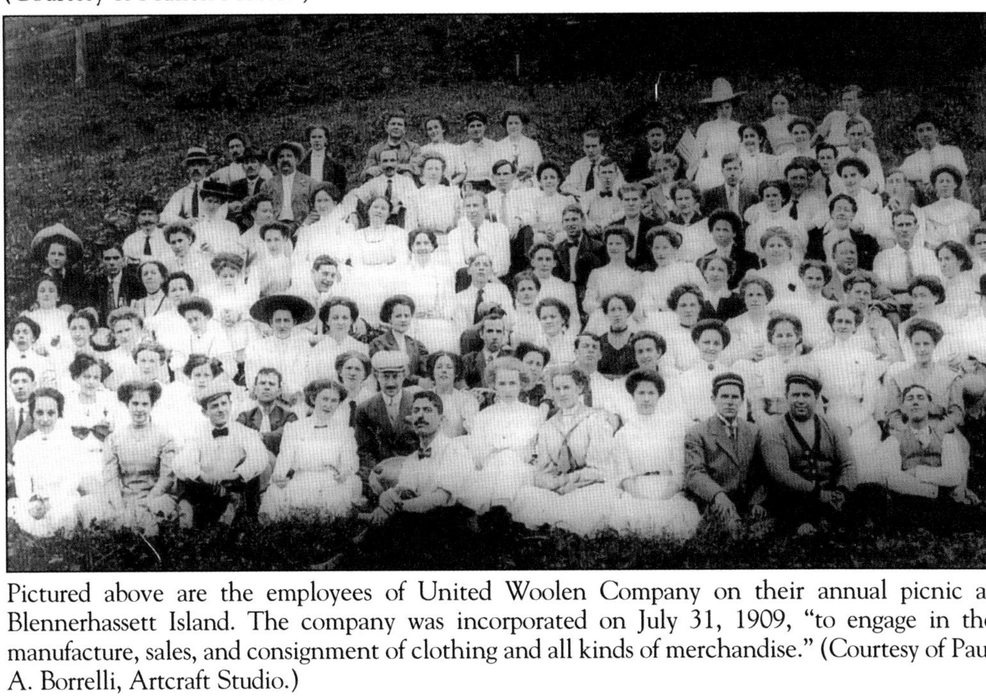

Pictured above are the employees of United Woolen Company on their annual picnic at Blennerhassett Island. The company was incorporated on July 31, 1909, "to engage in the manufacture, sales, and consignment of clothing and all kinds of merchandise." (Courtesy of Paul A. Borrelli, Artcraft Studio.)

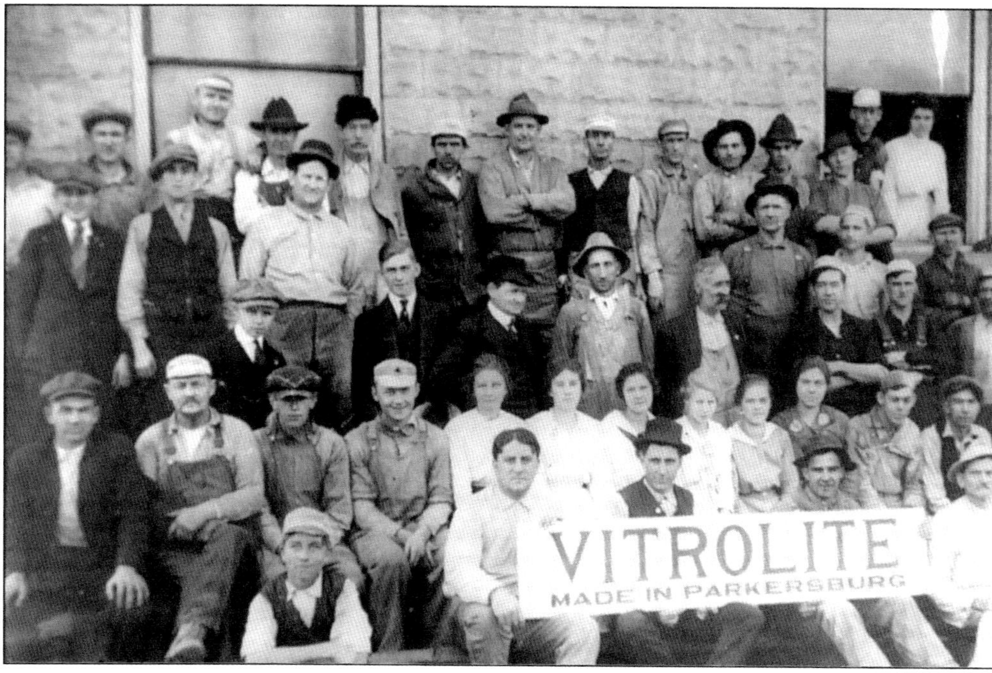

Meyercord-Carter Company, later known as the Vitrolite Company, began operation in Vienna in 1908. The company manufactured an opaque structural glass, an inexpensive substitute for marble called Vitrolite, that was used for storefronts, bathroom and kitchen walls, and table tops. In 1950 the plant, then owned by Libbey-Owens Ford Glass Company, produced fiberglass yarns and insulation. The plant operates today as part of the Johns-Manville Corporation. (Courtesy of R.E. Enoch.)

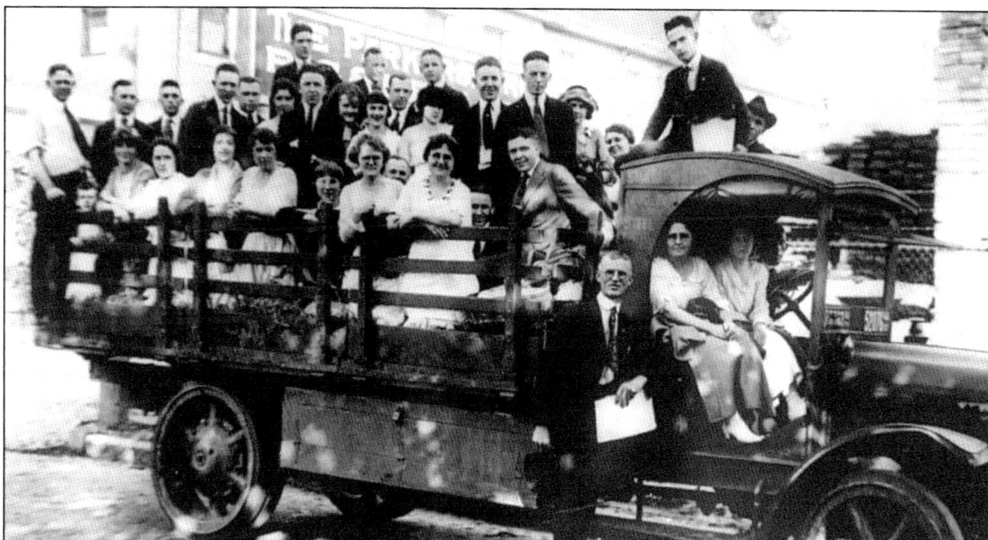

To supply the needs of the oil and gas companies, John M. Crawford, an Irish immigrant, started the Parkersburg Rig and Reel Company in 1897 in a frame building covered with sheet iron at the corner of Second and Green Streets. The company manufactured drilling rigs, machinery, and other equipment. During World War II Rig and Reel devoted all its facilities and manpower to producing war materials. (Courtesy of R.E. Enoch.)

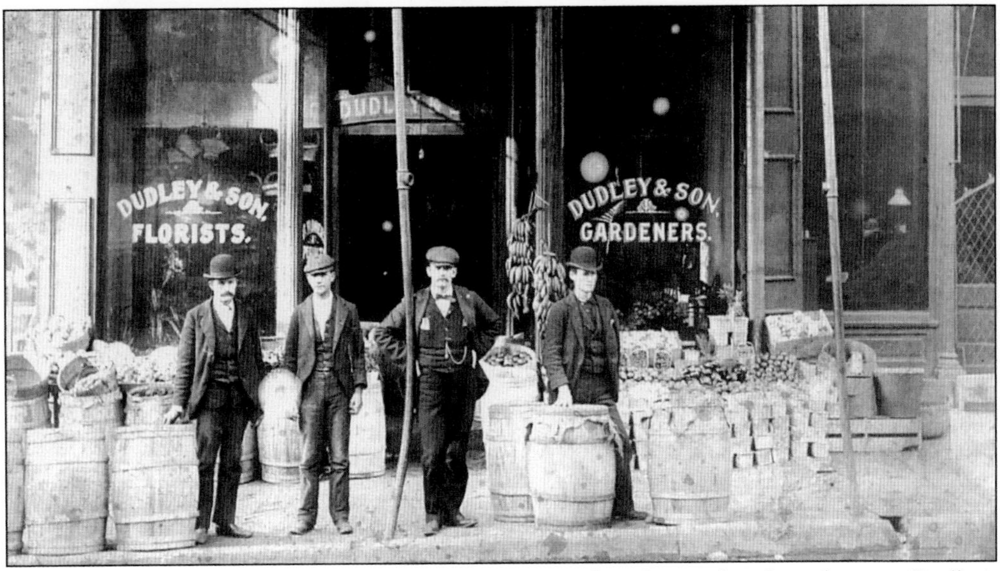

In 1863, John Dudley opened a produce store on Market Street that later became Dudley's Florists. Today, it is Wood County's oldest continuously operating retail business. Dudley Avenue in front of Parkersburg High School was named after the large Dudley's store and greenhouses that were located just north of the high school. (Courtesy of West Virginia State Archives.)

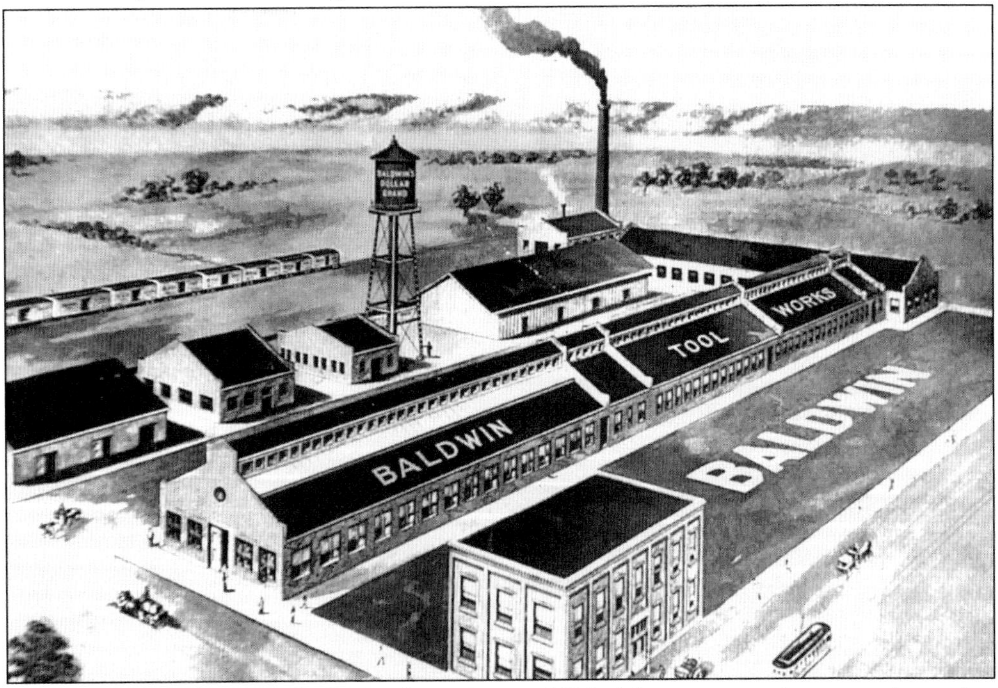

Baldwin Tool Works opened a Parkersburg plant in 1910. After a merger, the name changed to Ames Baldwin Wyoming Tool Works and, by 1952, to the O. Ames Company. To Parkersburg, however, it quickly became known as the Shovel Plant. Bernard P. McDonough, who worked at the plant as a teenager, purchased the plant in 1955. For many years, the company manufactured most of the shovels sold in America. O. Ames merged with the True Temper Company in July 2001 and closed one of the Parkersburg plants. (Collection of B. Leavengood.)

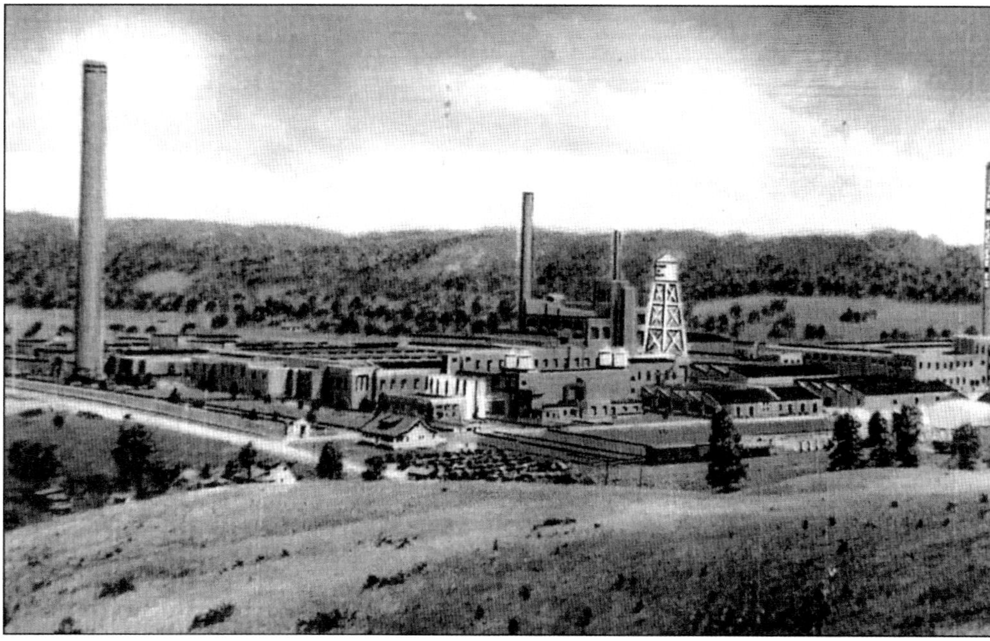

In June of 1925 the American Viscose Company announced that it would build a major plant employing 4,000 people south of the Little Kanawha River to manufacture a synthetic fiber called rayon. The plant, owned by a British firm, opened in 1927. By 1935, at the depth of the Great Depression, the Viscose employed 4,300 people. During World War II, its workforce numbered 5,500. The company closed in 1974. Former employees still gather at the Parkersburg City Park for an annual picnic. (Collection of B. Leavengood.)

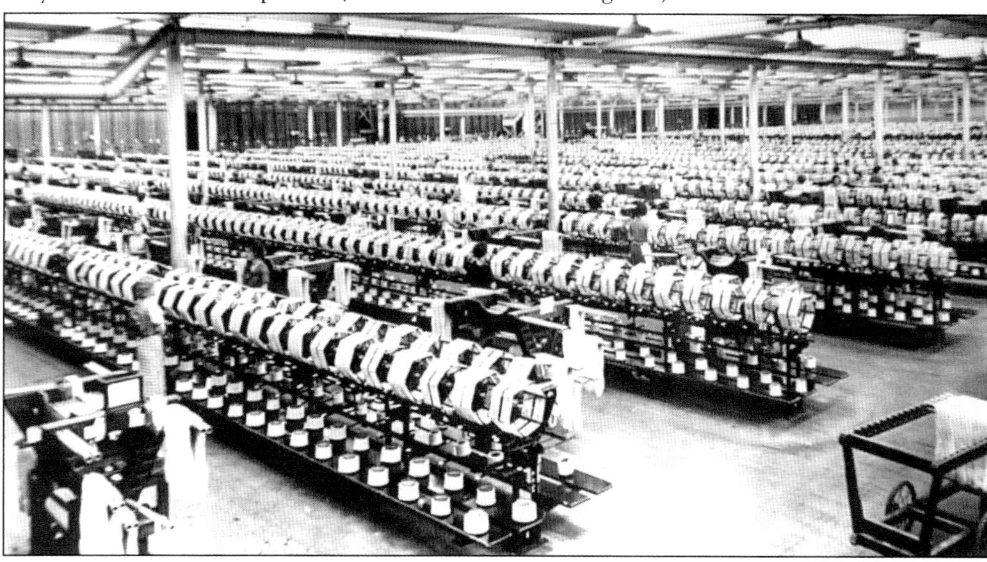

The spinning department of the Viscose Company spun the components of rayon into cakes—actually round off-white cakes with a hole in the center. The process used acids, which ate holes in the worker's clothing. After the spinning process, the cakes were sent to the reeling department where workers spun the cakes into skeins of rayon fiber. Next came the spooling department where the rayon fiber was wound onto spools. From there, the fiber was spun onto large cones and shipped all over the world. (Courtesy of R.E. Enoch.)

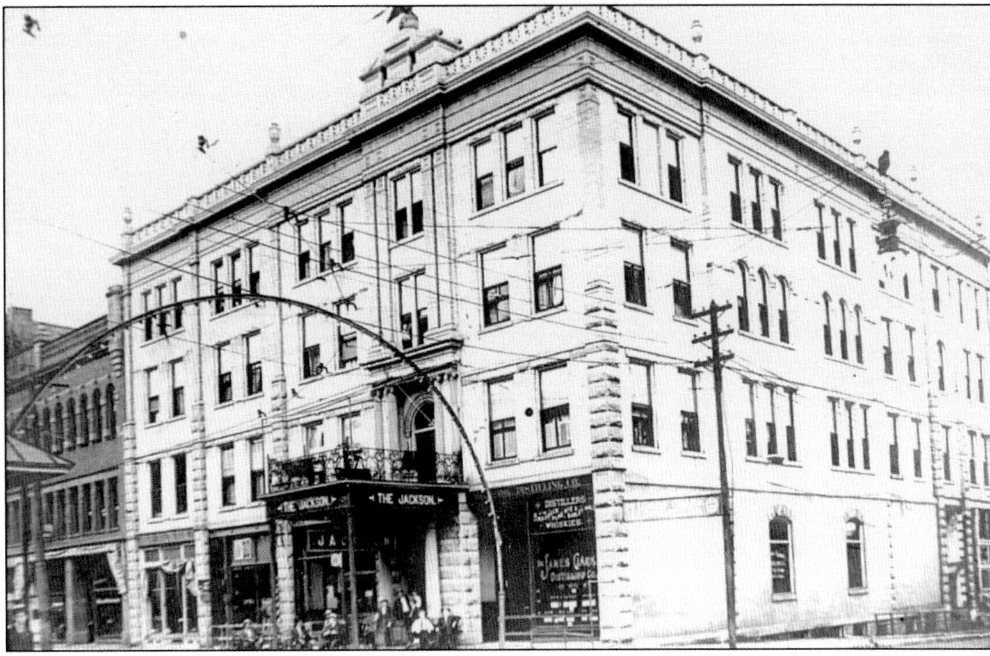

One of the better hotels in Parkersburg in the early 1900s was the Jackson Hotel at Third and Market Streets. The hotel served downtown until it was destroyed by fire c. 1920. (Collection of B. Leavengood.)

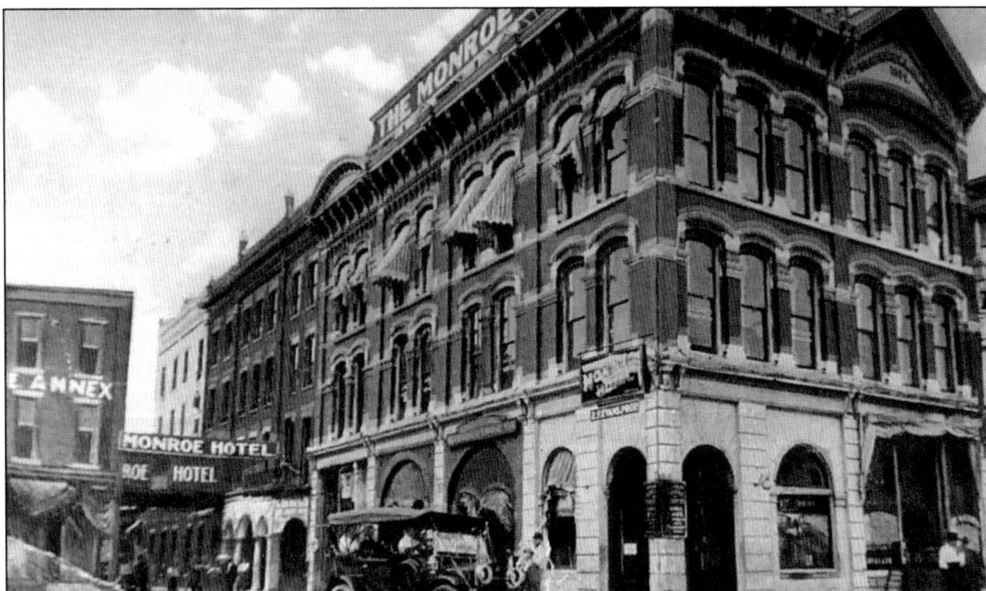

The Monroe Hotel, owned by Zeb F. Evans, stood in Court Square where the entrance to the Bureau of Public Debt is today. Rooms cost from $1 to $2 daily, depending on whether or not the room had a bath. In its earlier days the Monroe was considered one of Parkersburg's finest hotels. However, time did not enhance its reputation and by the 1950s the Monroe was at the center of the redlight district. The hotel was demolished by the Urban Renewal projects of the 1960s. (Collection of B. Leavengood.)

William C. Chancellor built the Chancellor Hotel on the corner of Seventh and Market in 1897. The hotel had 220 rooms, 136 with baths. Rates in the early 1900s ranged from $1.50 to $2 per day without a bath and from $2.50 a day with a bath. Chancellor, one of Parkersburg's foremost entrepreneurs, also built the Blennerhassett Hotel, which still operates in downtown Parkersburg. Unfortunately, the Chancellor was demolished in 1977. (Collection of B. Leavengood.)

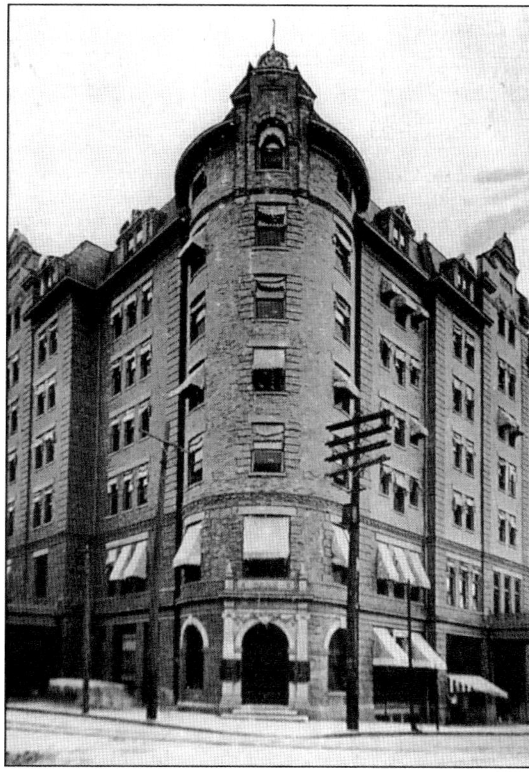

The January 2, 1893 *World's Fair Advocate* noted that the Blennerhassett Hotel was "the only first class hotel in Parkersburg." The hotel, built by William Chancellor in 1890, was, according to the *Advocate*, heated with steam, lighted by electricity, and had a good elevator. Today the Blennerhassett is Parkersburg's only remaining hotel. It is on the National Register of Historic Places. (Courtesy of West Virginia State Archives.)

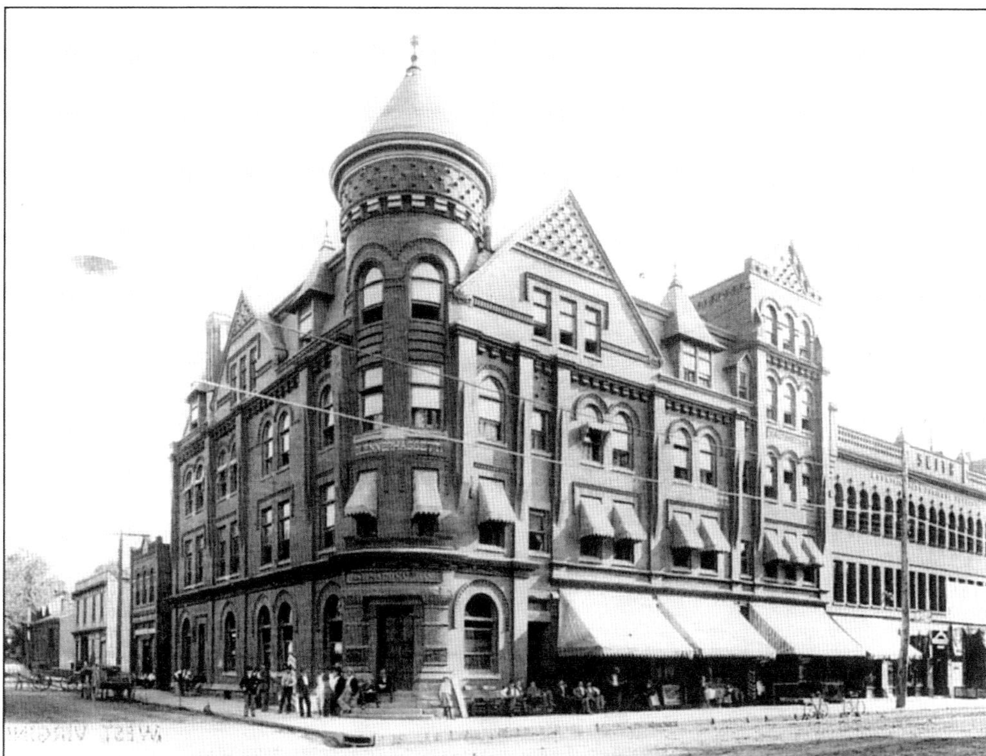

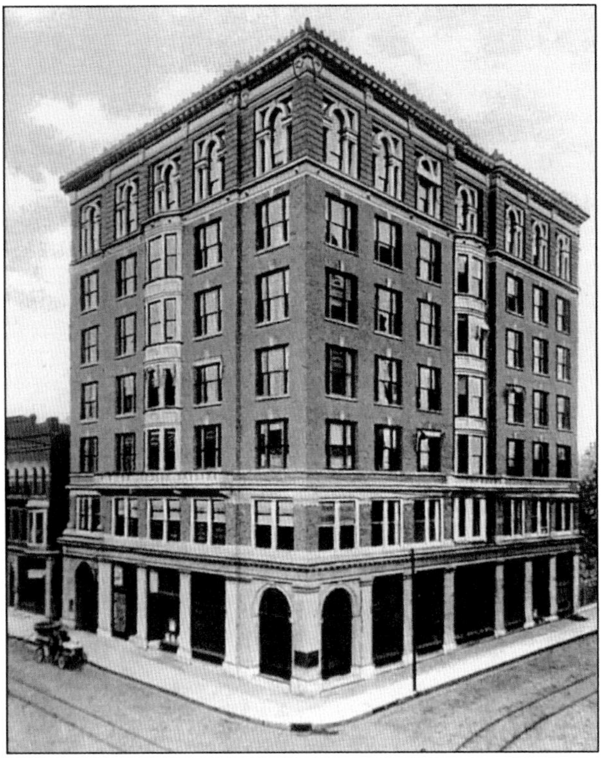

The Union Trust and Deposit Company was one of the leading financial institutions in Parkersburg. It was incorporated on April 22, 1903. On May l of that year the bank opened for business at 213 Fourth Street. On July 4, 1904 their offices were moved to the Union Trust Building on the corner of Market and Seventh Street. Johnson N. Camden was the first president of the bank. Today Mountain State Blue Cross-Blue Shield occupies the building. (Collection of B. Leavengood.)

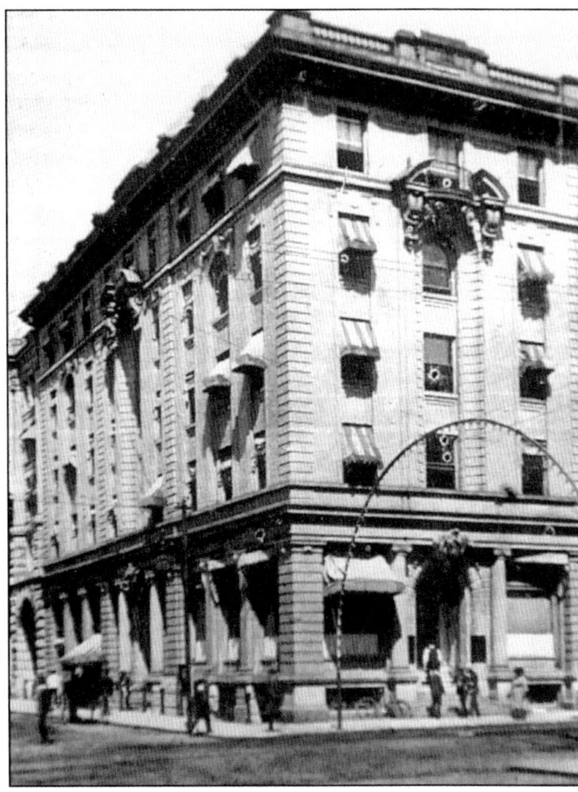

Citizen's Bank was incorporated on May 27, 1899. Charles Shattuck and J.M. Jackson Jr. were the major shareholders. The 1905 Parkersburg City Directory lists the Citizen's Bank at 225 Market Street as having $100,000 capital and a surplus of $185,000. Charles H. Shattuck was president of the bank. By 1907, the bank was Citizen's National Bank. The building, now vacant, still stands on the northwest corner of Market and Fourth Streets. Built in 1898, it is on the National Register of Historic Places. (Collection of B. Leavengood.)

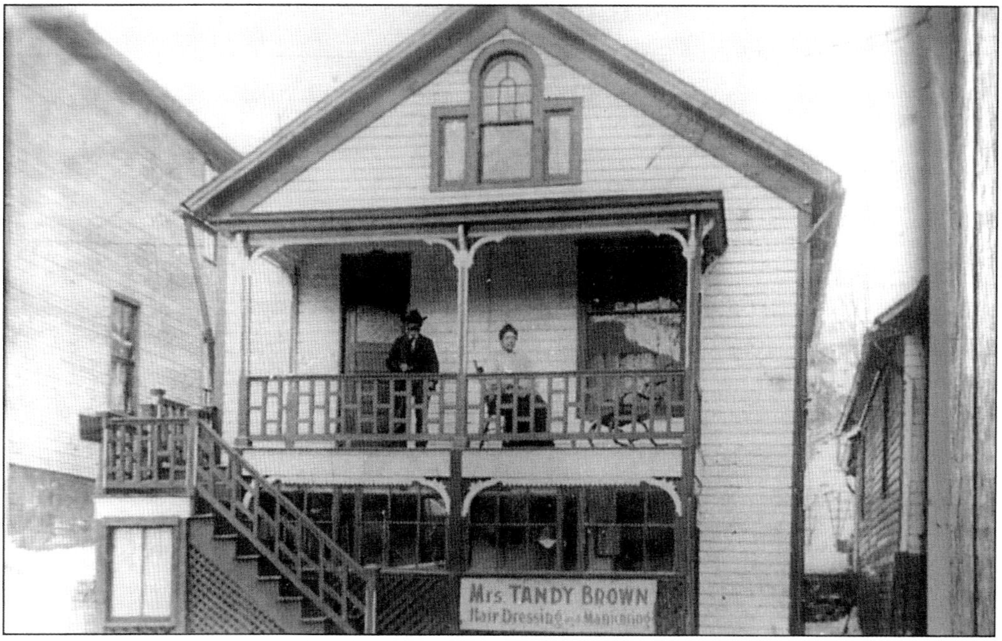

Mrs. Tandy Brown operated a beauty shop at 816 Clay Street in the early 1900s. Her advertisement in *A Souvenir of the City of Parkersburg*, published in 1907 by the William Barnes Directory Company, promised "Fashionable Hair Dressing, Manicuring, and Massage." In addition, Mrs. Brown did "all hair work made to order" and, if needed, "will call at residence." Mrs. Brown was well respected in Parkersburg as evidenced by the number of people who attended her funeral. (Courtesy of Sumnerite Museum, Rae Brown, curator.)

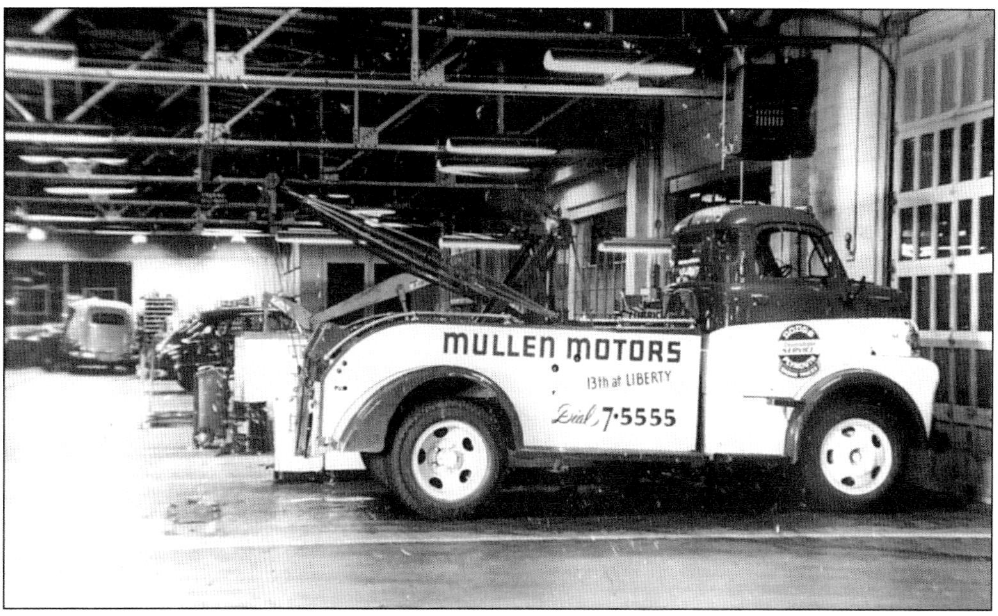

After Earl Oesterle's death in 1945, J. Vincent Mullen purchased the families interest in the firm. The company, now Mullen Motors, moved to their present quarters at Thirteenth and Liberty in 1948. Mullen Motors used this 1948 model tow truck in their wrecker service. (Courtesy of Mullen Motors.)

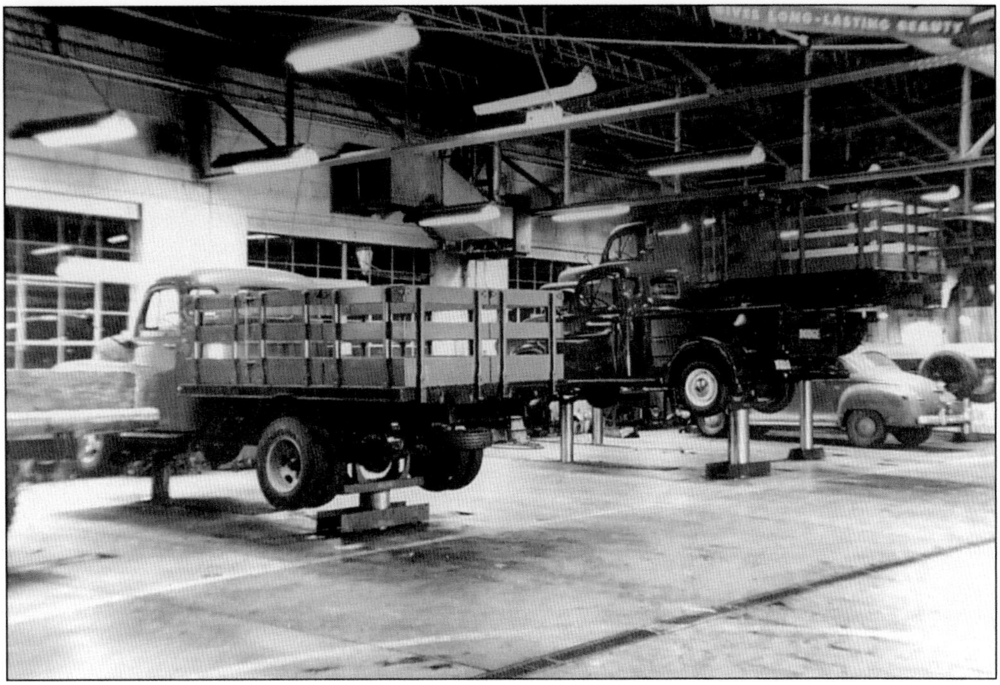

Mullen Motors new quarters at Thirteenth and Liberty featured the most up-to-date equipment. According to Jim Logan, who worked in the Mullen Motors Body Shop for 46 years, the hoist to lift up vehicles for service was very new at the time. Mullen Motors was one of the first car dealerships to have the hoists. (Courtesy of Mullen Motors.)

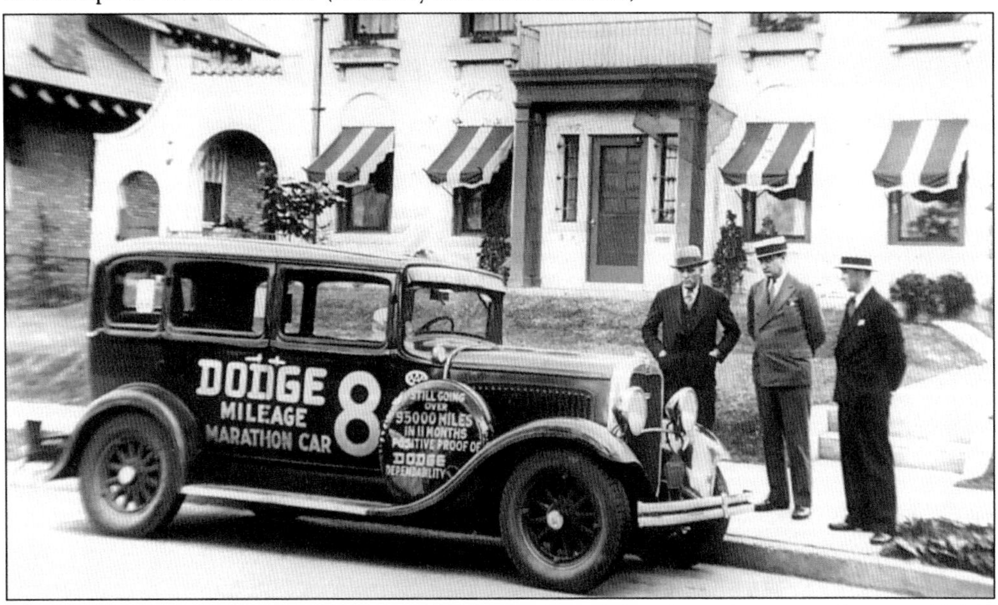

The 1930 four-door Dodge sedan—the Dodge Mileage Marathon Car—was driven 100,000 miles in one year as "positive proof of Dodge dependability." The car advertised one of Parkersburg's earliest car dealerships, Oesterle and Mullen, founded in 1923 by Earl Oesterle and J. Vincent Mullen. The three men stand in front of J. Vincent Mullen's house on upper Market Street. (Courtesy of Mullen Motors.)

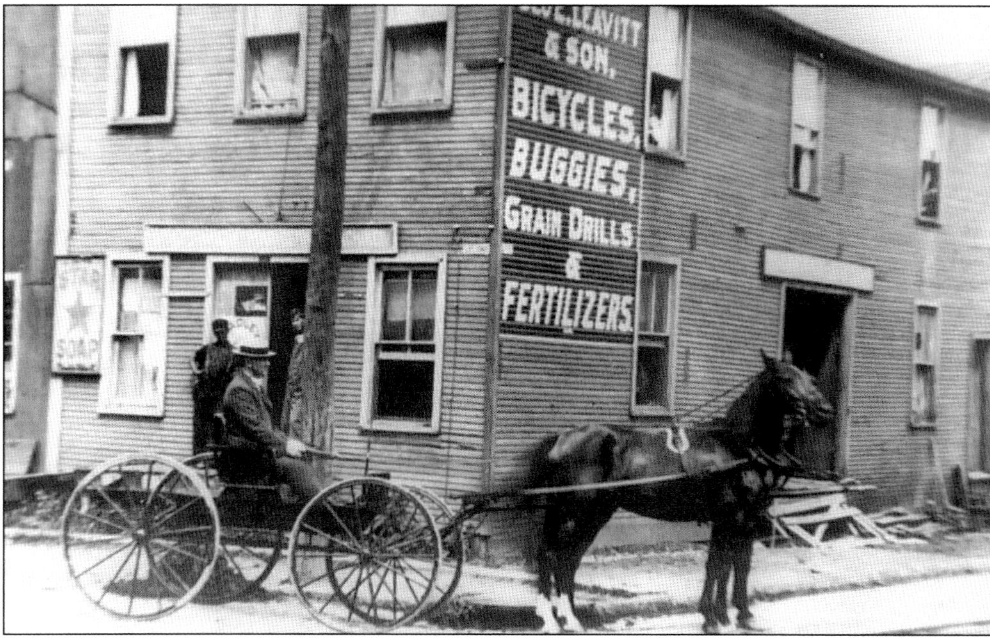

George E. Leavitt returned to his home in New England, West Virginia, after being discharged from the Union Army's First West Virginia Cavalry Regiment in 1865. He opened a barrel-making shop, but soon closed it to open a general store. Knowing that he was an excellent carpenter, people often asked him to build coffins. The Leavitt family dates the beginning of the Leavitt Funeral Home to 1882, the year of the first recorded coffin sale found in the store's account books. While continuing to operate the New England business, G.E. Leavitt opened the Leavitt General Store, pictured above, in Parkersburg in 1898 at Second and Juliana Streets. (Courtesy of Leavitt Funeral Services.)

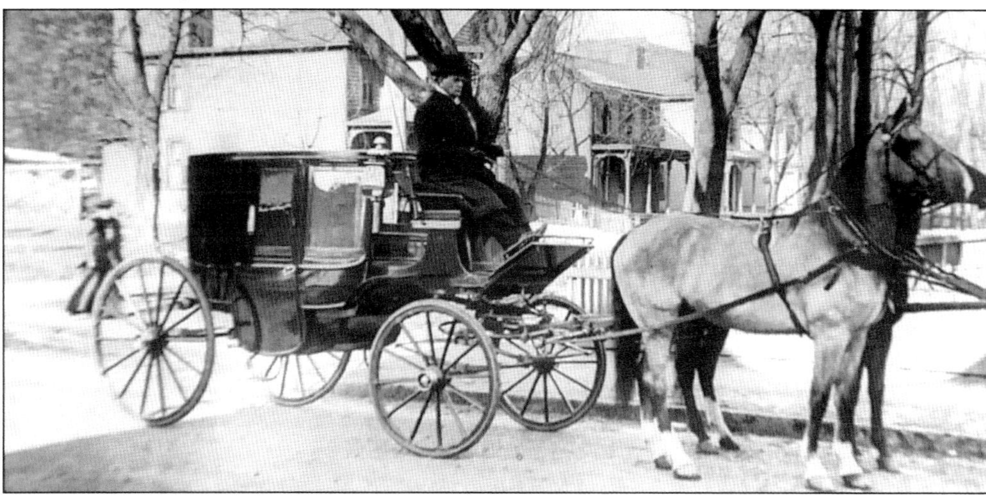

George E. Leavitt's son, Carr T. Leavitt, got his start in the business when a family asked George to deliver a coffin. He said, "I can't leave the store, but my boy, Carr, will." Thus began the transfer of leadership from generation to generation. Today, Jon and Stephen Leavitt, fifth-generation Leavitts, are owners and funeral directors of Leavitt Funeral Services. The business has undergone many changes since George E. rented the funeral carriage pictured above to transport coffins. (Courtesy of Leavitt Funeral Services.)

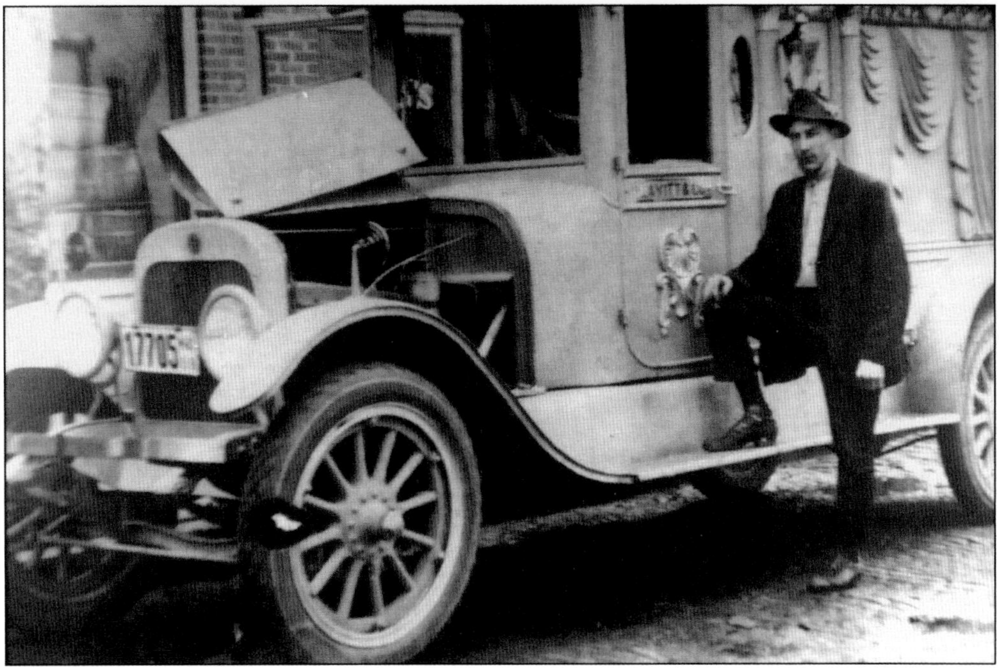

In the late 1920s, C.T. Leavitt and his son, Charles, went to Cincinnati to purchase a motorized hearse from the Sayers and Scovial Company. The vehicle shown above had a horse-drawn hearse body that was placed on an Oldsmobile Chassis. Although this was the beginning of the end for horse-drawn hearses, people still occasionally request a horse-drawn carriage. (Courtesy of Leavitt Funeral Services.)

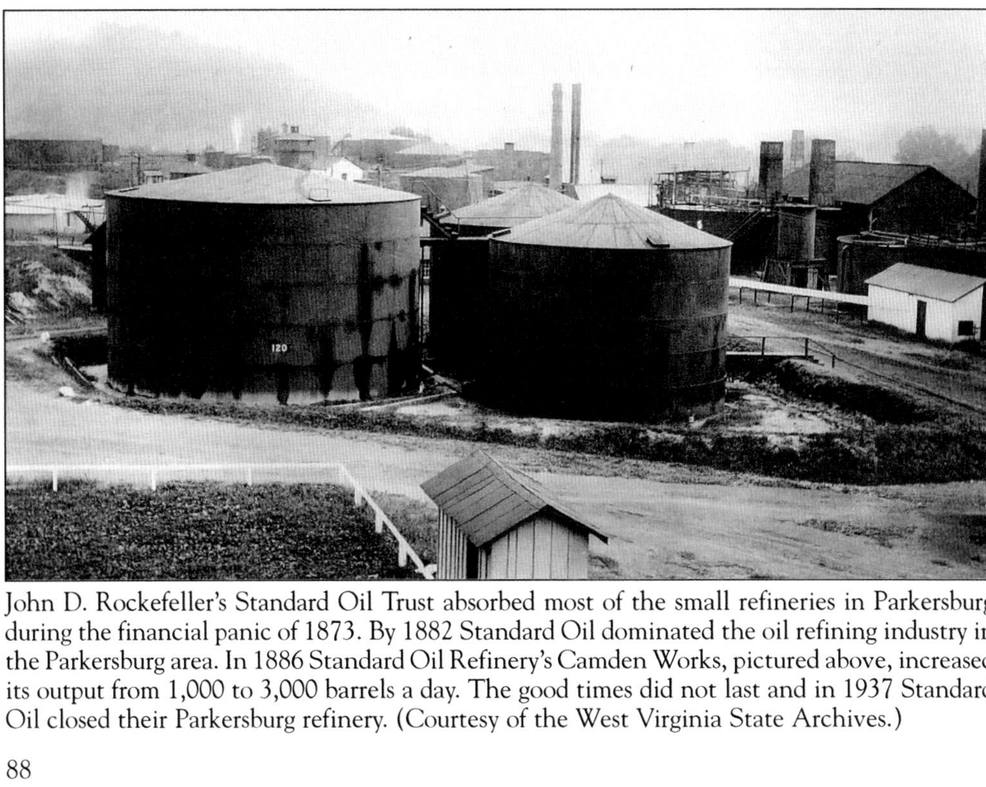

John D. Rockefeller's Standard Oil Trust absorbed most of the small refineries in Parkersburg during the financial panic of 1873. By 1882 Standard Oil dominated the oil refining industry in the Parkersburg area. In 1886 Standard Oil Refinery's Camden Works, pictured above, increased its output from 1,000 to 3,000 barrels a day. The good times did not last and in 1937 Standard Oil closed their Parkersburg refinery. (Courtesy of the West Virginia State Archives.)

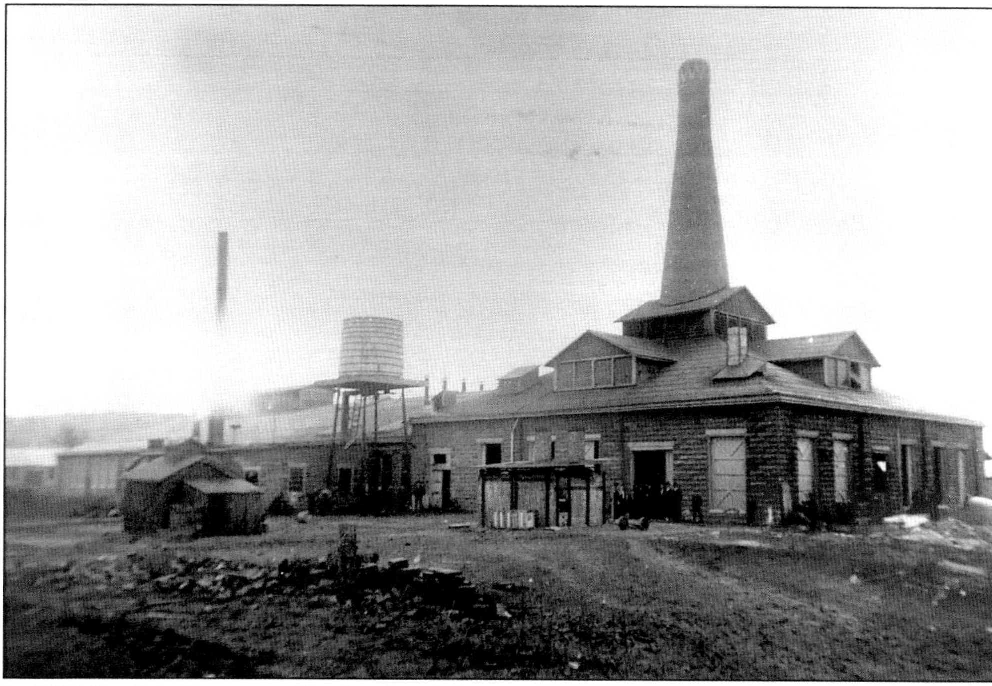

In 1905 Frank L. Fenton and his brother, John, pooled their resources—a total of $284.86—and began the Fenton Art Glass Company as a decorating firm in Martin's Ferry, Ohio. About a year later, unable to buy the glass they needed, they decided to build their own plant in Williamstown. The company, pictured above, produced its first glass crystal—crystal creamers in pattern number 8—on January 2, 1907. (Courtesy of Fenton Art Glass Co.)

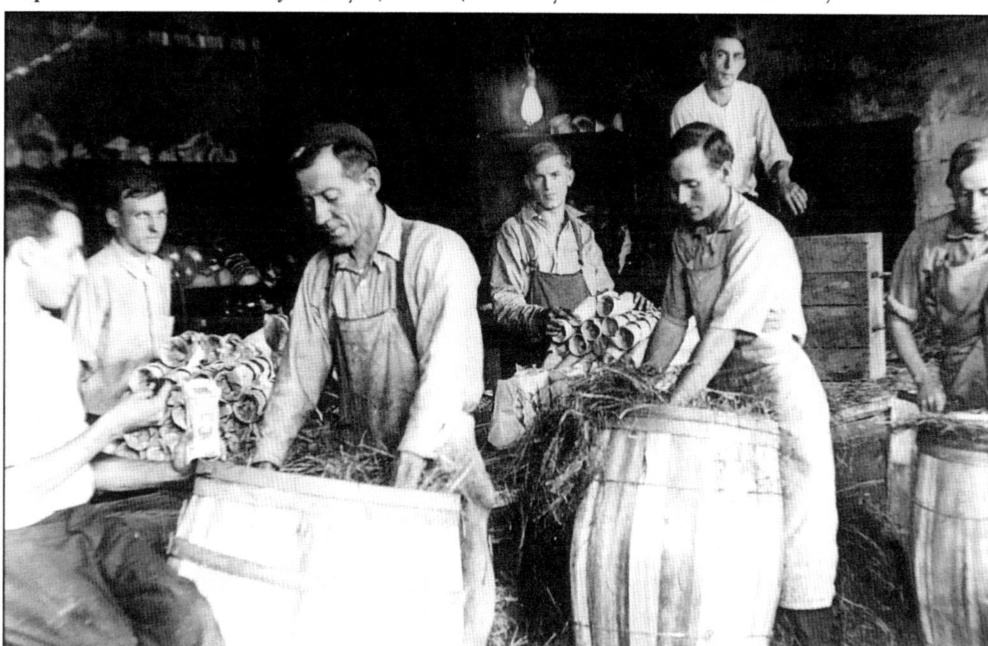

In 1910 workers in the Fenton Art Glass packing department fill barrels with glassware and straw for shipping. (Courtesy of Fenton Art Glass Co.)

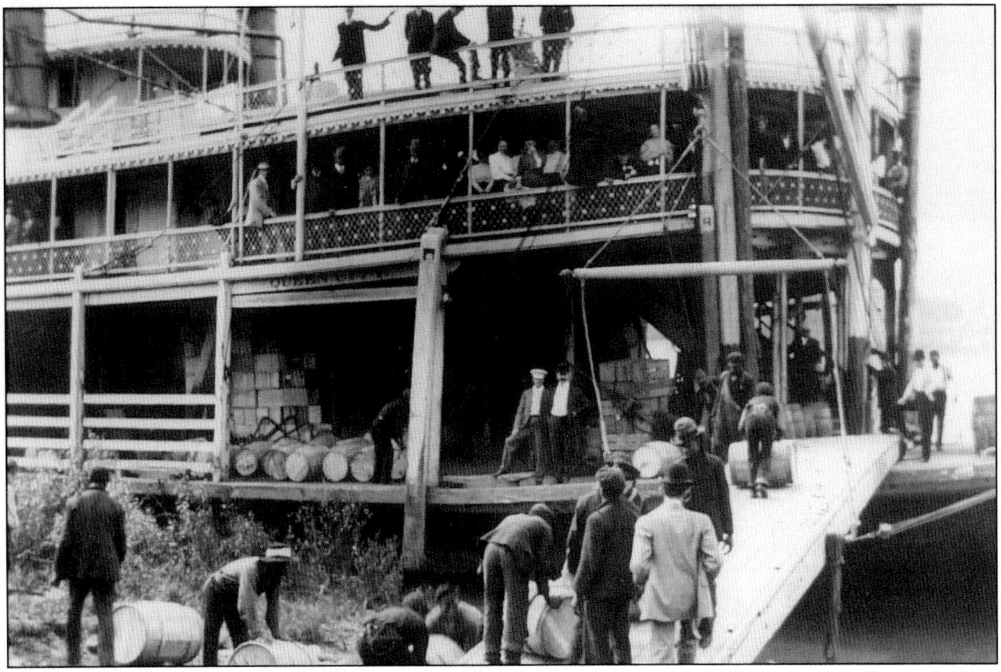

In the early years of production Fenton Art Glass was sometimes loaded on steamboats plying the Ohio and Mississippi Rivers to reach markets from Pittsburgh to New Orleans. The man in the light suit in the lower right corner of the gangplank is company founder Frank L. Fenton. (Courtesy of Fenton Art Glass Co.)

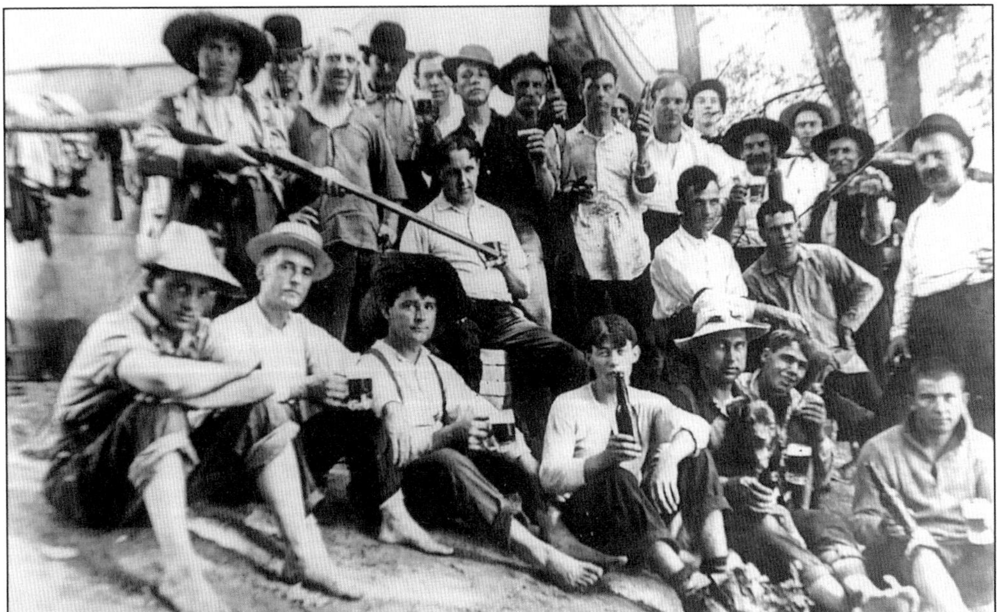

In the early 20th century, Fenton and other glass companies stopped production for six weeks from mid-July until the end of August. Many men camped by the Ohio River during this time, fishing, hunting, and otherwise amusing themselves. Tradition had it that they did not bathe or shave during the entire six weeks. (Courtesy of Fenton Art Glass.)

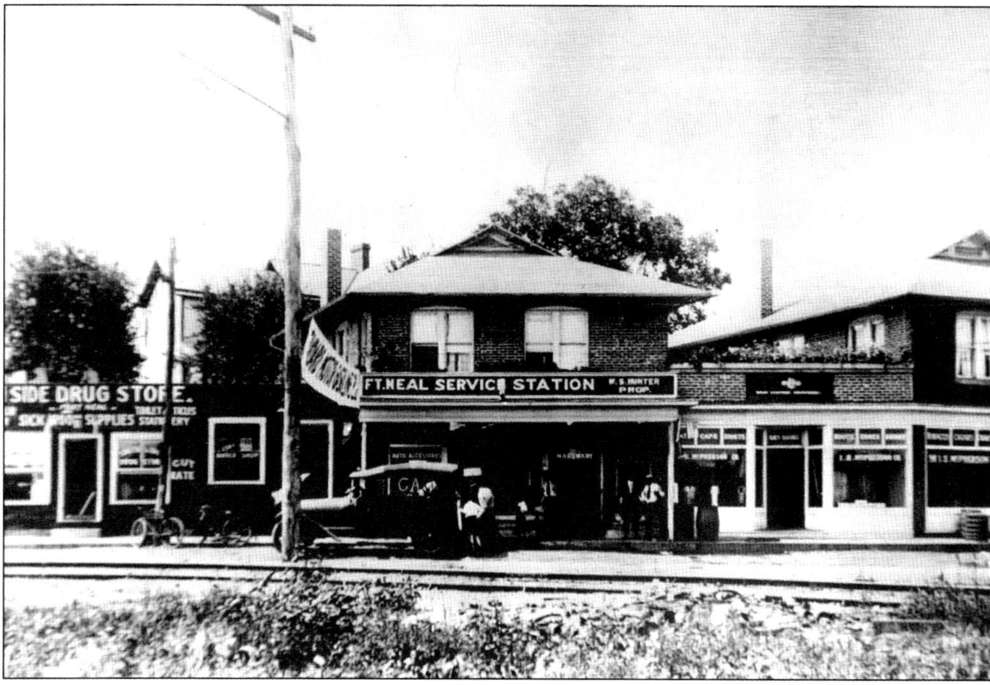

The Fort Neal Service Station in South Parkersburg was one of the early service stations in the area. In the 1924 Parkersburg Directory the station advertised "Gas, Oil, Grease, Accessories, Battery Charging and Repairing." (Courtesy of R.E. Enoch.)

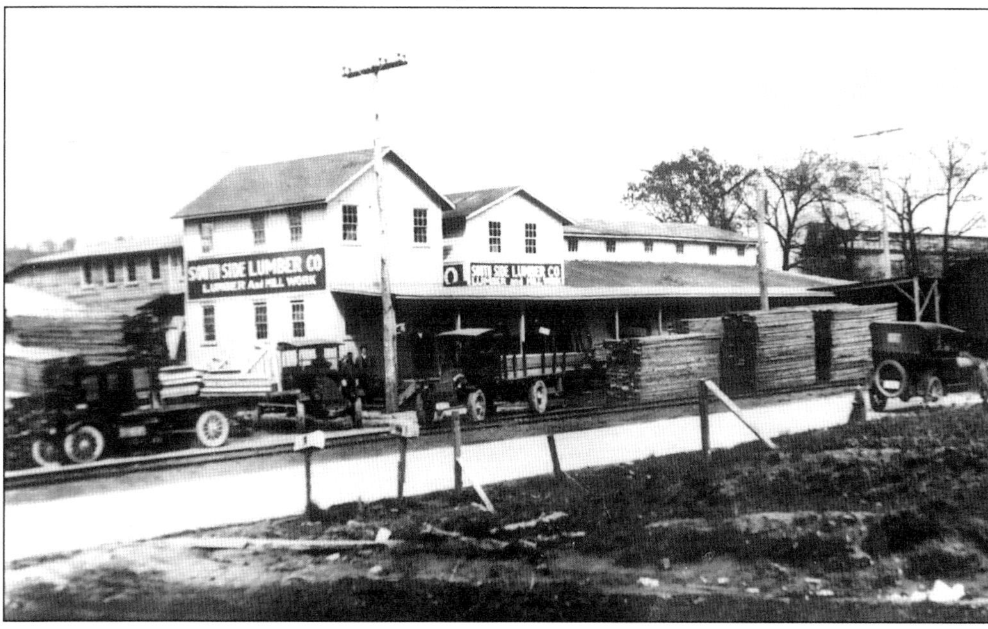

Frank Badger started selling lumber in Elizabeth, West Virginia, in the late 1800s. He moved his business to Parkersburg in 1922 and opened under the name of Southside Lumber. A few years later he changed the name to Badger's Lumber. Paul Ferrell purchased the business and name in 1991. Badger's Lumber is the only privately owned lumber company in Parkersburg. (Courtesy of R.E. Enoch.)

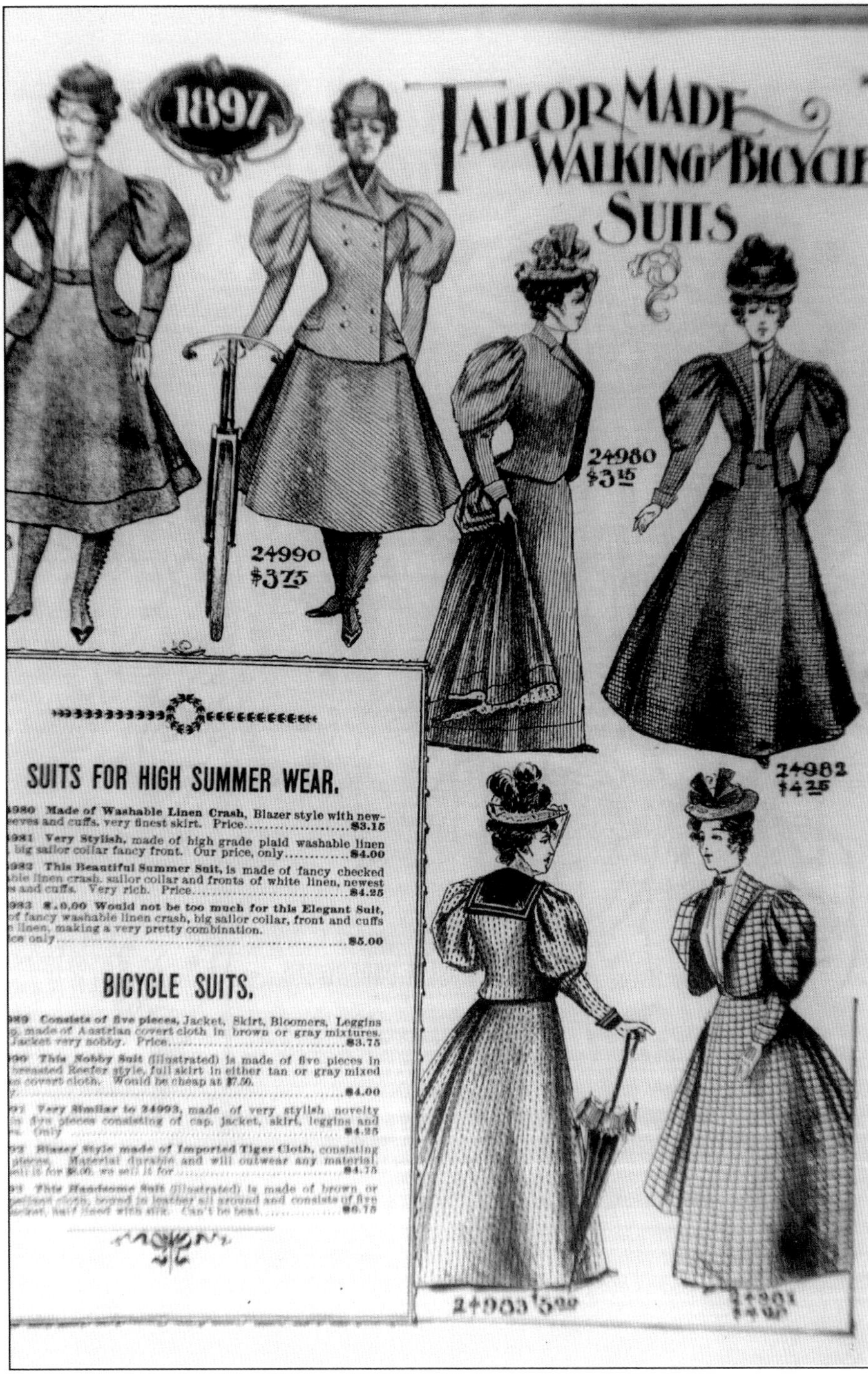

The Sears Catalog reached most homes in Wood County. Rural areas of the county in particular relied on the catalog to supply their needs. This page from the 1897 catalog shows the latest in lady's fashions, including the proper attire for riding that newfangled machine, the bicycle. It was not until 1932 that Sears opened a store in Parkersburg. (From the Sears 1897 Catalog.)

Six

Bad Times and Good Times

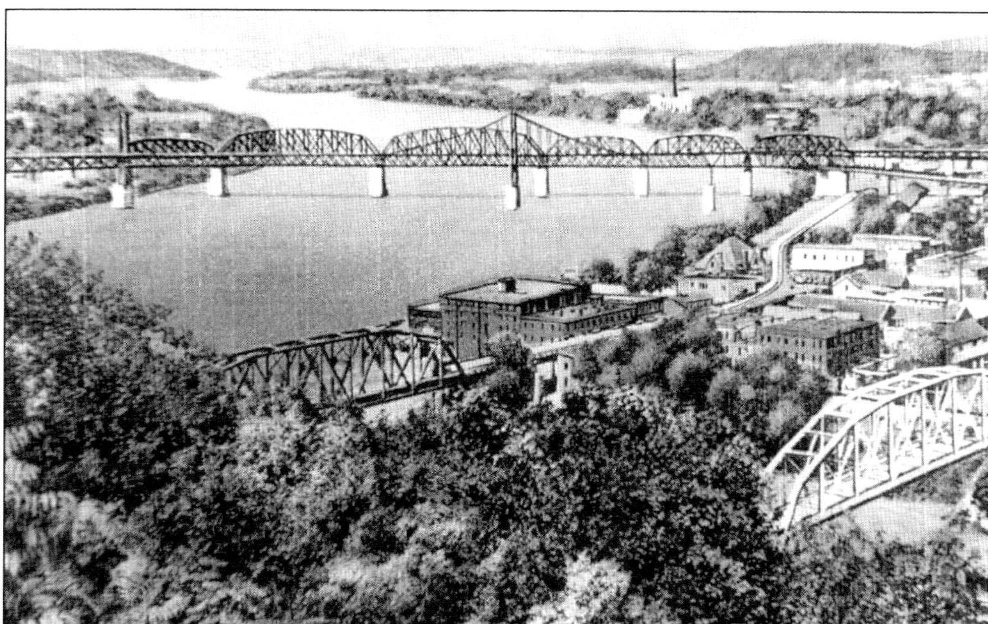

This postcard view of Parkersburg from Fort Boreman Hill taken *c.* 1917 shows the four main Parkersburg bridges. The railroad bridge across the Ohio River was completed in January of 1871. In 1916 the Parkersburg-Belpre bridge opened to wagon, carriage, and "horseless" traffic. The railroad bridge spanning the Little Kanawha River was constructed in 1886 and the bridge for horses, wagons, and later horseless carriages across the Little Kanawha was built in 1891. (Collection of B. Leavengood.)

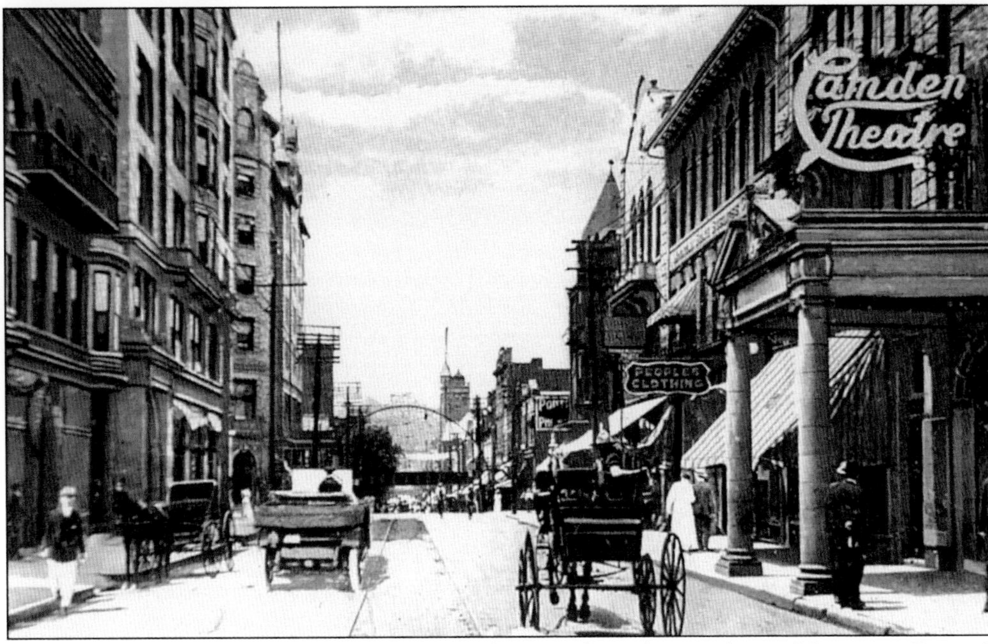

This postcard view of Market Street shows the Camden Theater, located between Seventh and Eighth Streets on the west side of Market Street. The theater had seating for 1,400 people on the main floor in addition to the balcony and private boxes. Built by Sen. Johnson Nelson Camden's Opera Block Investment Company, the Camden featured minstrel shows, vaudeville, and such plays as *Ten Nights in a Barroom* and *She Stoops to Conquer*. The theater burned on November 30, 1929. (Collection of B. Leavengood.)

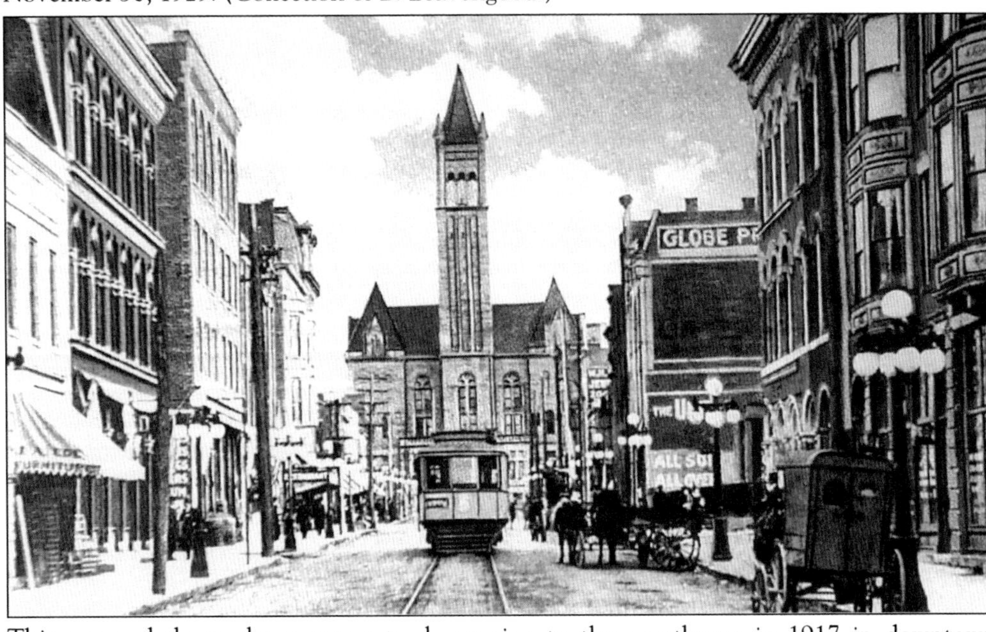

This postcard shows the streetcar track running to the courthouse in 1917 in downtown Parkersburg. Streetcars, horses and buggies, and automobiles shared the streets, but in a few years horses would no longer be seen. The last streetcar line ceased operation on May 25, 1947. The automobile survived and congests our streets today. (Collection of B. Leavengood.)

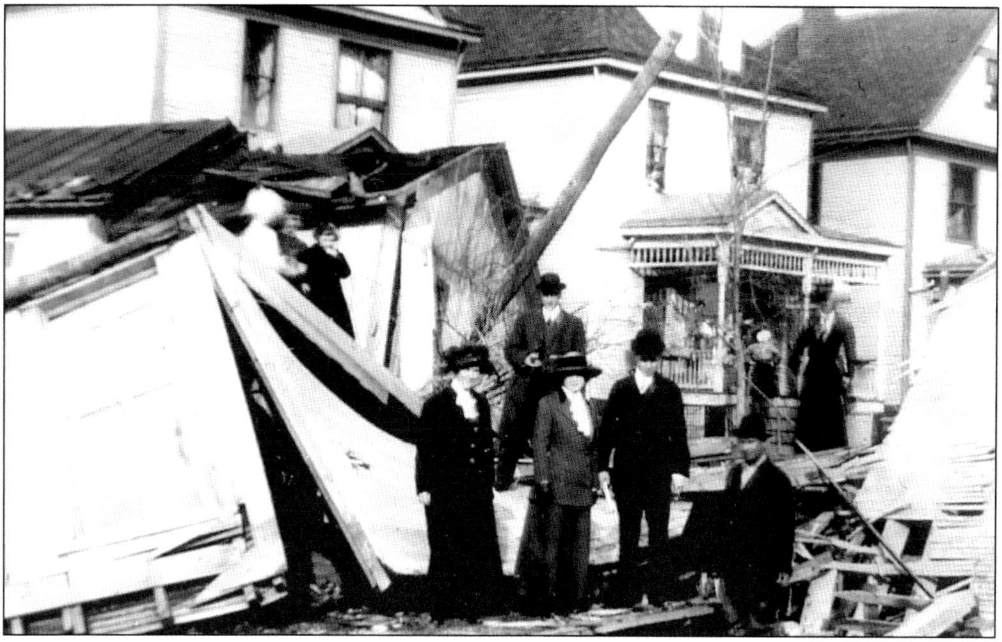

At 5:10 a.m. on March 19, 1909, two City of Parkersburg reserve water tanks on the top of Prospect (now Quincy) Hill burst, sending two million gallons of water down the hill and destroying everything in its path. A small cottage on the hillside above Avery Street at Tenth crashed down the hill, killing the occupants—a newly married couple named Wigal—instantly. (Courtesy of the family of Ruth Schoolcraft Murphy.)

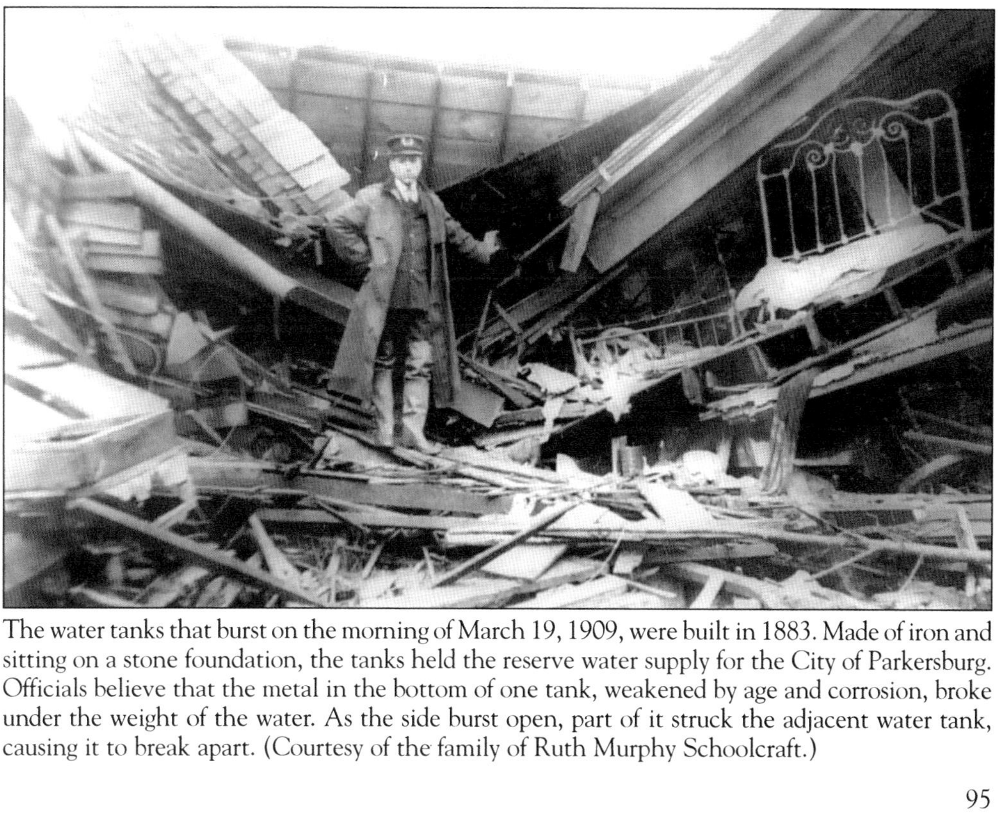

The water tanks that burst on the morning of March 19, 1909, were built in 1883. Made of iron and sitting on a stone foundation, the tanks held the reserve water supply for the City of Parkersburg. Officials believe that the metal in the bottom of one tank, weakened by age and corrosion, broke under the weight of the water. As the side burst open, part of it struck the adjacent water tank, causing it to break apart. (Courtesy of the family of Ruth Murphy Schoolcraft.)

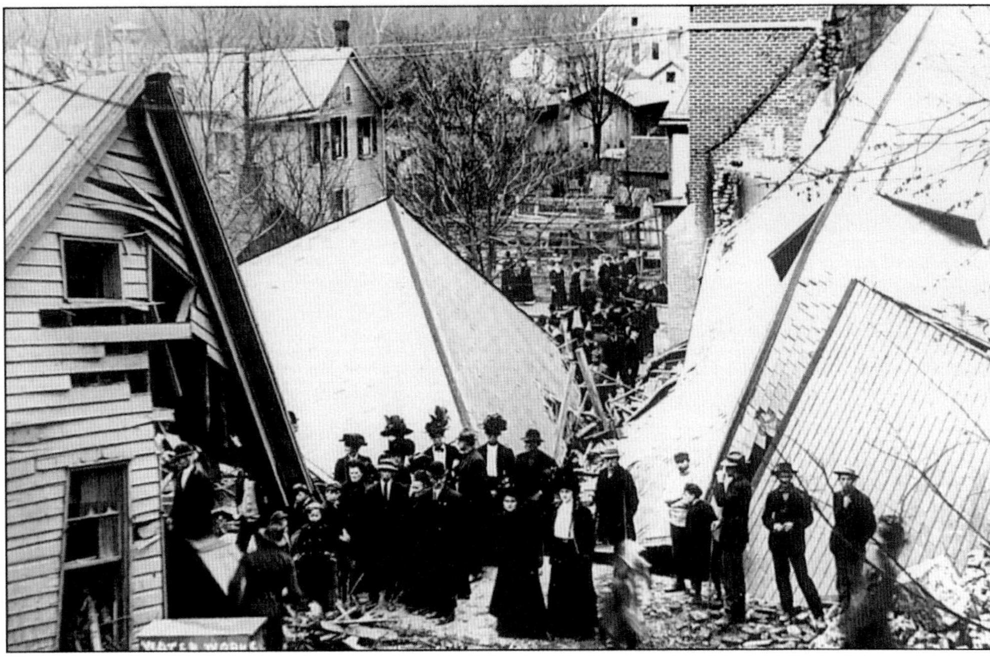

Water from the tanks caused extensive damage. The back walls of St. John's Lutheran Church, at the corner of Ninth and Avery Streets, collapsed, causing the ceiling to cave in. A stable, set below ground on William and Mary Streets, flooded, drowning a cow. Trees from the hillside came down with such force that they penetrated the brick walls of Sumner School. (Courtesy of the family of Ruth Murphy Schoolcraft.)

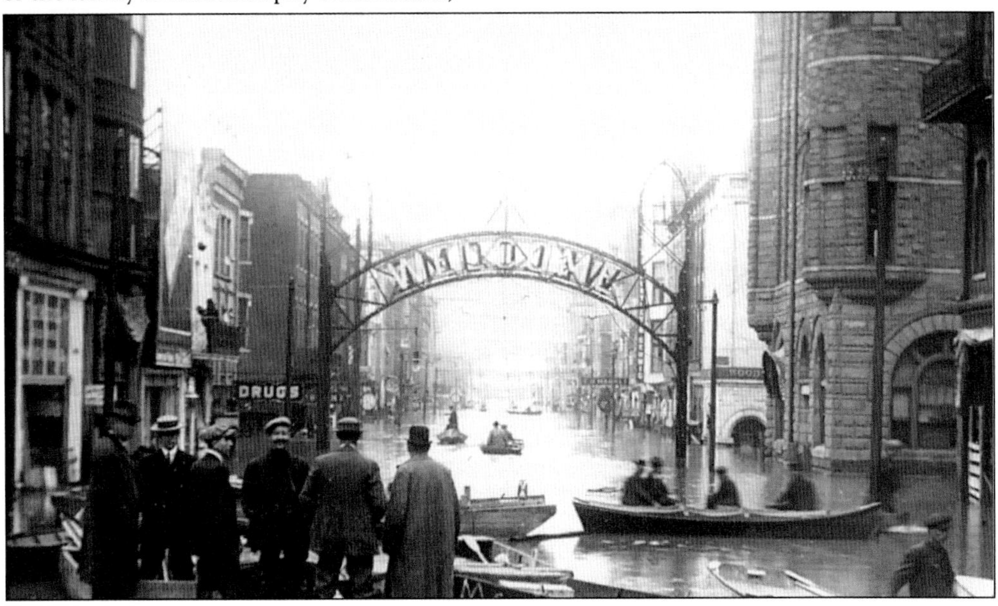

On Wednesday, March 26, 1913, *The Parkersburg Sentinel* warned merchants in the lower sections of town to remove merchandise from their stores as the river was "rising rapidly." The next day weather forecasters predicted an Ohio River crest of 55 feet. Saturday's paper warned, "The Ohio Valley is experiencing the greatest flood in history," and predicted a crest of 58 feet. (Courtesy of the family of Ruth Murphy Schoolcraft.)

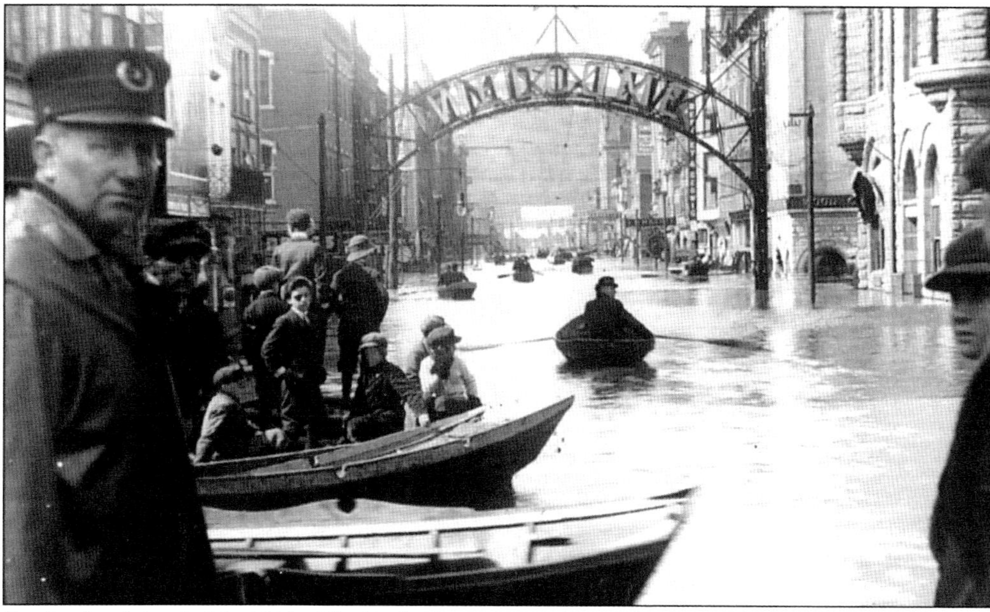

On Friday, March 28, 1913, *The Parkersburg Sentinel* stated, "Parkersburg is isolated without rail or wire communication from the outside." More rain fell and the Ohio River kept rising. Firemen evacuated their building and moved the fire engines up Market Street just above the water line. Samuel Whitlatch fell out of his skiff on Juliana Street below Third and drowned. (Courtesy of the family of Ruth Murphy Schoolcraft.)

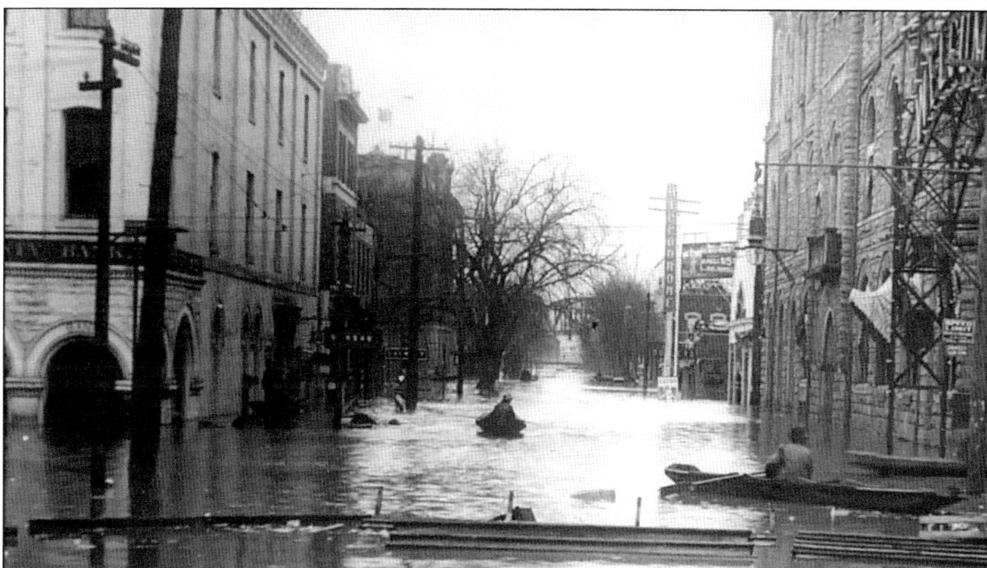

The Ohio River crested at Parkersburg at 58 feet and 5 inches at 11:00 a.m. on March 29, 1913, causing widespread damage. All the furniture inside the Trinity Episcopal Church on Juliana Street, including the $5,000 pipe organ, was ruined. As a result of the flood, some of the numbered pews are no longer sequential. The flood waters rose too rapidly to allow downtown merchants to remove all of their merchandise. Thousands visited the flooded area, many going to the top of Prospect (now Quincy) Hill for a better view. (Courtesy of the family of Ruth Murphy Schoolcraft.)

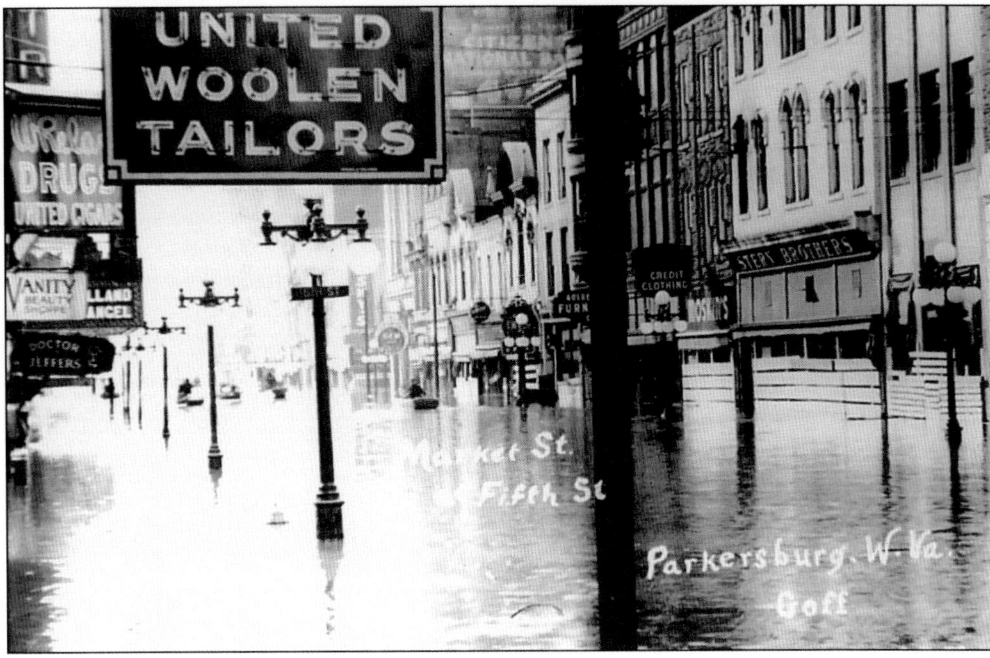

The Ohio River crested at Parkersburg at 55 feet and 4 inches on January 26, 1937. All roads leading to the city were closed. The Baltimore and Ohio Railroad could not enter or leave the city. Streetcar service to Marietta was canceled. Four hundred families were evacuated in the city. The four families living on Blennerhassett Island were brought out by skiff as the island flooded. (Courtesy of the family of Ruth Murphy Schoolcraft.)

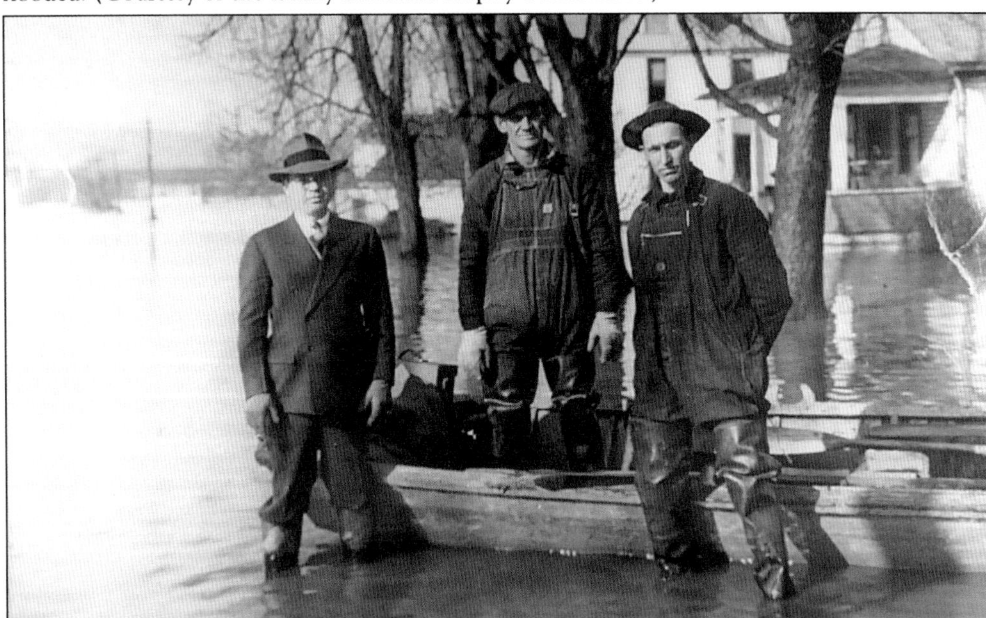

Charles Newman (left), manager of Parkersburg Iron and Steel Company, with the help of Ernest Miracle (middle) and W. Frank Miracle (right) ferried employees back and forth to the plant on Twenty-ninth Street and Beechwood, off Murdoch Avenue during the flood of 1937. (Courtesy of Jacquelyn Miracle Goodman.)

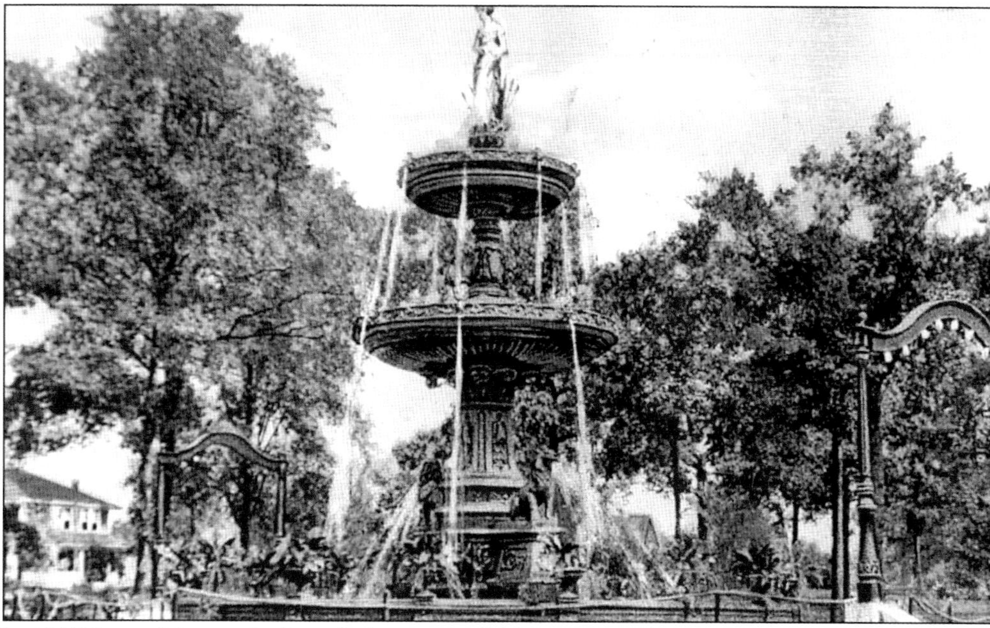

In 1905 James Monroe Jackson Jr. bequeathed $5,000 to purchase a fountain in memory of his father, Judge James Monroe Jackson. The $5,000 was to be taken from his estate before any other funds were removed. William Willard Jackson purchased the fountain on his wedding trip to New York. Originally the fountain had three tiers; one tier has been removed because of aging. The main features of the fountain are the lions with water coming out of their mouths and Parkersburg's "Lady of the Lake" on top of the fountain. The fountain was erected in 1906 at the main entrance to the Park. Arches with electric lights originally illuminated the fountain. (Collection of B. Leavengood.)

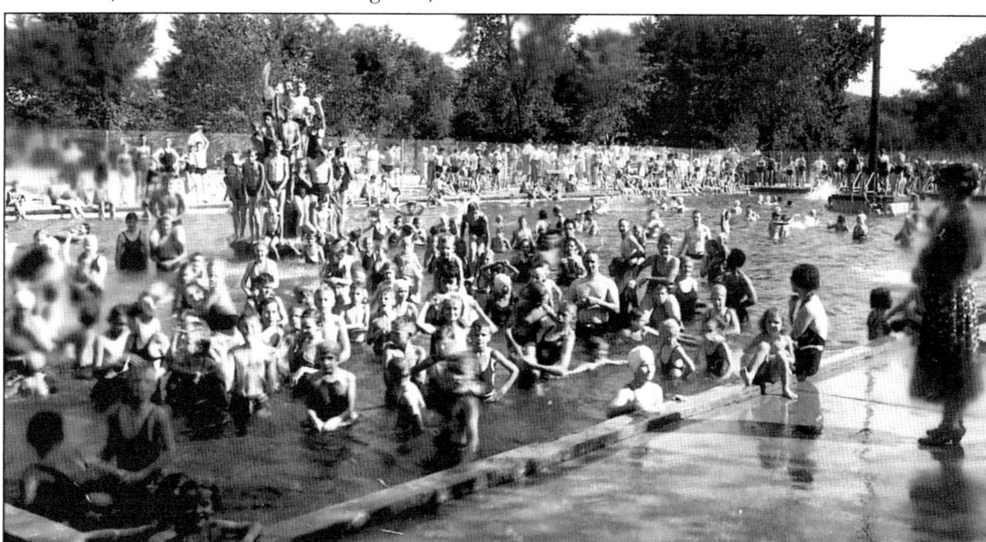

In 1897 the City of Parkersburg purchased 42 acres near Twenty-third Street to develop a city park, first named Oakwood Park. The city council officially changed the name to "City Park" in 1911. Many improvements were made over the years including two lily ponds, tennis courts, a band shell, and, in 1936, a swimming pool. (Courtesy of Paul A. Borrelli, Artcraft Studio.)

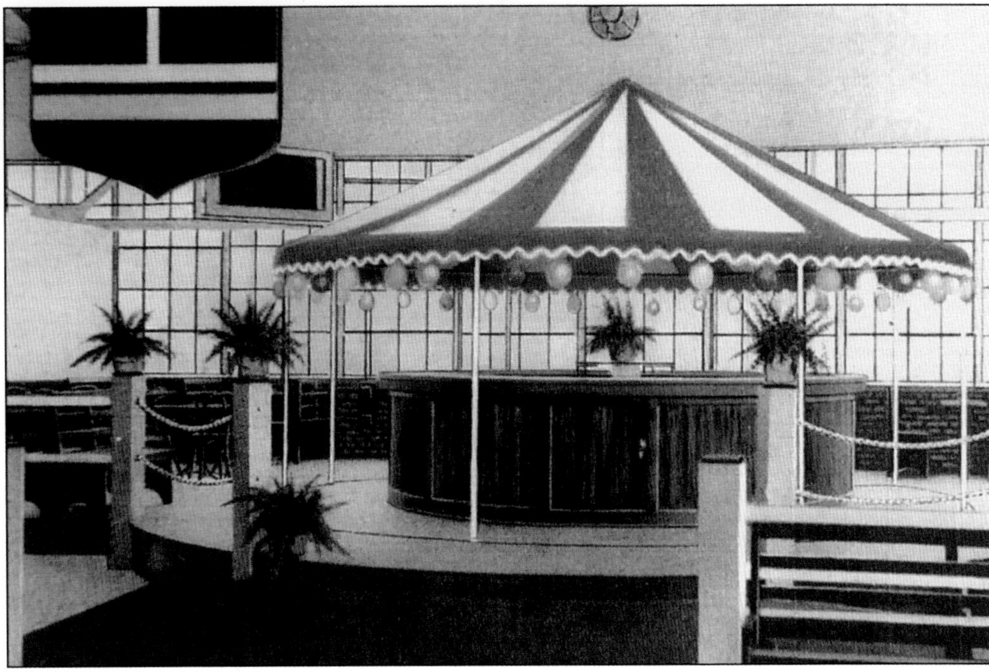

In the 1930s Sherman Dils turned the second floor of his Motormart Ford dealership into a dance floor and called it the "Coliseum." Big name bands provided music including Guy Lombardo, Tommy Dorsey, and Glenn Miller. Guests enjoyed sitting at the revolving carousel bar, pictured above, drinking 3.2 beers. Dils adapted a Ford Model T motor to turn the carousel. Today Warner Pontiac occupies the former Coliseum. (Collection of B. Leavengood.)

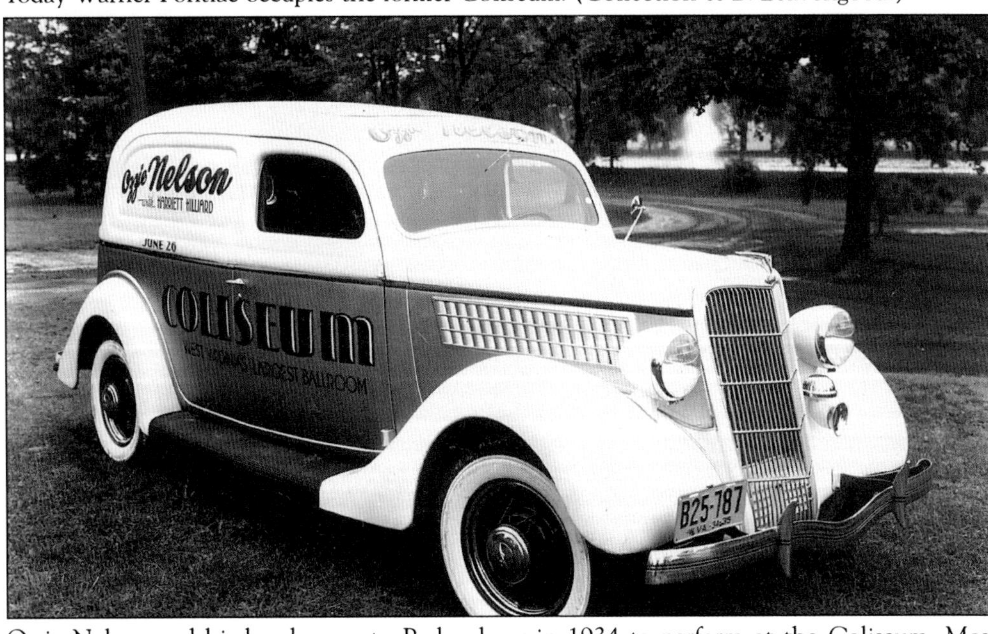

Ozzie Nelson and his band came to Parkersburg in 1934 to perform at the Coliseum. Most people remember Nelson for the 22-year run of the radio, and the television series *Adventures of Ozzie and Harriet*. Few know that in the 1930s, Nelson had his own band that performed in small towns across America. (Courtesy of Paul A. Borrelli, Artcraft Studio.)

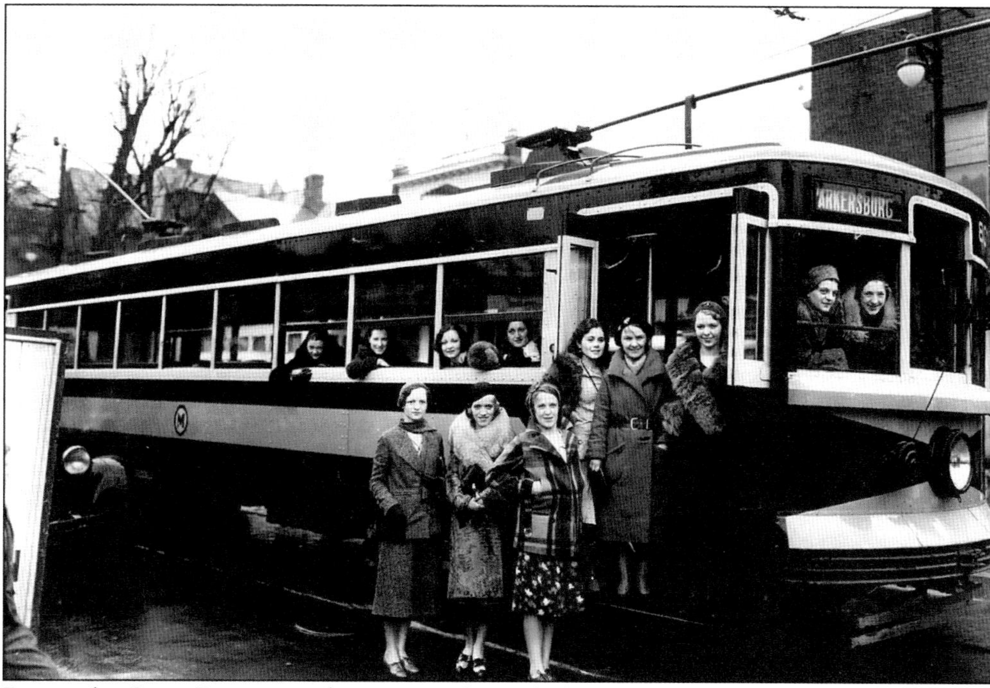

During the Great Depression theater attendance declined all over the United States. Warner Brothers sent this group of young actresses around the country to give shows and promote attendance at theaters that had contracts with Warner Brothers. The group appeared in Parkersburg in 1931 at the Smoot Theater. (Courtesy of Paul A. Borrelli, Artcraft Studio.)

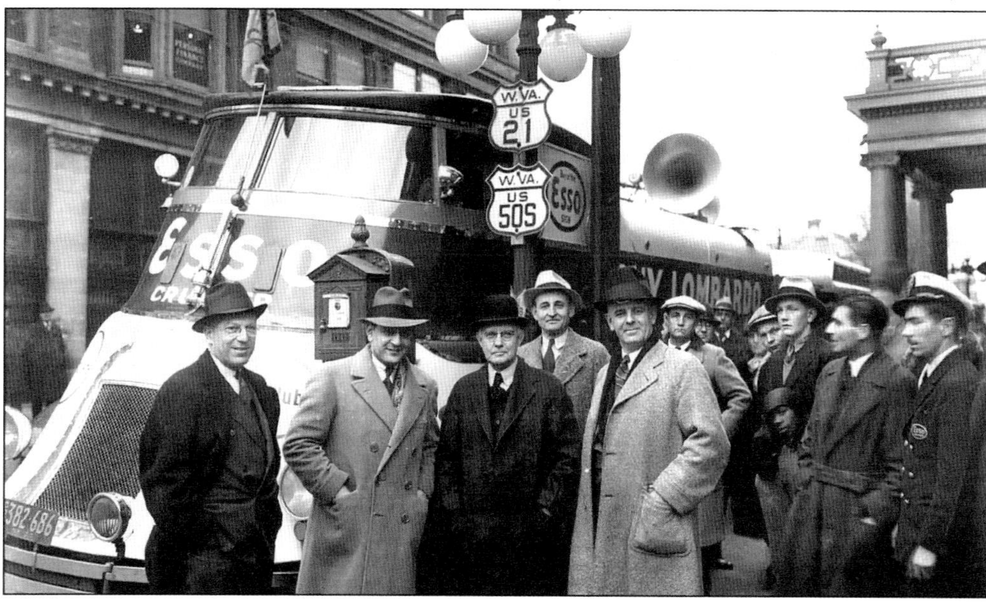

Famous big band leader Guy Lombardo (second from the left) came to Parkersburg in 1934 to perform at the Coliseum ballroom. One of seven children of a musically minded tailor, Lombardo and his brothers began performing while still in school. He sold over 100 million records. Lombardo and his band traveled at least 6,000 miles a year, performing at colleges and in small towns across the country. (Courtesy of Paul A. Borrelli, Artcraft Studio.)

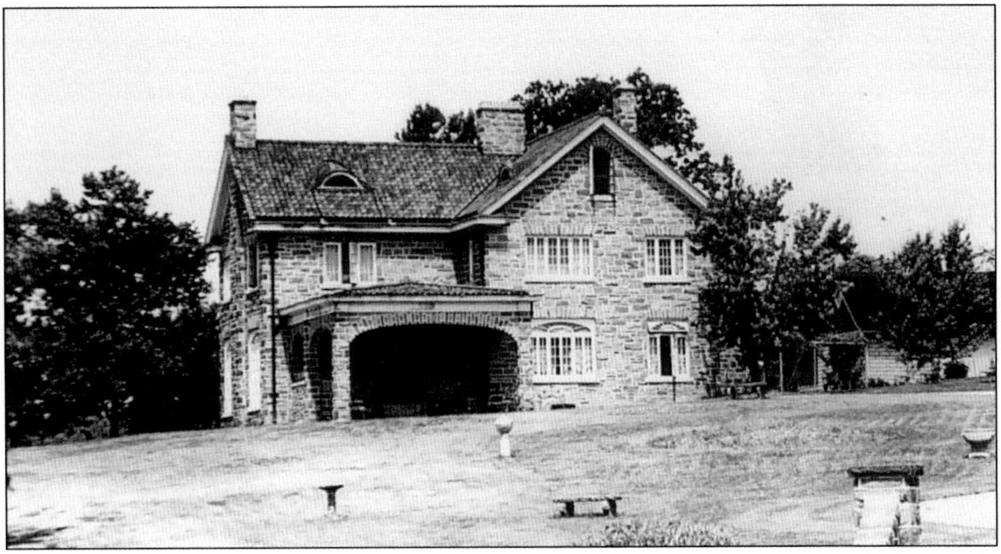

William H. Bickel made a fortune in the oil fields and he shared that fortune with the people of Wood County. His 368-acre estate in what is now the Larkmead section in southern Wood County hosted thousands of families. "Uncle Wig," as his friends called him, provided ponies for children to ride and a private zoo, which included groundhogs, deer, peacocks, and buffalo. He sponsored a horse show every year and revived the sport of sulky racing. "Uncle Wig" died at a square dance on November 28, 1946. (Collection of B. Leavengood.)

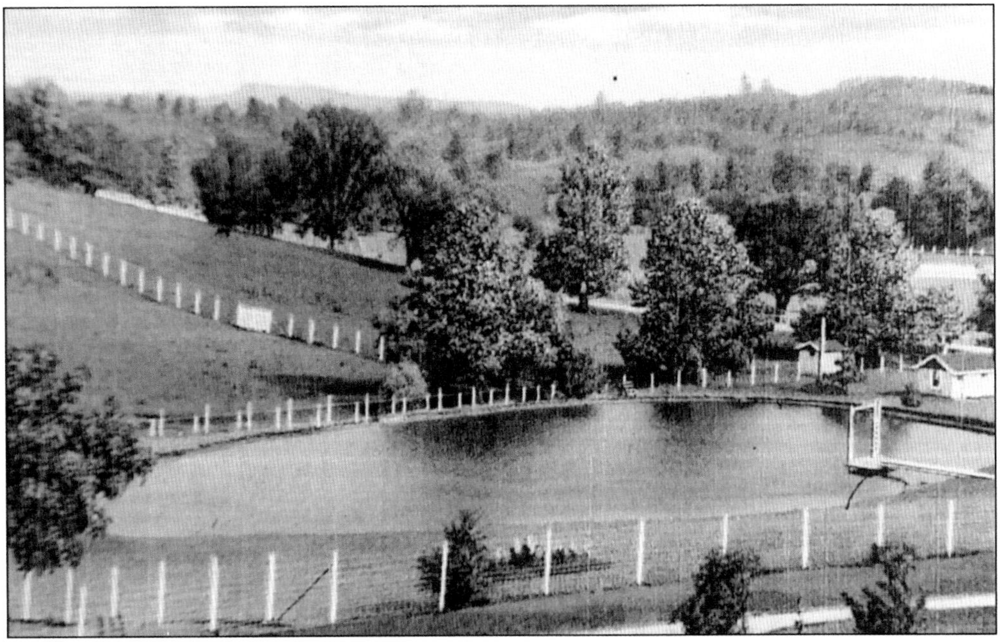

Families enjoyed watching swans and ducks swimming on this large pond on William H. Bickel's estate. Other attractions included Bickel's white Arabian and Percheron work horses and his pedigreed Dalmatian coach dogs. Uncle Wig occasionally entertained area organizations with his performing turkeys, bantam hens, pigeons, and Rhode Island Chickens. The turkeys played dead, laying on their backs and hanging their heads over the table, while other feathered flock performed various tricks. (Collection of B. Leavengood.)

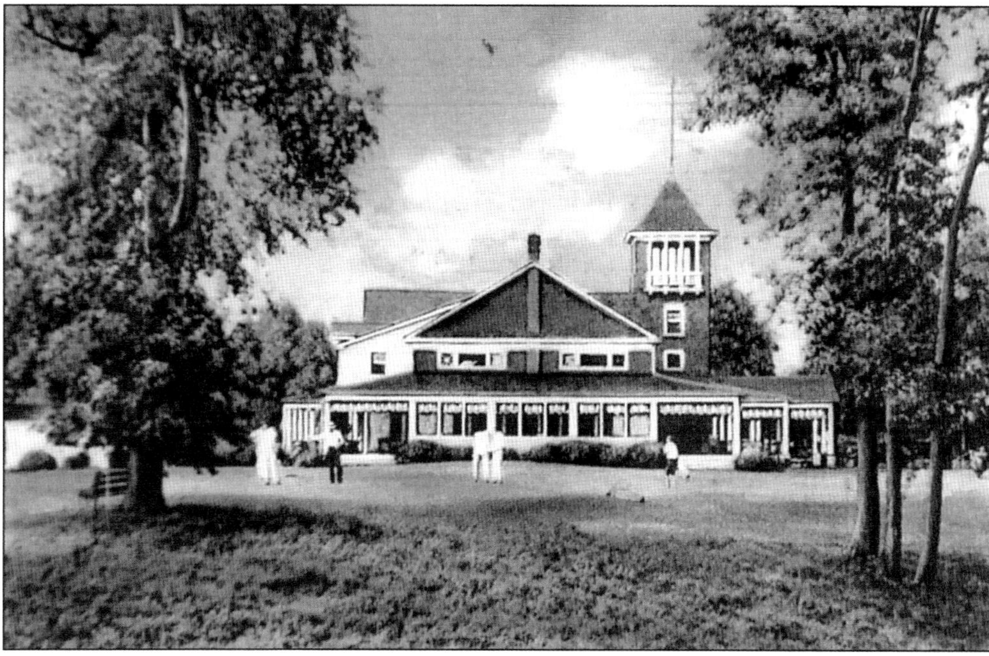

The State of West Virginia chartered the first country club in the state in Parkersburg on June 26, 1902. Club officers purchased land in upper Vienna and built a clubhouse where fine dining, dancing, tennis, and billiards were available to members. In 1905 a six-hole golf course and a swimming pool were added. A fire consumed the clubhouse on May 25, 1936. The present clubhouse opened in 1939. (Collection of B. Leavengood.)

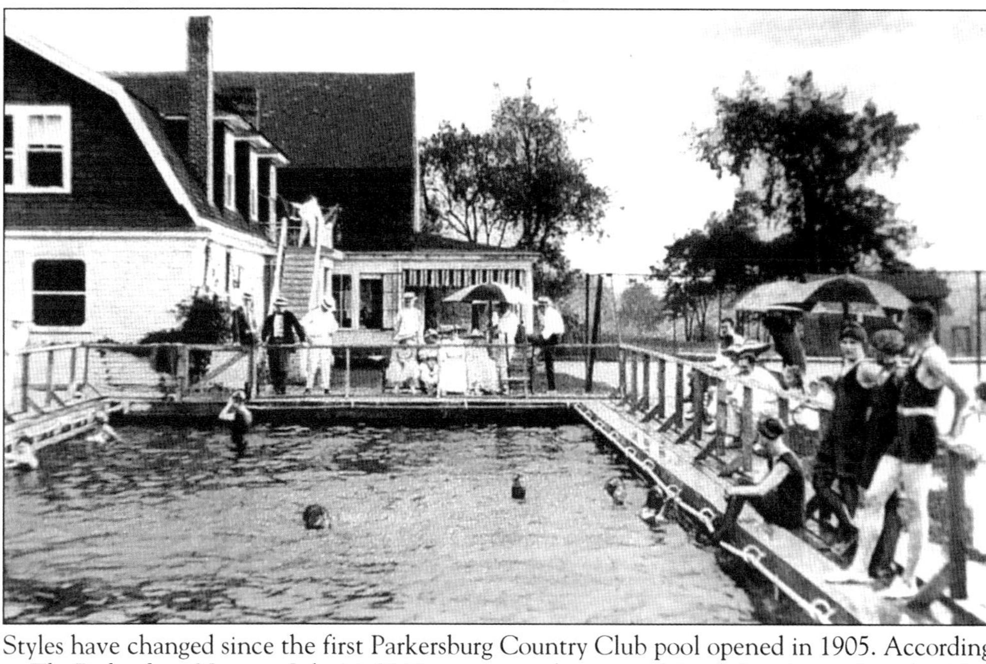

Styles have changed since the first Parkersburg Country Club pool opened in 1905. According to *The Parkersburg News* on July 14, 2002, many members complained that the pool was "cold as ice." The present pool was built in 1980. In the summer of 2002 the Parkersburg County Club celebrated a "century of excellence." (Collection of B. Leavengood.)

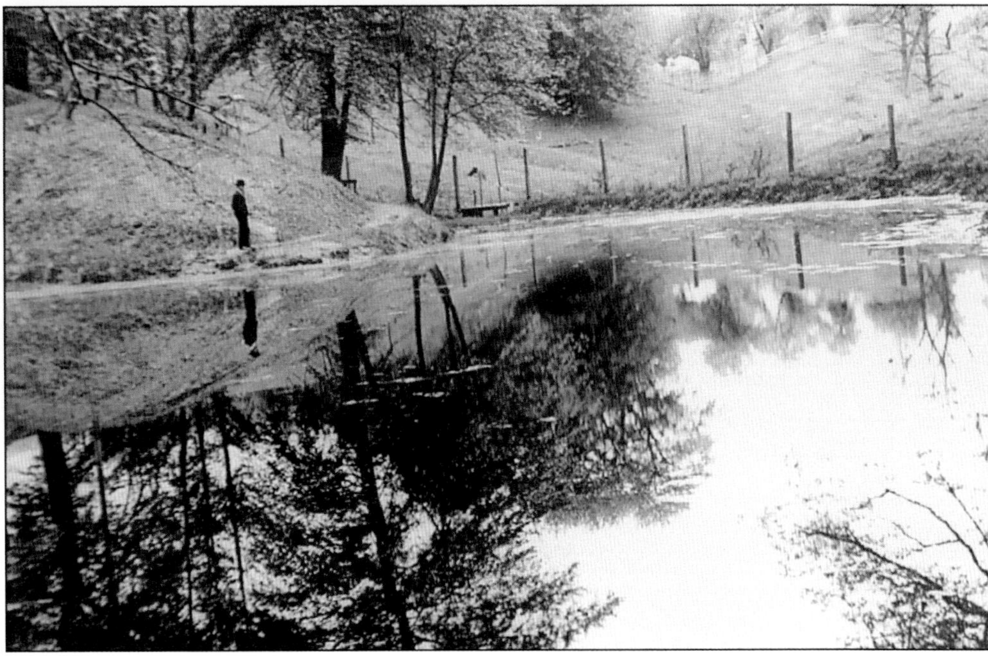

In 1898, Charles H. Shattuck, president of the Parkersburg Electric Power and Street Railway, decided to build a trolley park, a company-owned park along one of the streetcar lines to attract riders. Shattuck purchased land on the outskirts of Parkersburg at Dudley Avenue and Twenty-fifth Street and began construction of what he called Terrapin Park. One of his first improvements was to dam a stream to create a small lake. (Collection of B. Leavengood.)

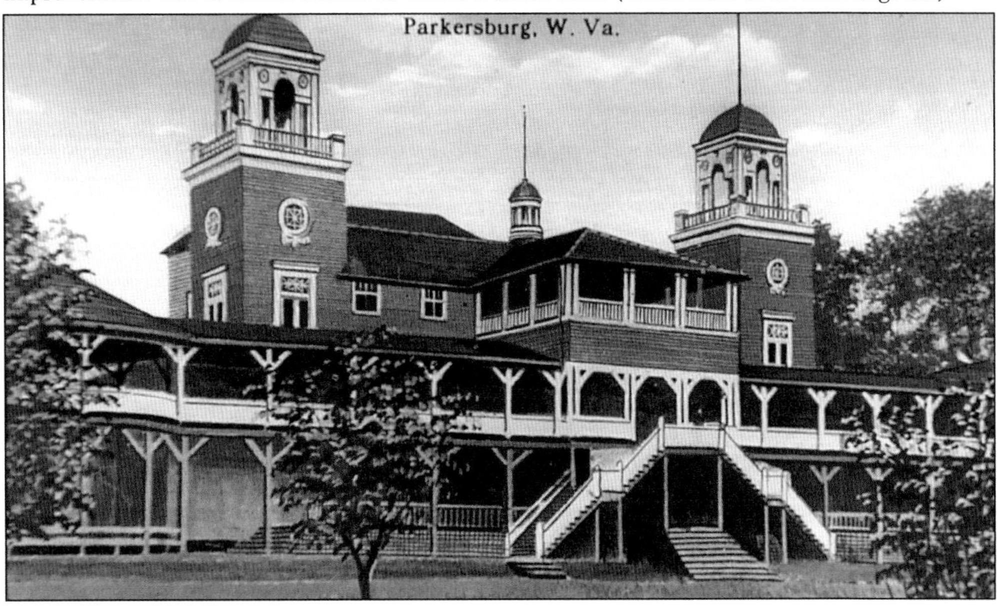

Built in 1899, the Terrapin Park Casino was not a gambling casino as we use the term today, but a large multi-purpose building. The casino featured a café, cigar stand, and confectionery, but it was the 2,000-seat auditorium that drew the crowds. People stood in line to get tickets for plays, musical entertainment, vaudeville, and moving pictures plus performances by the Amazing Canadian Diving Elks and Dare Devil Jack. (Collection of B. Leavengood.)

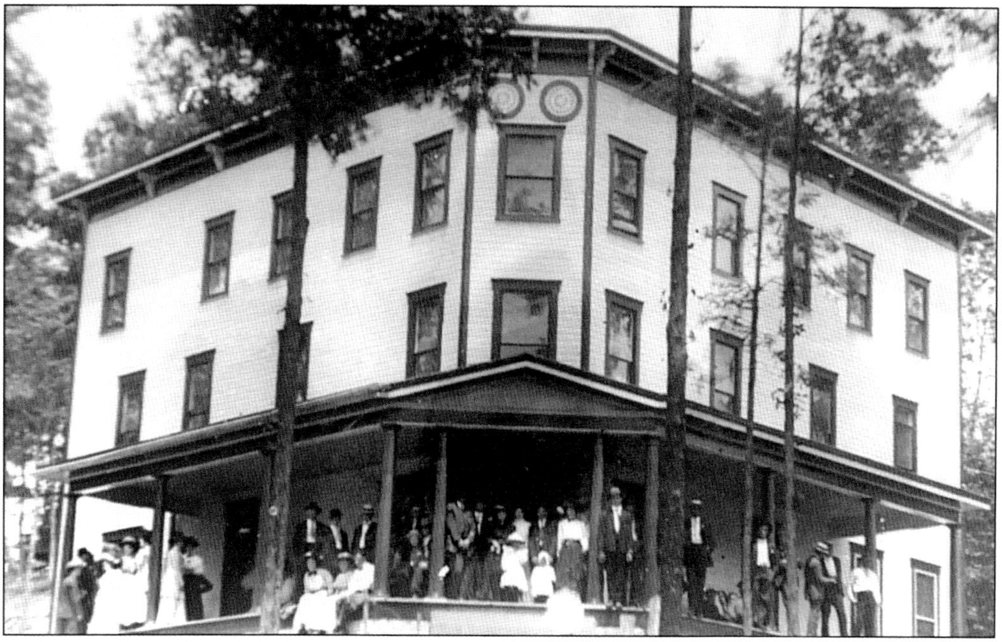

Built in 1910 by Dr. J.W. Grimm of St. Marys, West Virginia, the Borland Springs Hotel sat on 240 acres on the Wood and Pleasant County line. The three-story hotel had sixty-two rooms. Rates, which included all meals, were $12 to $14 weekly. The main attraction of the hotel was its inexhaustible supply of mineral waters thought to have healing powers. For several years, the hotel sold bottled mineral water. (Courtesy of the family of Mary Reece Dunlap.)

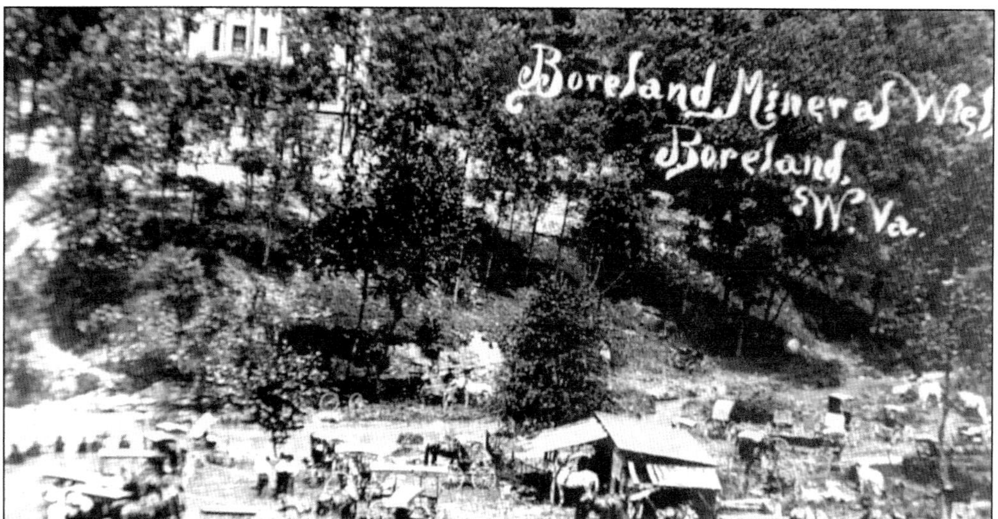

People came to Borland Springs Hotel to bathe in the mineral waters believed to have health restoring powers. C.T. Leavitt of Parkersburg purchased the hotel from Dr. J.W. Grimm in 1932. Leavitt spent two years renovating the hotel and making repairs to the spring house. He operated the hotel from 1934 until 1938 and again from 1940 to 1941. The hotel closed for good shortly after the outbreak of World War II. In 1952, the hotel was used to raise chickens. As many as 12,000 chickens lived in the once elegant hotel. In 1967, fire destroyed the hotel. (Courtesy of R.E. Enoch.)

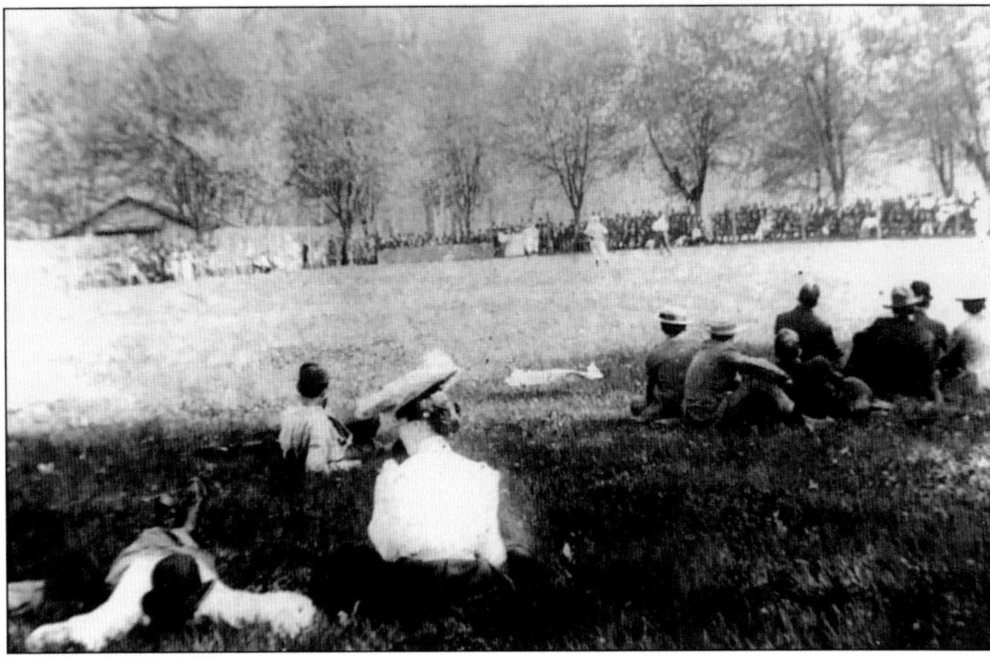

From 1886 until the 1913 flood, Amos W. Gordon's park on Blennerhassett Island attracted as many as 15,000 visitors each year. The 10-acre park on the head of the island featured a baseball diamond, boxing ring, bowling alley, large dance pavilion, and special events such as an annual Fourth of July celebration that attracted up to 5,000 people. Baseball drew crowds to the island where they spent afternoons watching the Cincinnati Reds, Brooklyn Dodgers, Pittsburgh Pirates, and local teams play. (Courtesy of Blennerhassett Island Historical State Park.)

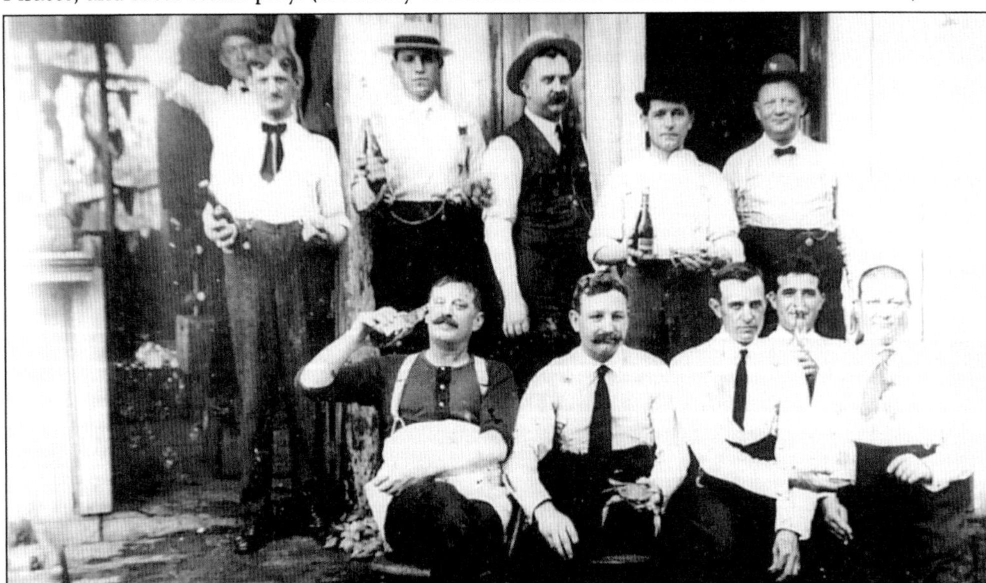

Fries Park on the west side of Fort Boreman Hill was a favorite place for families to picnic on a weekend. Gustavus Fries operated the park during the 1930 and 1940s. Crowds turned out on weekend nights to dance in the dance hall or to feast on crabs and beer as the men are doing in the photograph above. (Courtesy of R.E. Enoch.)

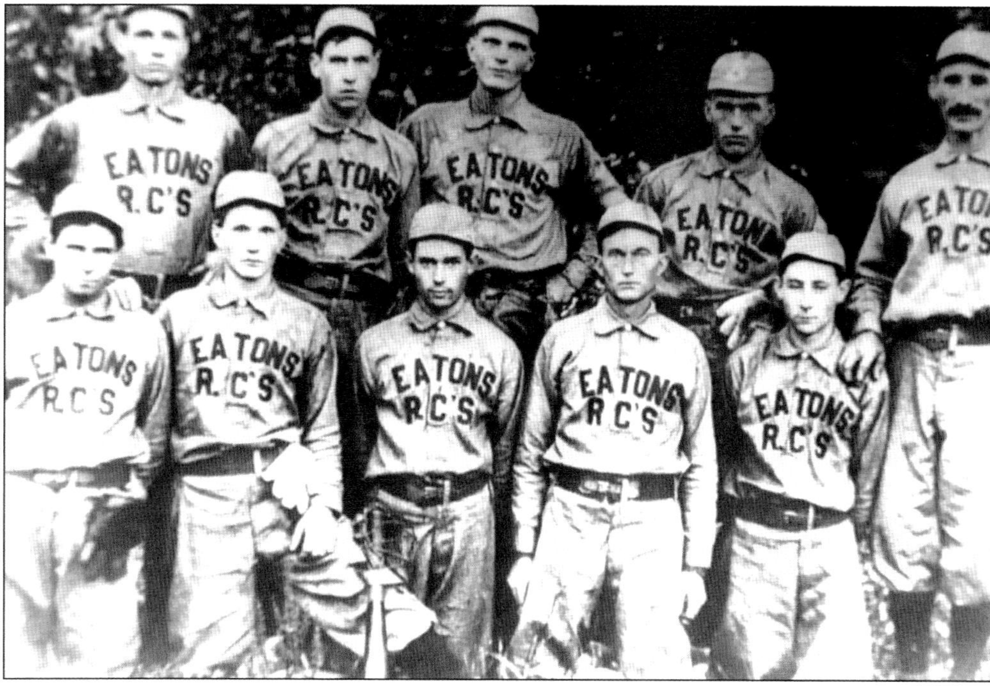

In the early years of the 20th century, each community had its own baseball team. Pictured above is the Eaton's Team, *c.* 1912. Members are, from left to right, (front row) Herbert Spears, Limen Reynolds, Lee Sprout, Tom Reynolds, and Karl Sprout; (standing) George Reynolds, Bill Spears, Seward Bush, Ves Reynolds, and Aaron Swearingen. (Courtesy of R.E. Enoch.)

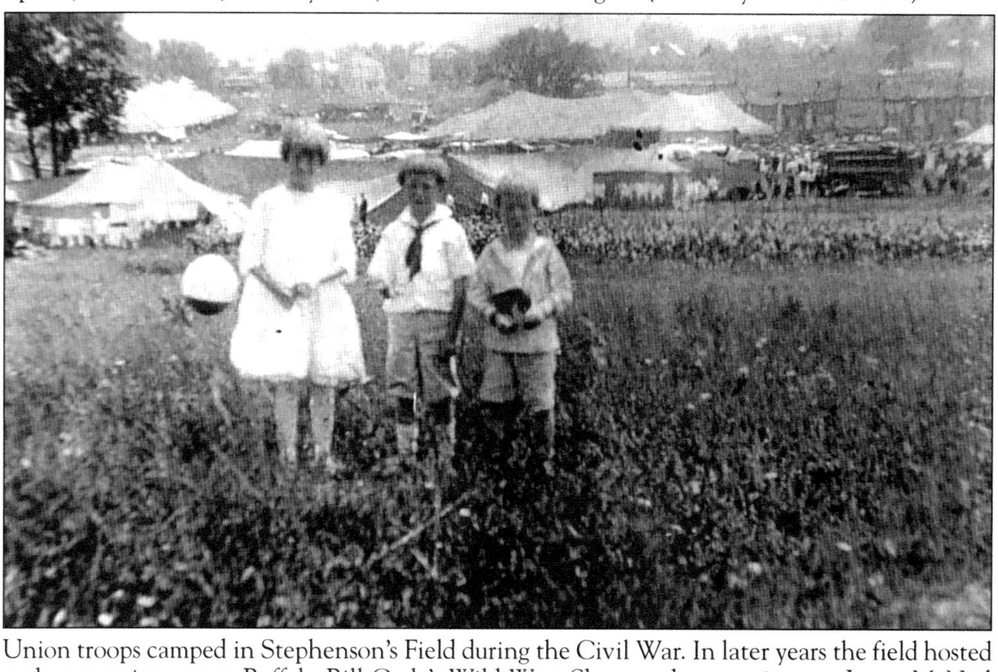

Union troops camped in Stephenson's Field during the Civil War. In later years the field hosted such entertainment as Buffalo Bill Cody's Wild West Show and many circuses. James McNeil Stephenson, one of Parkersburg leading citizens in the 19th century, owned the field. Today several automobile dealers occupy what was Stephenson's Field. (Courtesy of R.E. Enoch.)

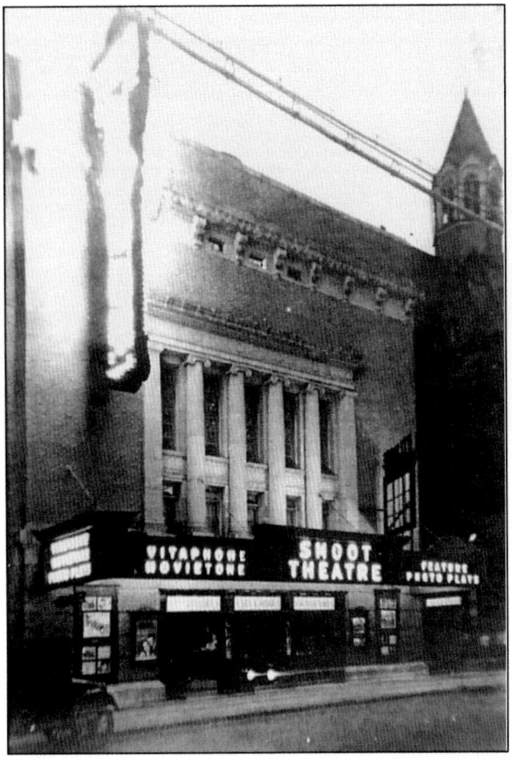

The Smoot Theatre, built at a cost of $200,000 by the Smoot Amusement Company, opened on October 18, 1926, at its present location on Fifth Street. The theater featured vaudeville and photoplays, seated 1,100 persons, and used the latest equipment. For years the Smoot was the place to go on a Saturday night, but competition from television led to its closing in 1974. Plans were made to demolish the theater in 1989, after it sat vacant for many years. However, three weeks before the scheduled demolition, a group of volunteers launched an effort to save the theater. They formed the Smoot Theatre Cooperation and raised funds from state and private sources to restore the Smoot to its former glory. Today, thanks to the dedicated volunteers and the skilled leadership of artistic director Felice Jorgenson, the Smoot features first-rate performances by touring Broadway productions and such artists as Wynton Marsalis, Vince Gill, and Shirley Jones. (Courtesy of the Smoot Theatre.)

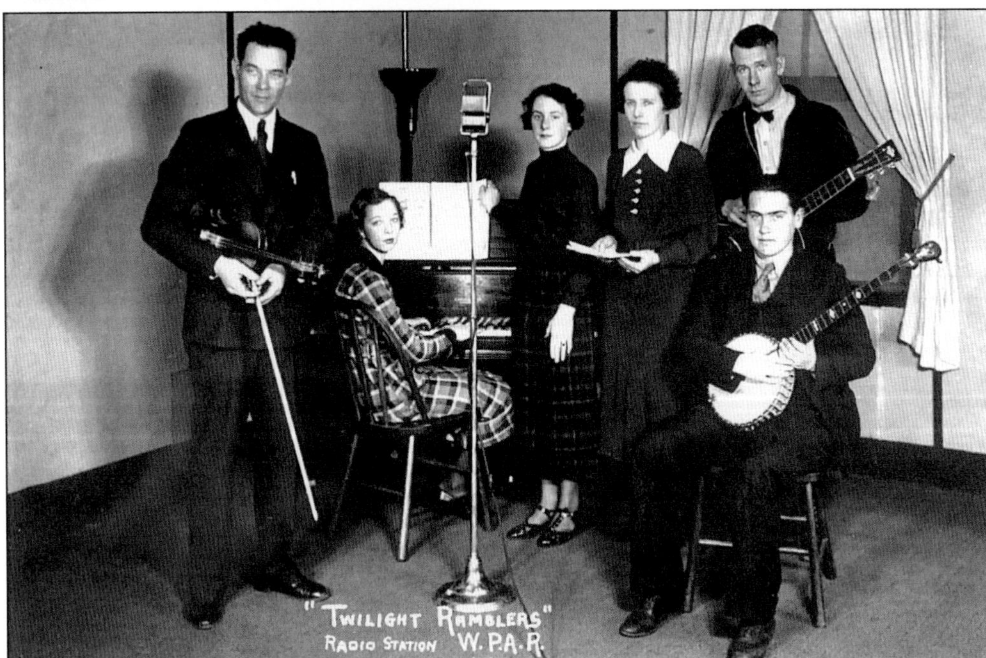

In the mid-1930s the Twilight Ramblers band entertained Wood Countians on WPAR, Parkersburg's premier radio station. The Ramblers appeared on the Farm Chat Program. Pictured above, from left to right, are Sidney Fadely, Allegra Fadley, Mrs. Henry Carpenter, and Henry "Hank" Carpenter. (Courtesy of the West Virginia State Archives.)

Seven

Around the County

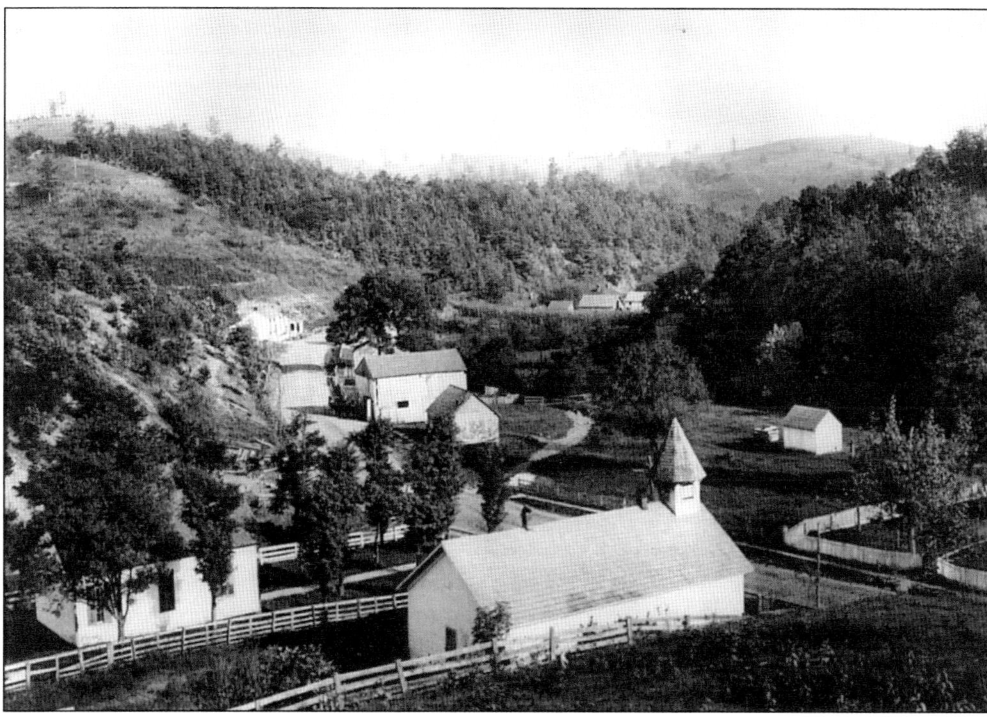

Francisco Murphy rode into the Little Kanawha Valley in 1860 looking for a suitable place to build a sawmill. He settled in a valley six miles east of Parkersburg near what is now Route 50. A town grew up around the mill and became known as Murphy's Mill. In 1891 oil was discovered nearby and the town grew rapidly. The name was changed to Murphytown, pictured above c. 1910. By 1920 the oil field had been depleted and the town returned to being a peaceful rural community. (Courtesy of the West Virginia State Archives.)

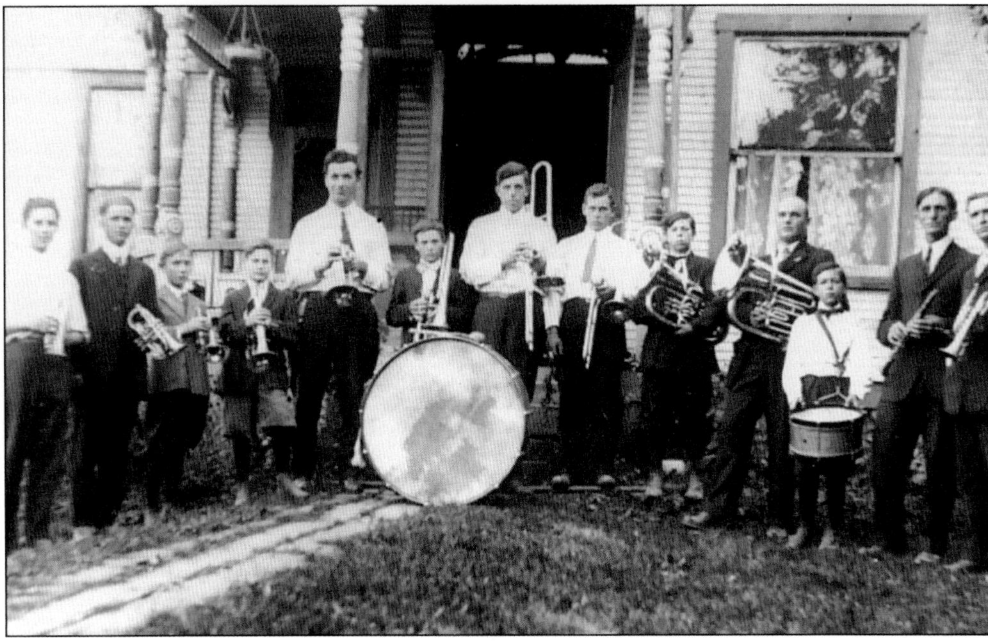

Most communities had community bands. Murphytown's band entertained at local occasions and participated in county-wide events. On October 5, 1899, they marched in the Wood County Centennial celebration parade. *The Parkersburg Sentinel* reported, "The Murphytown Band may not be the best musical organization in the county, but they attracted as much attention as the other bands." (Courtesy of R.E. Enoch.)

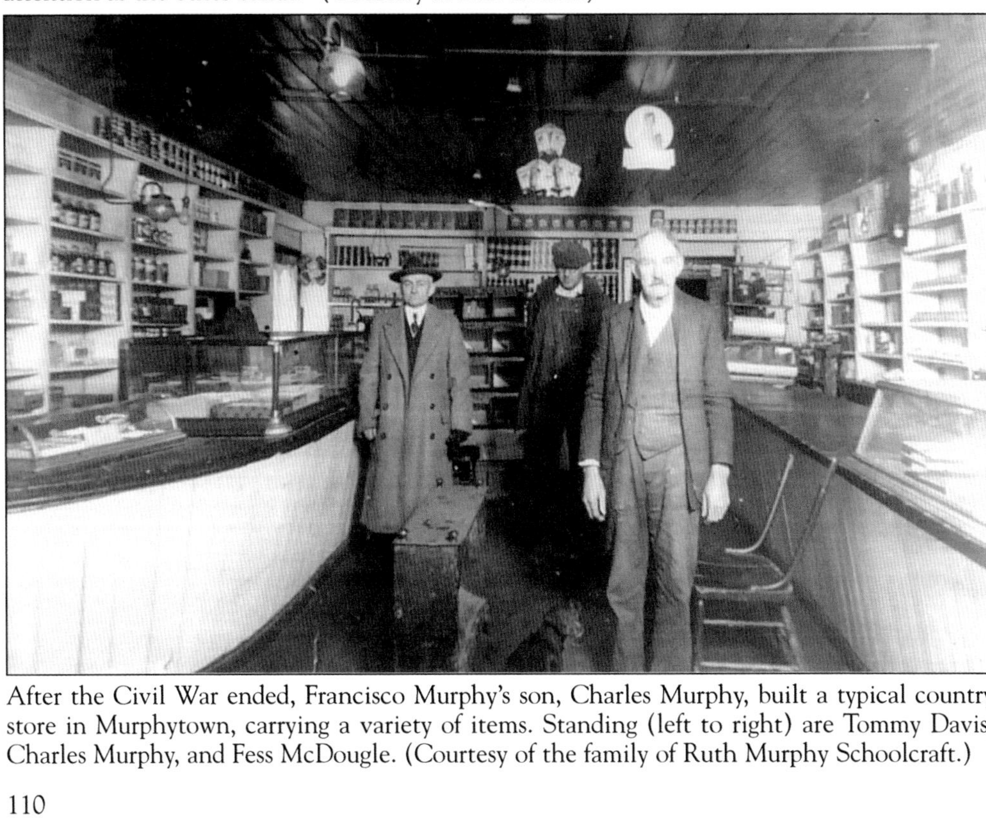

After the Civil War ended, Francisco Murphy's son, Charles Murphy, built a typical country store in Murphytown, carrying a variety of items. Standing (left to right) are Tommy Davis, Charles Murphy, and Fess McDougle. (Courtesy of the family of Ruth Murphy Schoolcraft.)

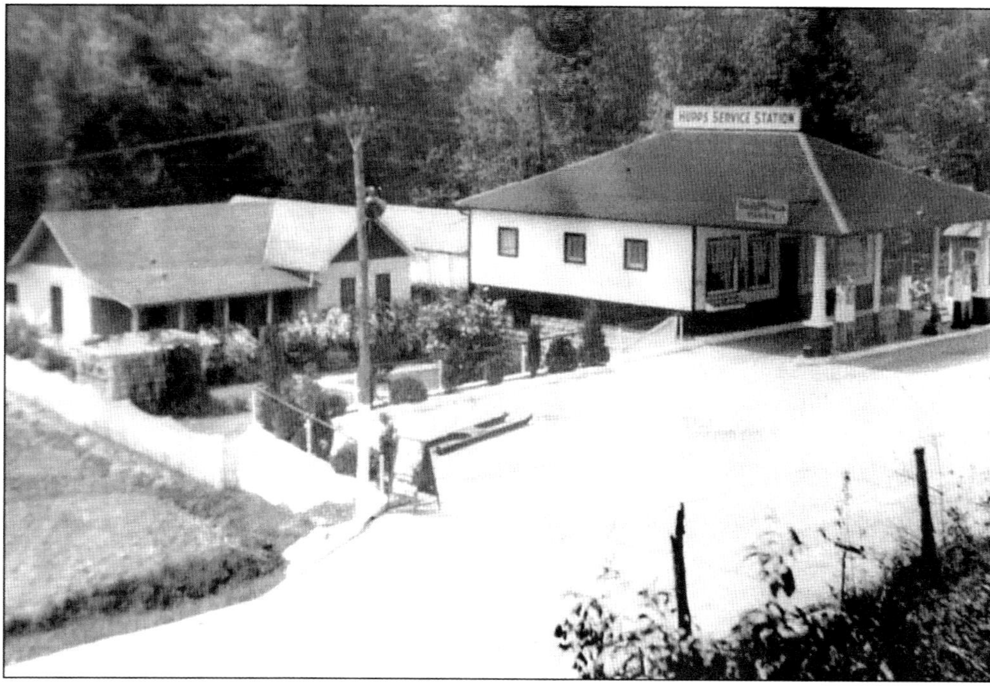

In 1918, after serving in World War I, Virgil Hupp returned home to Murphytown to build one of the first service stations along Route 50. He ran the station from 1926 until 1945, when he sold it to Okey Dilly. Dilly operated the station until 1970. The store was vacant until Darrell and Terry Deem purchased it in February 2000. They have converted it into a diner, deli, and grocery called Hops Country Store and Diner. (Courtesy of Darrell and Terry Deem.)

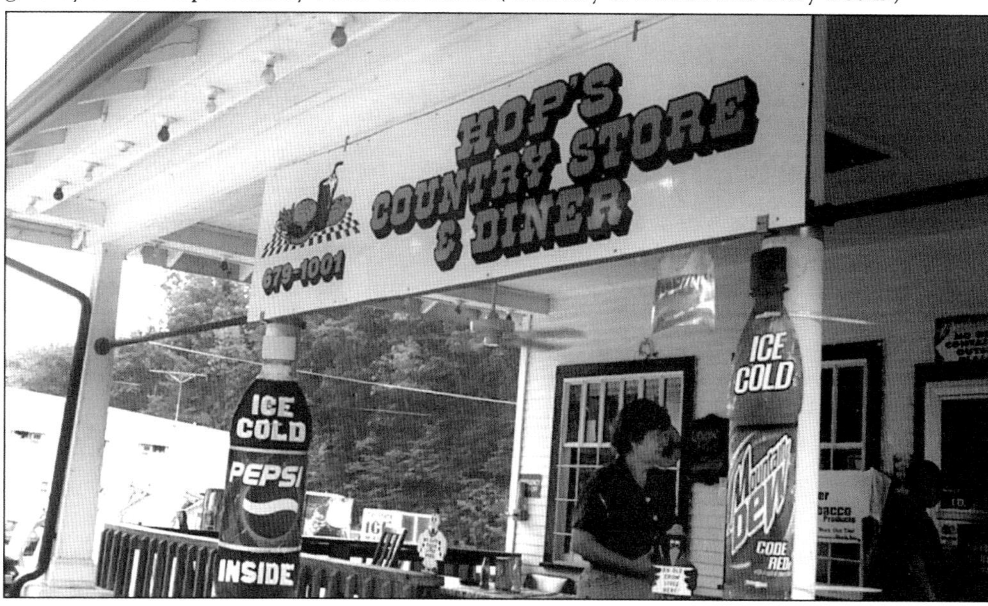

Customers gather on the porch of Hops Country Store and Diner in August 2002. A "good old-fashioned country store" where friends gather to share a meal, pick up groceries, or find out what is happening in the neighborhood, Hops Country Store and Diner sponsors a Murphytown homecoming each fall. (Photograph taken by Fred Cornwell.)

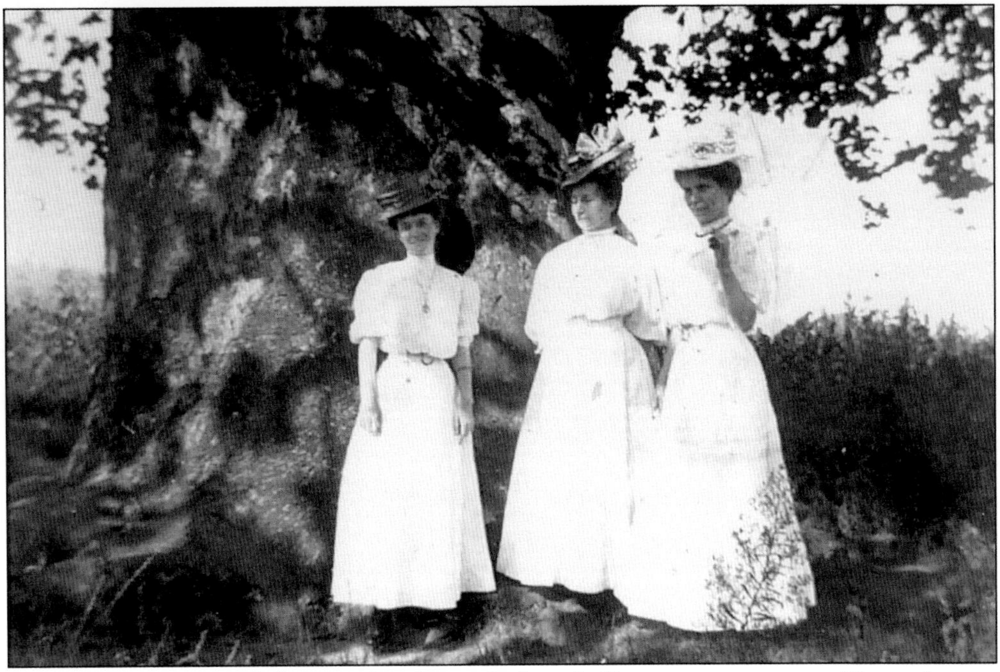

Three lovely Victorian ladies stand in front of a large hollow sycamore tree on Blennerhassett Island, c. 1890. The tree had a circumference of 37.5 feet, making it one of the largest Ohio Valley. Tales abound of American Indians and early settlers hiding in the hollow of this tree. When it was destroyed by fire in 1953, the sycamore was estimated to be 400 years old. (Courtesy of Blennerhassett Island Historical State Park.)

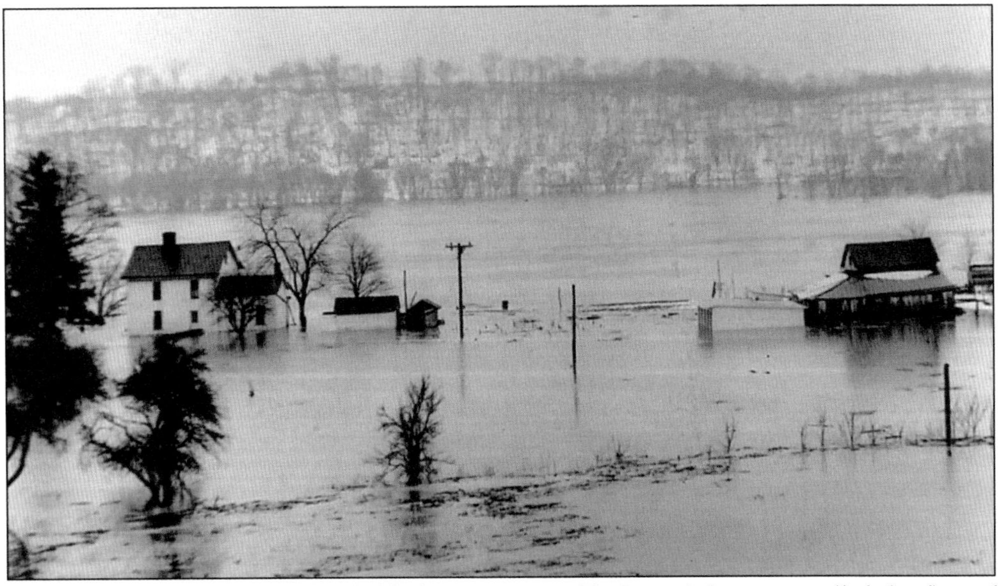

Blennerhassett Island often flooded before a system of locks and dams controlled the flow of the river. During the 1913 and 1937 floods, residents of the island were rescued by boats. Their cattle, however, were not as fortunate. Many tried to swim to shore and drowned. When the Blennerhassett Mansion was restored, planners made the foundation six feet higher than the original to protect it from floods. (Courtesy of Blennerhassett Island Historical State Park.)

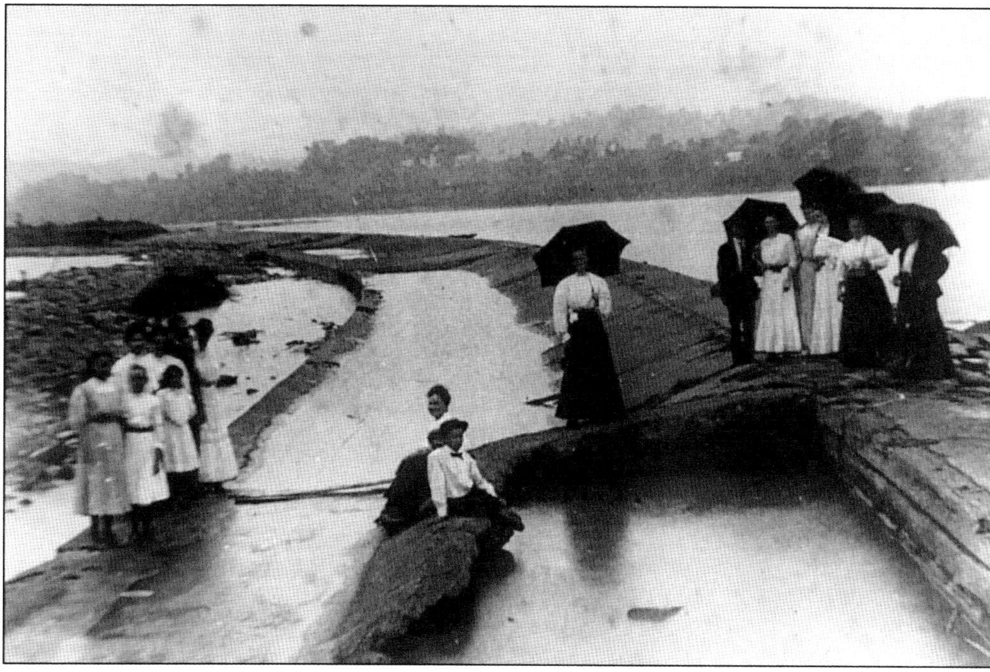

To improve navigation on the Ohio River, the United States Army Corps of Engineers built a wing dam in the 1840s that extended from the Virginia (now West Virginia) side of the river to the head of Blennerhassett Island. When the river was low, people enjoyed walking out on the dam, as shown in this c. 1906 photograph. When Lock 19 at Little Hocking was completed, the wing dam was covered with 10 feet of water. (Courtesy of Blennerhassett Island Historical State Park.)

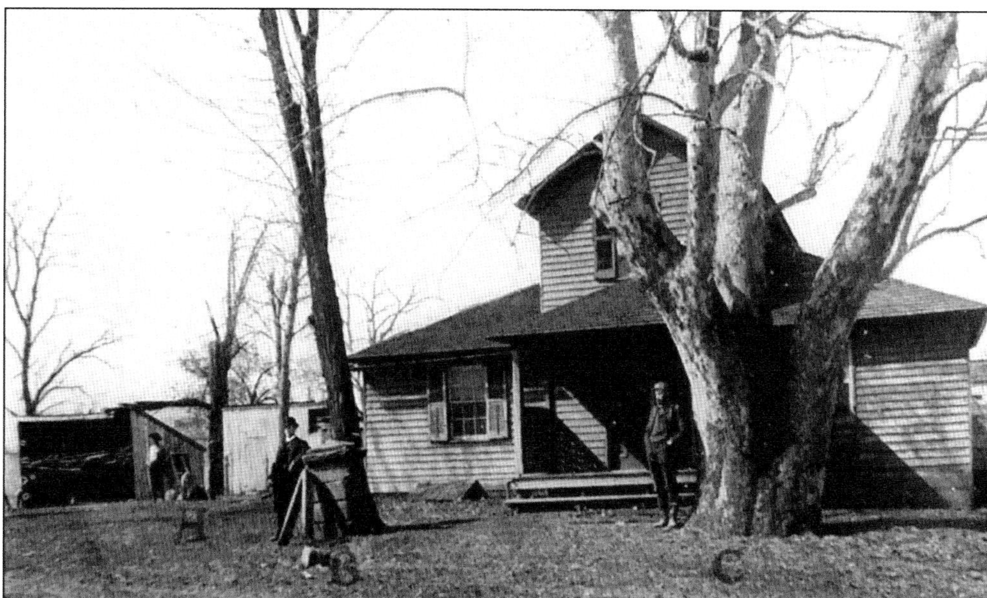

This house on Blennerhassett Island was the Gordon bungalow. The center part was built in 1834. It stood on the site of the north wing building of the mansion. Two boys who escaped from the Union Mission burned the bungalow in 1952. (Collection of B. Leavengood.)

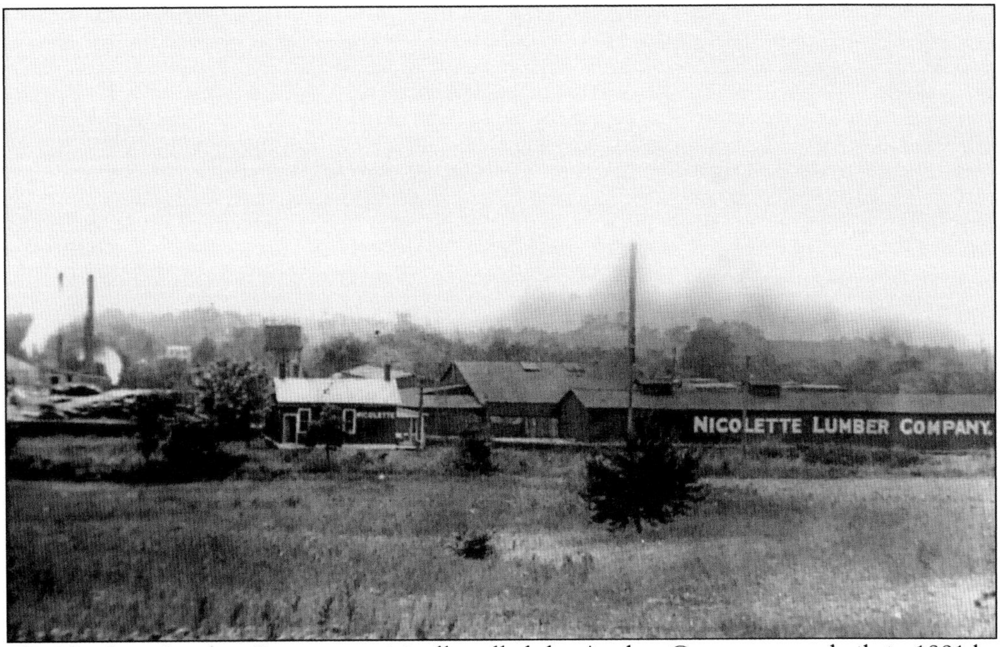

The Nicolette Lumber Company, originally called the Anchor Company, was built in 1881 by two Pennsylvania businessmen, W.H. Ewing and William Croft. The mill, the second largest in Wood County, was powered by steam. The mill soon became the largest producer of oak timber in the United States. The Nicola Brothers—Austin and Frank—purchased the mill in 1892. They changed the name of the mill to Nicolette Mill and incorporated the village that had grown up around the mill as Nicolette. (Courtesy of R.E. Enoch.)

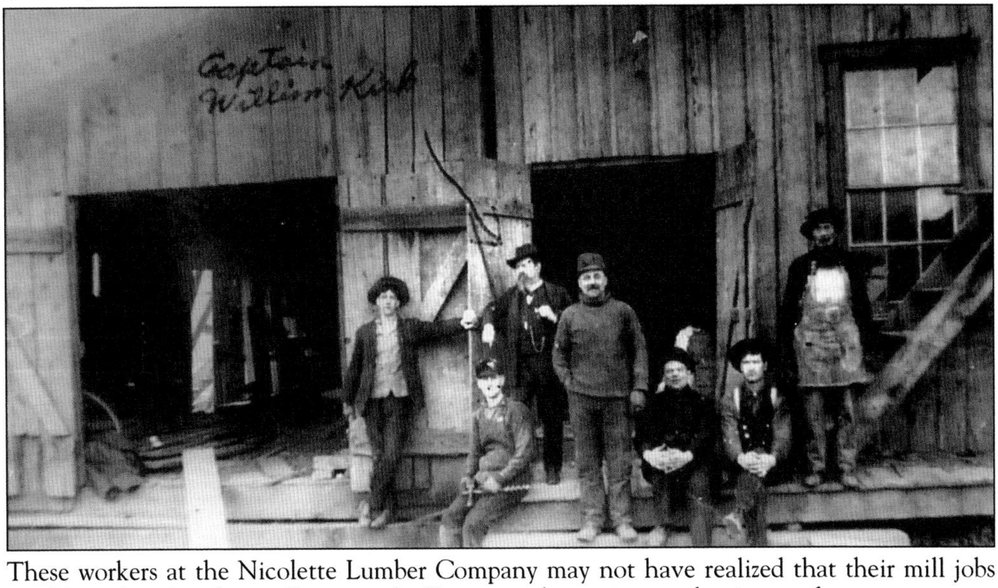

These workers at the Nicolette Lumber Company may not have realized that their mill jobs would not last. Lumber mills across the East were decreasing production, and some were even closing. It was only a matter of time before the Nicolette Lumber Company would face the same problems. The company closed in 1917 because of an inadequate supply of logs. When the mill shut down, most families moved away. By 1920 only nine families remained in Nicolette. (Courtesy of R.E. Enoch.)

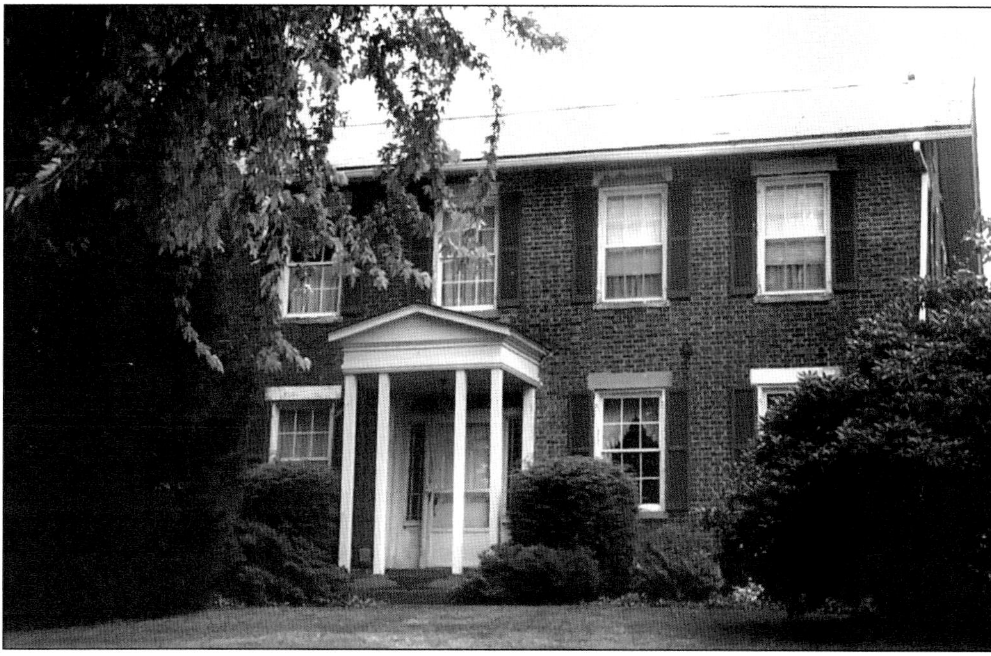

The earliest attempt at settlement in what is now Wood County was made near present-day Williamstown by Joseph Tomlinson Sr. and his son Samuel in 1769. Indian attacks forced the Tomlinsons and other settlers to return to their homes in the East or seek safety in one of several forts on the frontier. It was not until after the Revolutionary War that the Tomlinsons returned to Wood County to stay. In 1839 Joseph Tomlinson III built this Colonial-style brick mansion. It is the oldest home in Williamstown. (Photograph taken by Fred Cornwell.)

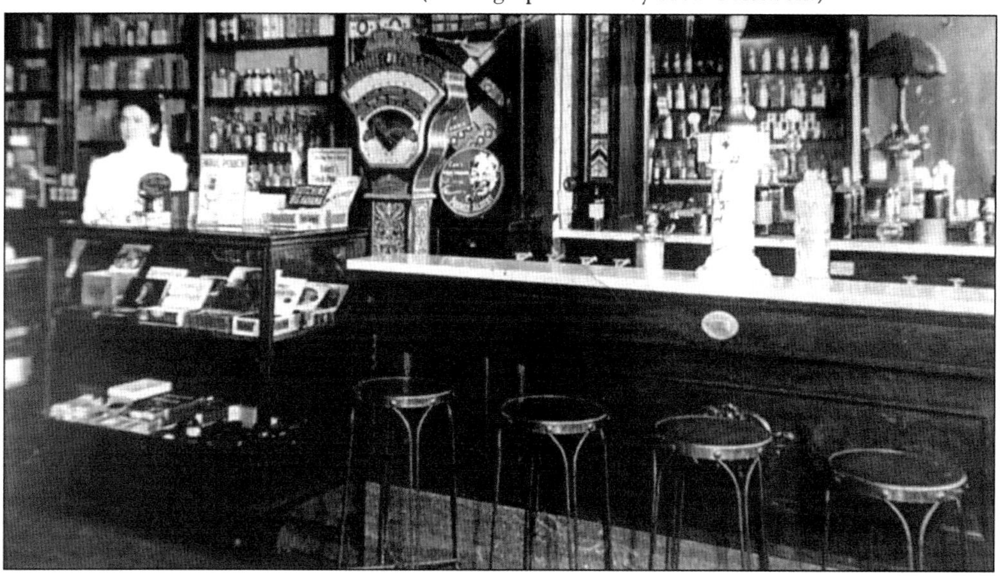

Sipping an ice cream soda at the corner drugstore is only a memory now. Old-timers in Williamstown remember Sadie Haught's drugstore at Highland Avenue and Second Street. Her secret chocolate syrup recipe was much in demand. Ms. Haught dispersed prescriptions along with sodas, and she was the first registered female pharmacist in the state of West Virginia. (Courtesy of Pat Peters.)

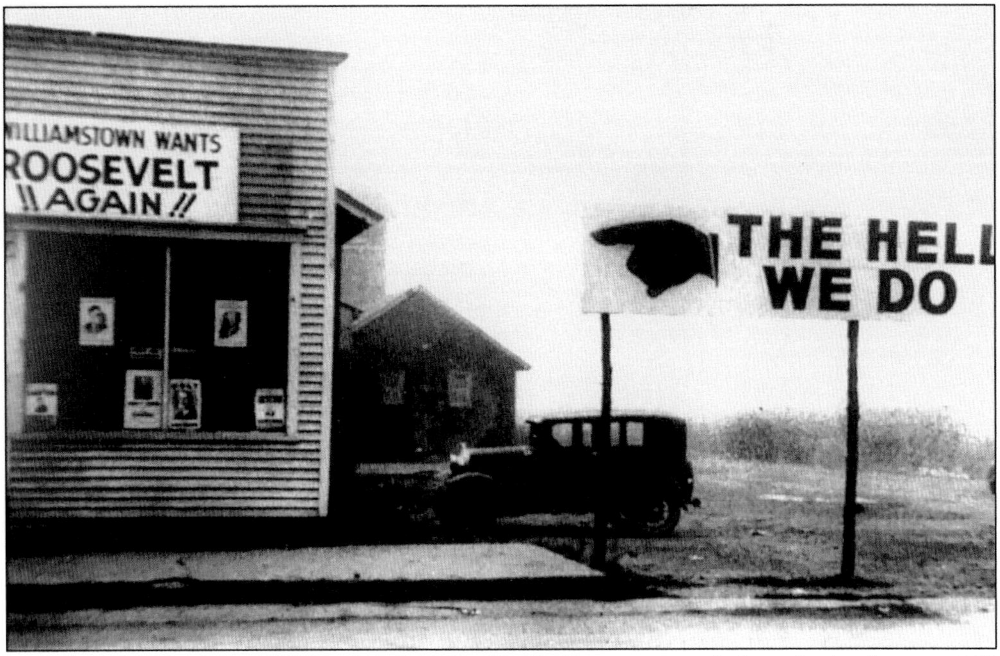

Kenneth "Red" Bever and his brother, O. Frank Bever, opened their barbershop at 208 Highland Avenue in 1935. Franklin Roosevelt's third run for the presidency generated some heated discussions in the late 1930s as the signs show. The building was later moved across the street to 209 Highland Avenue. It was torn down in the 1950s to make way for Schultheiss Furniture. (Courtesy of Pat Peters.)

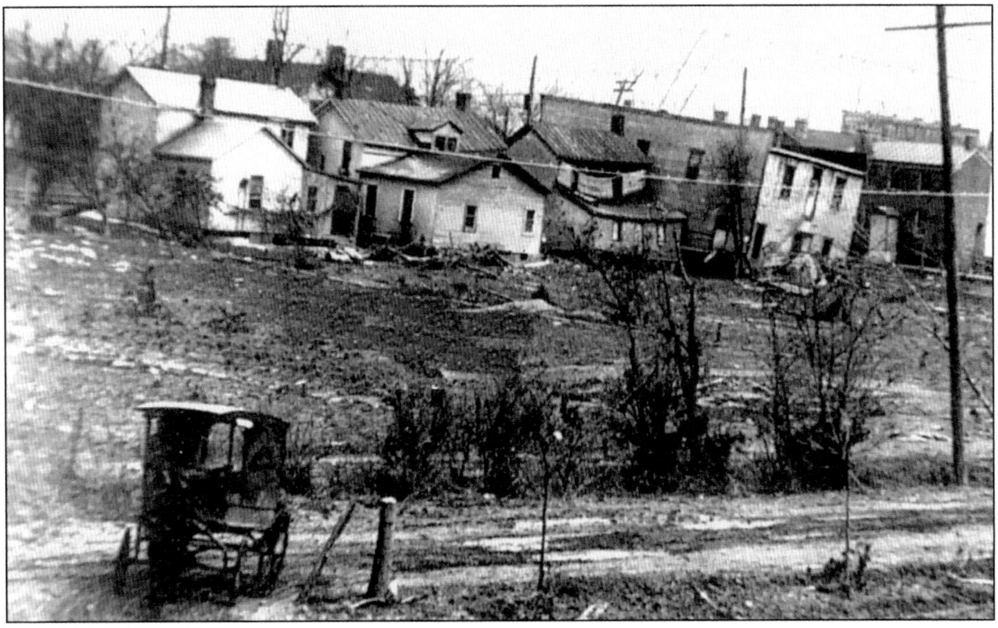

The 1913 flood damaged houses in lower Williamstown along Parkersburg Road, now called State Route 14. Eleven inches of rainfall fell over a 24-hour period, causing the Ohio River to crest at 45 feet. Most of the buildings pictured above were too badly damaged to restore and were eventually demolished. (Courtesy of Pat Peters.)

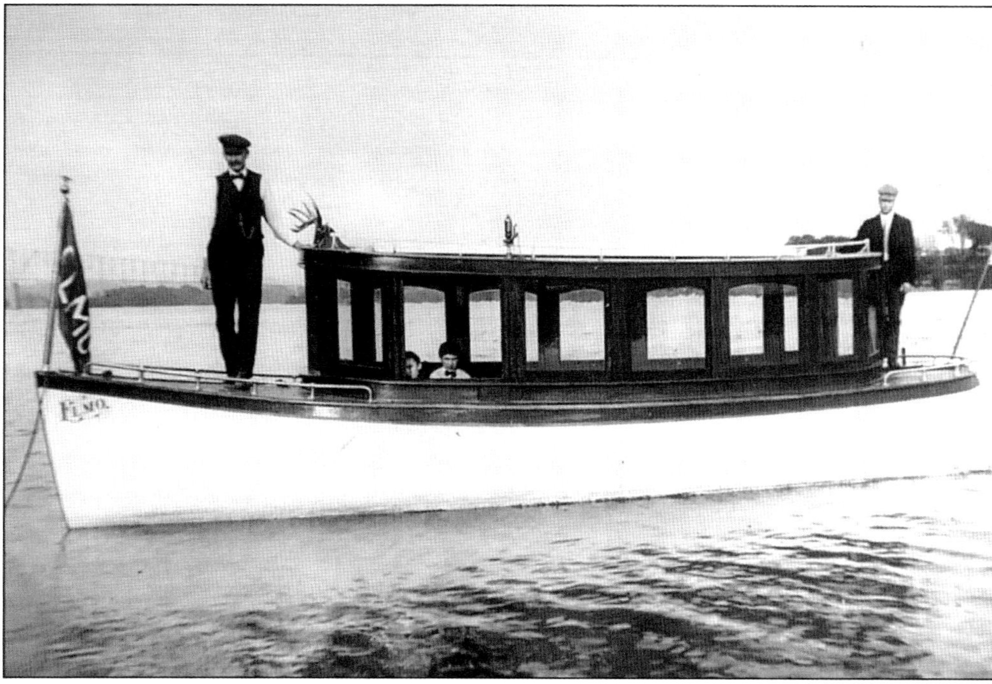

The *Elmo* was built by the Parmalee Boat Company in Williamstown. Owner Charlie Anderson named the boat for his son, Elmo. In this 1905 photograph the sleek boat is testing its seaworthiness in the Ohio River. (Courtesy of Charles D. Alden.)

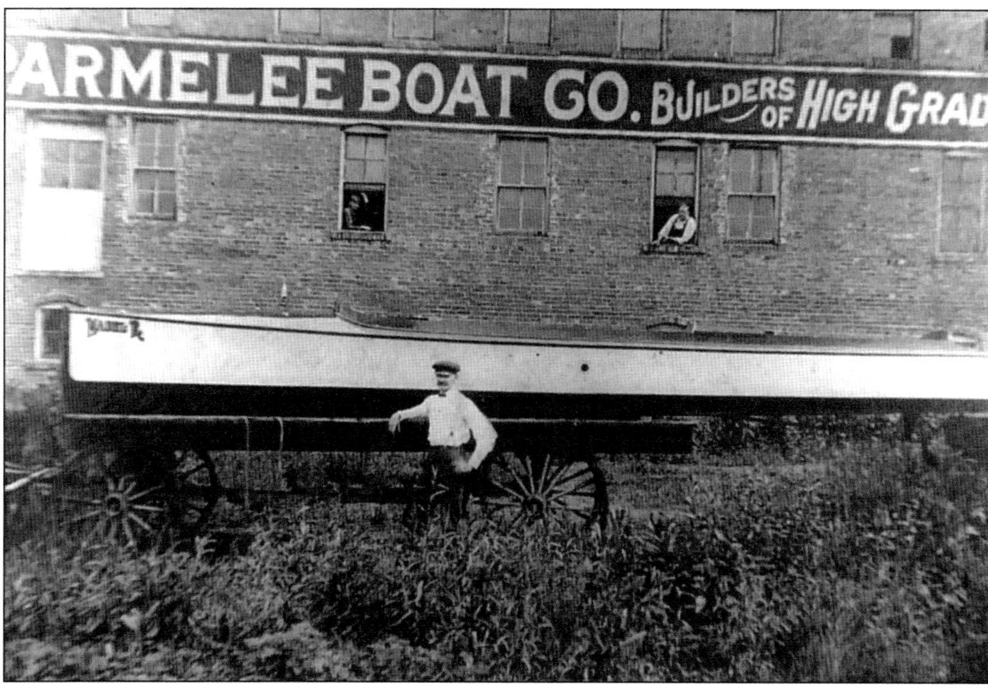

Charlie Reynolds owned the Parmalee Boat Company, builders of High Grade Pleasure Boats, located up river from Highland Avenue near the railroad in Williamstown. He named the boat beside the building *Mable R* for his daughter. (Courtesy of Charles D. Alden.)

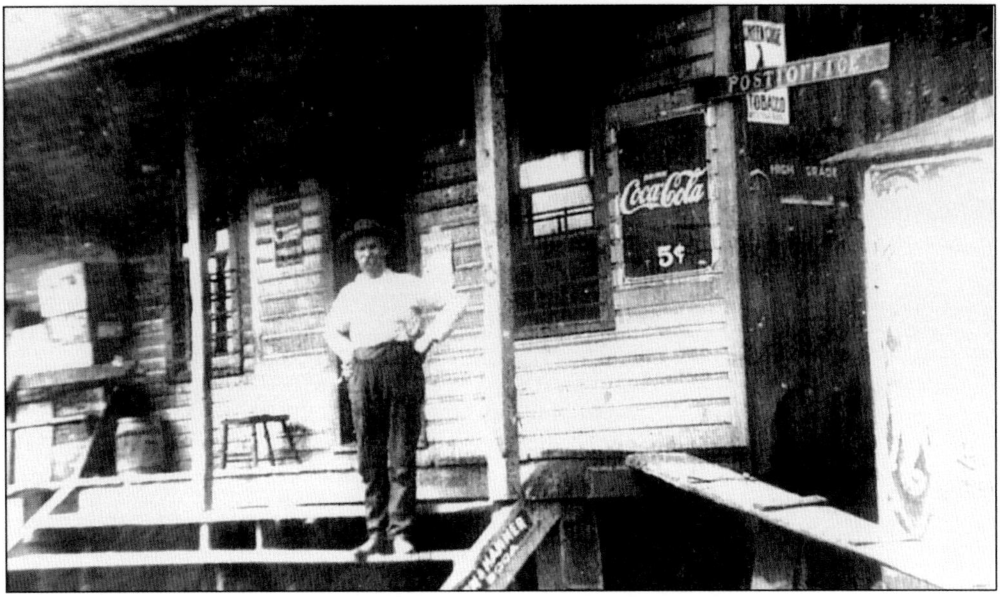

Kanawha Station was a booming town prior to the Civil War. Besides being a train stop, Kanawha Station had an oil refinery and a cooper shop that made barrels for the refinery. Small businesses, such as the grocery store/post office pictured above, flourished. During the Civil War raiders destroyed Burning Springs oil field. After the war, Kanawha Station, which was dependent on business related to the Burning Springs oil field, lost most of its population and all of the businesses closed. Today nothing remains but a few summer homes. (Courtesy of Sally Wyatt, researching Kanawha Station, West Virginia.)

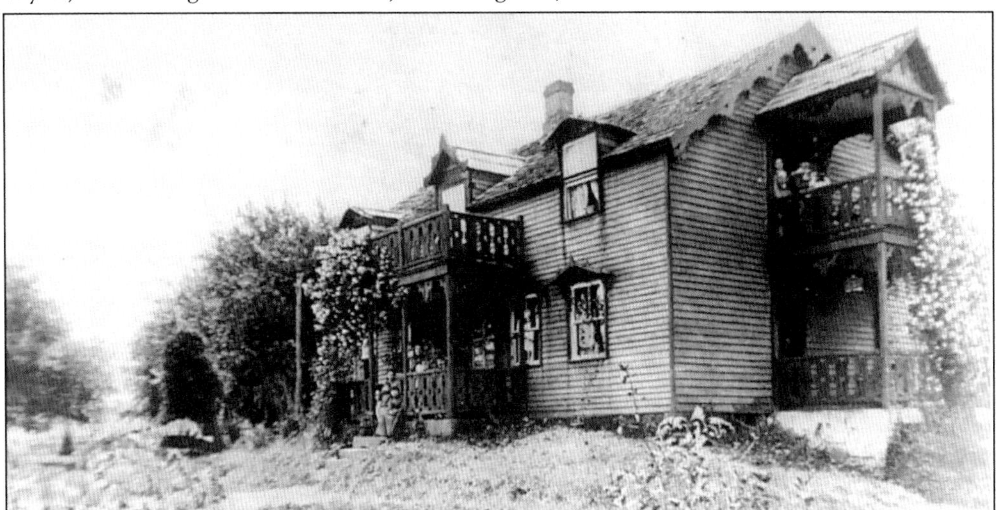

Emil Meldahl, a Dane who had worked for the King of Denmark, and his wife, Caroline, came to America in the late 1840s. They settled in Cleveland, but the cold wind off Lake Erie affected Mrs. Meldahl's asthma. After contacting their friends the Munchmeyers in Washington Bottom, the Meldahls moved to Washington Bottom and purchased part of the Munchmeyer farm. Although Mr. Meldahl had little experience in farming, he did well and built the home pictured above in 1860. The home burned in the late 1890s. (Courtesy of Blennerhassett Island Historical State Park.)

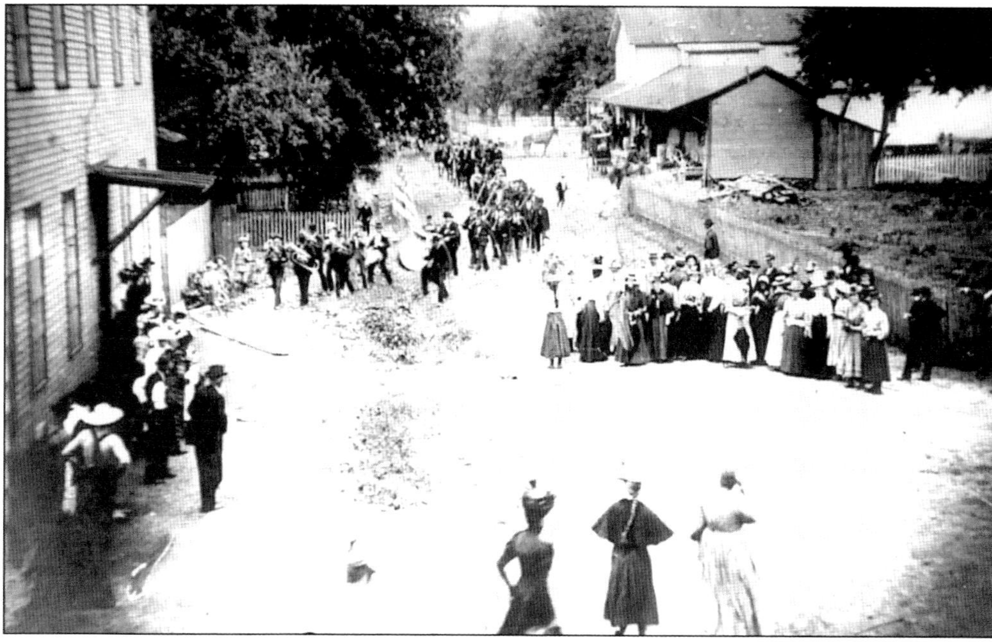

Nearly everyone in Belleville and the surrounding farms came to town to celebrate Memorial Day. This picture shows the parade, probably between 1896 and 1900, winding its way down the main street. The first horn player on the left is E.W. Crooks, born in 1874. (Courtesy of Dr. Robert D. Crooks.)

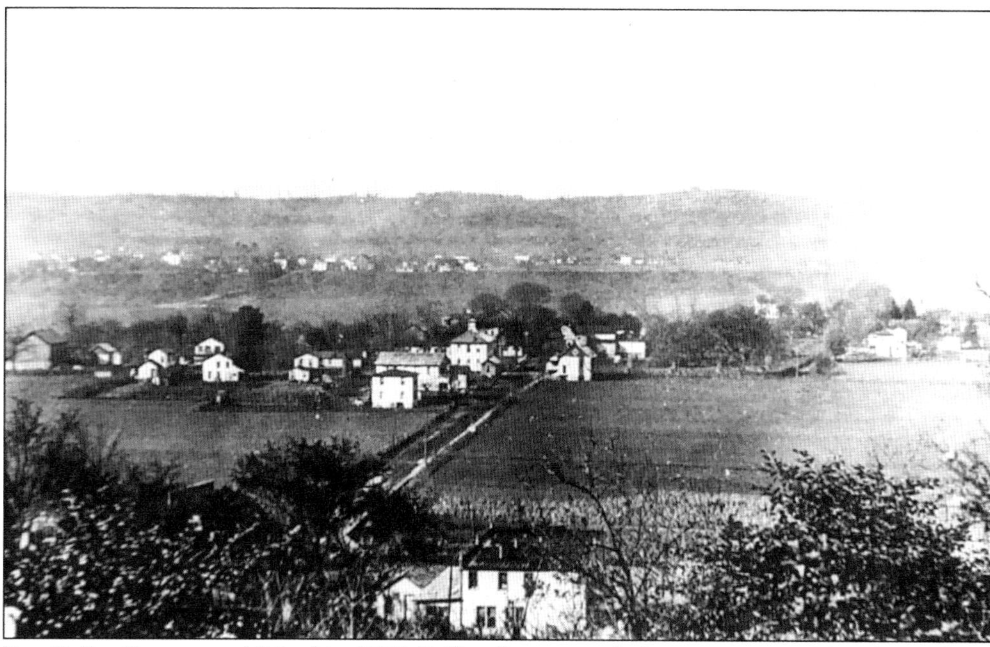

Fort Belleville was established in 1785. Belleville, pictured above prior to 1922, is located one mile south of the original fort. In this picture the Methodist church, built in 1908, stands on the northeast corner of the Main Street. The school is on the southeast corner, and the Methodist parsonage is on the left of the street leading to the river. The picture was taken from a hill east of Belleville. (Courtesy of Nadine Hofmann.)

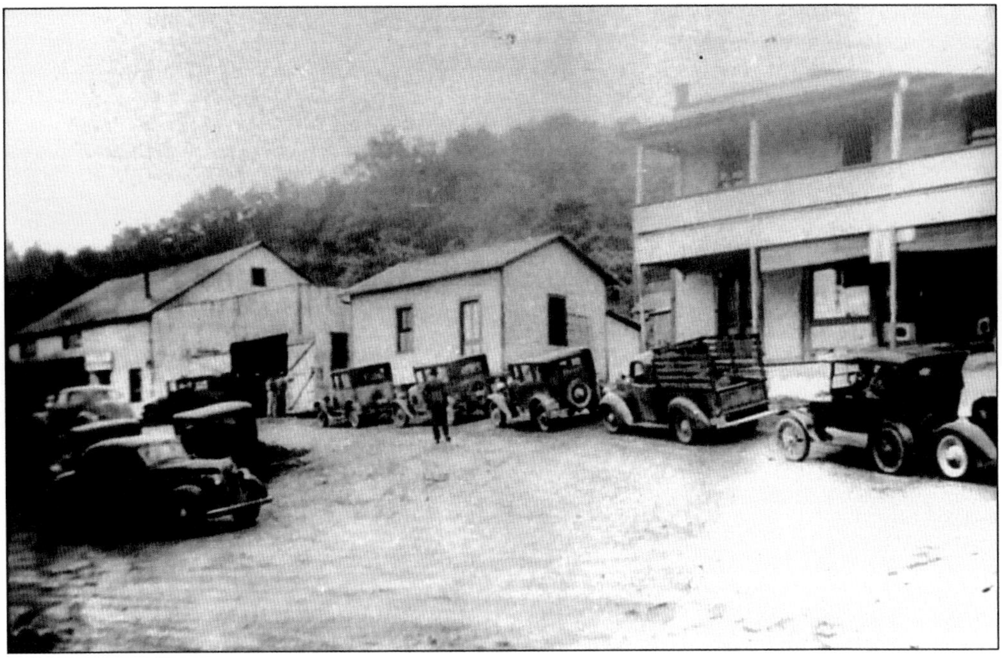

Farmers brought their wool to Belleville to sell after shearing their sheep. This day was called "Wool Day." (Courtesy of Nadine Hofmann.)

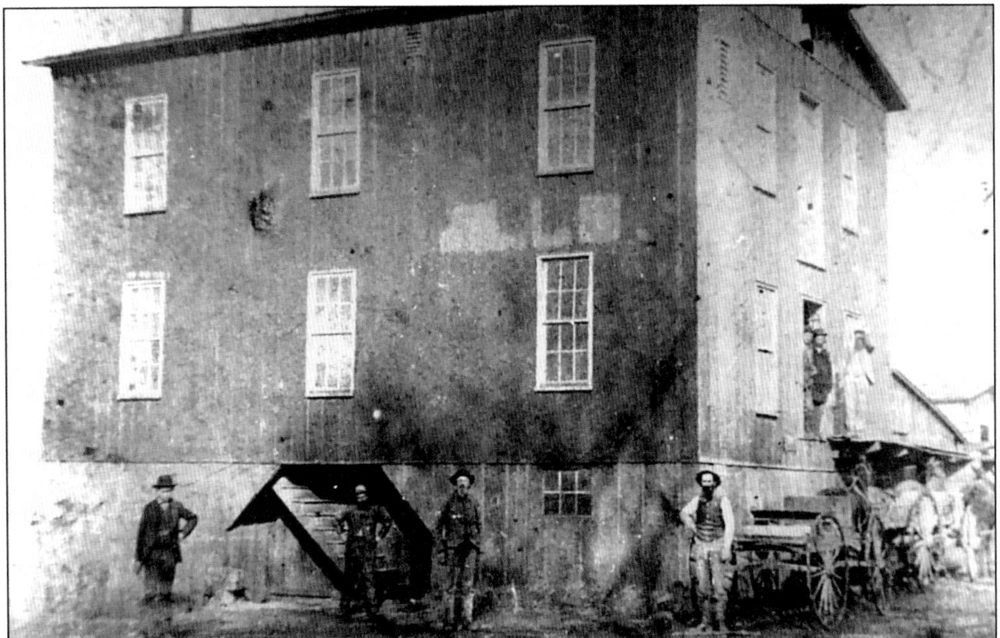

Jacob Adams built this steam mill at the foot of Second Street near the Ohio River in Belleville for H.H. Pennybacker and a Mr. Wells sometime before 1886. This is the only remaining picture of the mill, which was known as the "Big Red Mill." Farmers brought their wheat to the mill to be ground into flour, which was shipped in barrels made by the local cooper plant. The flood of 1913 damaged but did not remove the mill. However, the proprietors were not able to make the mill operational again and it was dismantled. (Courtesy of Mrs. Forrest Adams.)

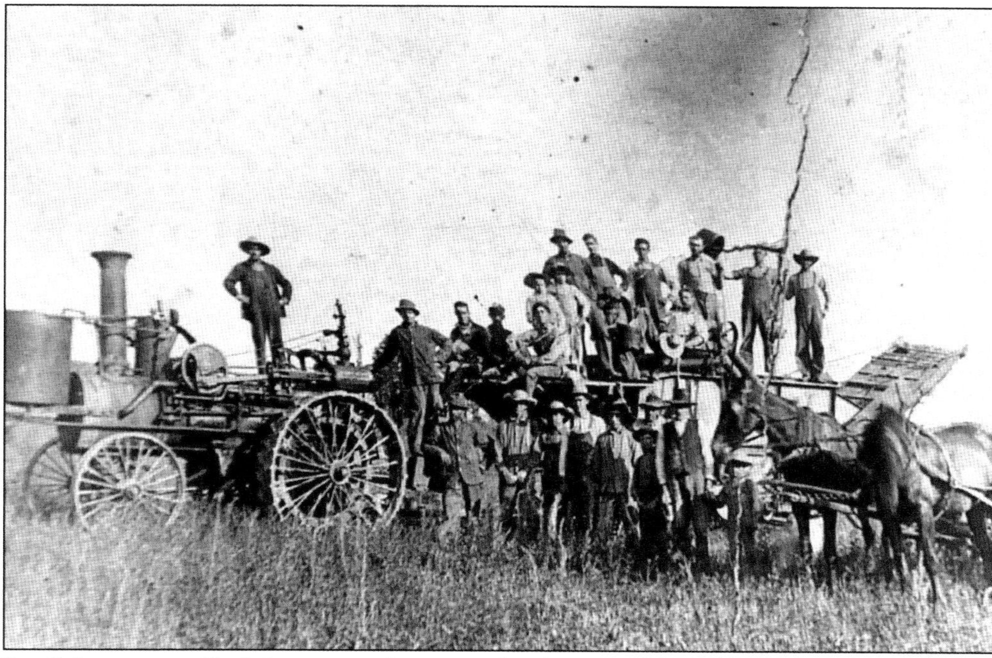

Small farmers usually did not own their own threshing machine, shown above. Instead, they hired a thresher man to bring his rig to their field. When all was ready, the farmer and his neighbors went out into the field to load shocks of wheat onto a horse-drawn wagon. After the wagon was filled, the wheat was brought to the threshing machine and pitched onto the threshing machine's bundle feeder, where the grain was separated from the stalk. (Courtesy of Nadine Hofmann.)

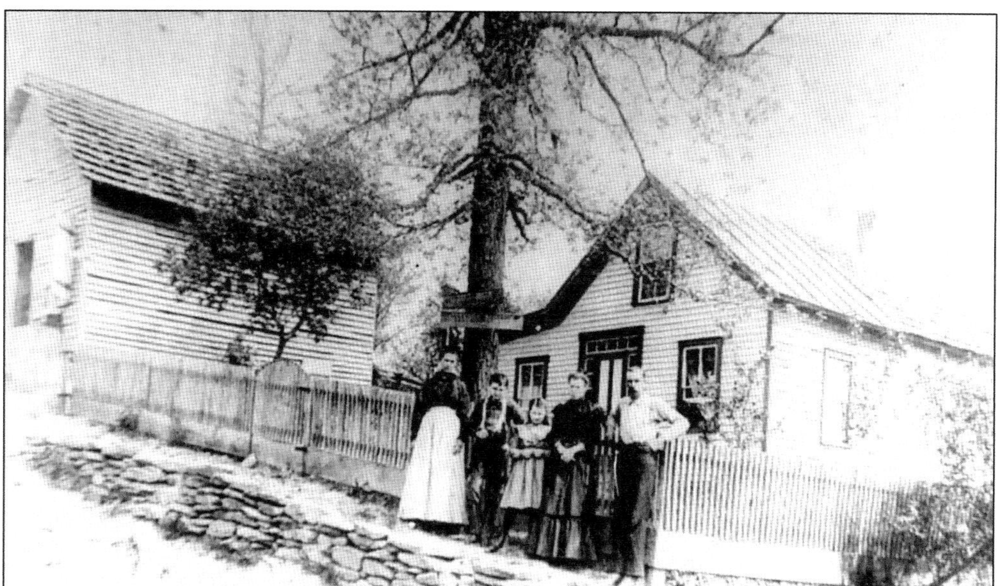

This photograph shows the Thomas Dugan family standing in front of their home at Renuis, two and a half miles northeast of Belleville. The post office and store were on the left of the road passing in front of the house. The post office existed from 1887 to 1906. One of the postmasters was Cyrenius Burdette. (Courtesy of Nadine Hofmann.)

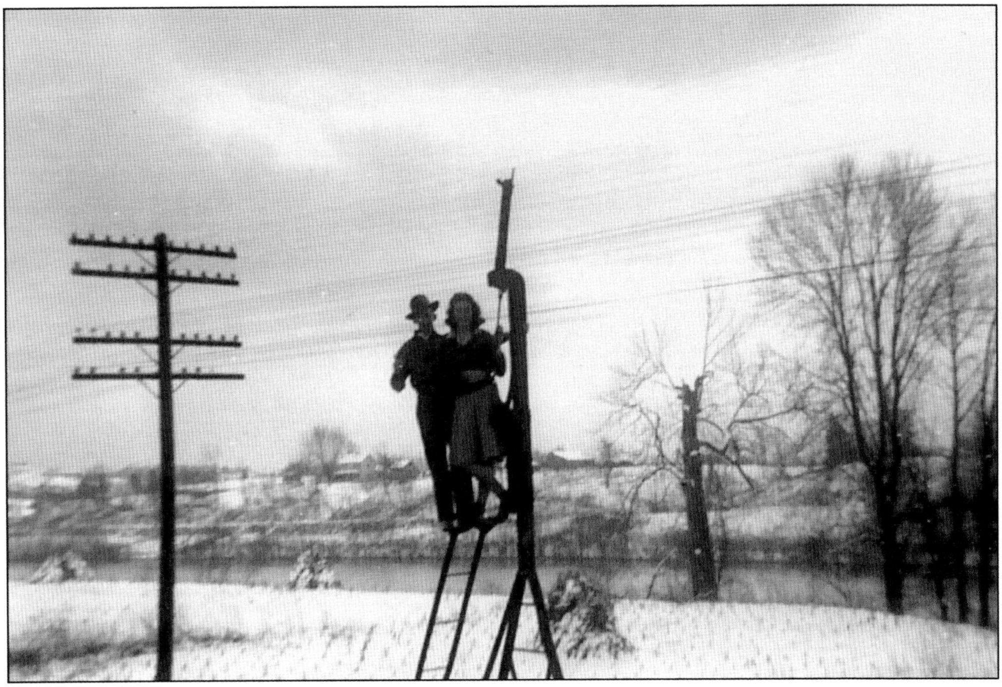

On this dark and gloomy winter day in 1942, a young couple climbed the Davisville mail drop to either wait for the mail or just to have their picture taken. The postmaster in Davisville hung a sack of mail on the hook to be picked up by the train. (Courtesy of Nadine Hoffman.)

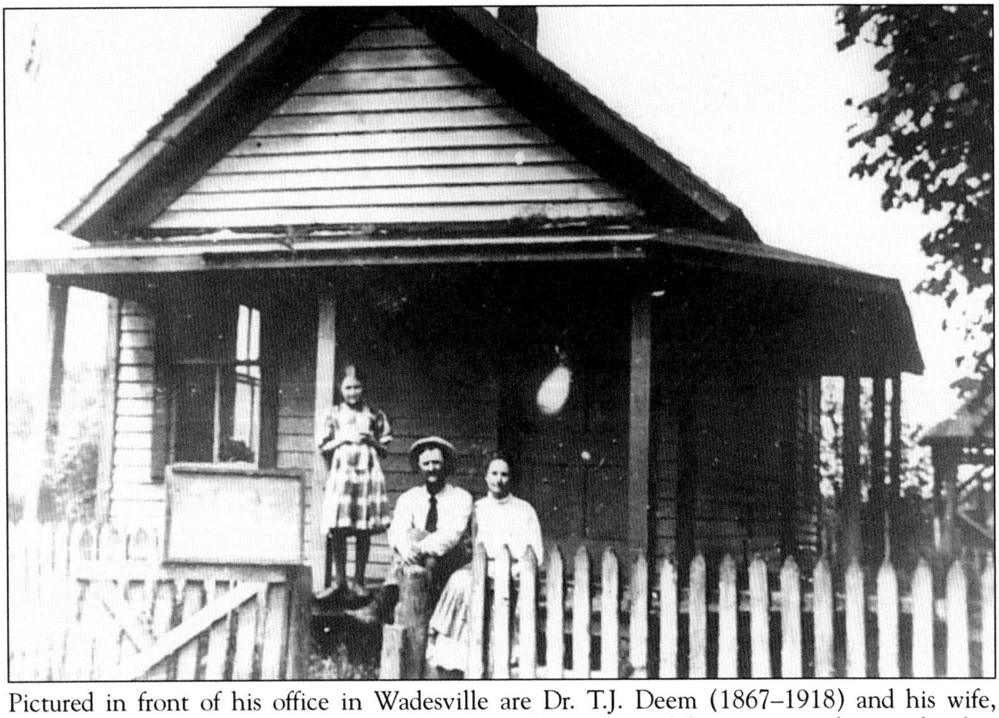

Pictured in front of his office in Wadesville are Dr. T.J. Deem (1867–1918) and his wife, Victoria; daughter Georgia is standing on the porch. Doctors of that era treated entire families and dealt with everything from chicken pox to heart failure. (Courtesy of Nadine Hofmann.)

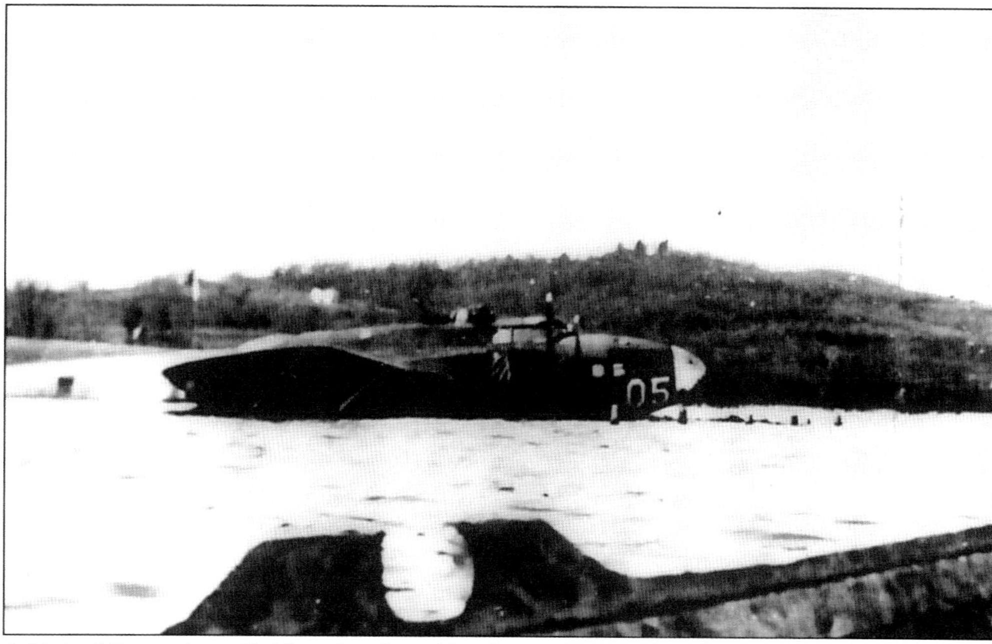

A United States Army B-17 made a forced landing on December 18, 1942, on Charles Lowthers farm at Belleville because of low gas. The crew told neighbors that they had "about 40 gallons of gas left, just enough to go around the corner." Crew members remained on board overnight and took turns standing guard over the ship. A heavy snowstorm followed by warm weather that made the field muddy, plus a flood kept the plane grounded until January 14, 1943. (Courtesy of Nadine Hofmann.)

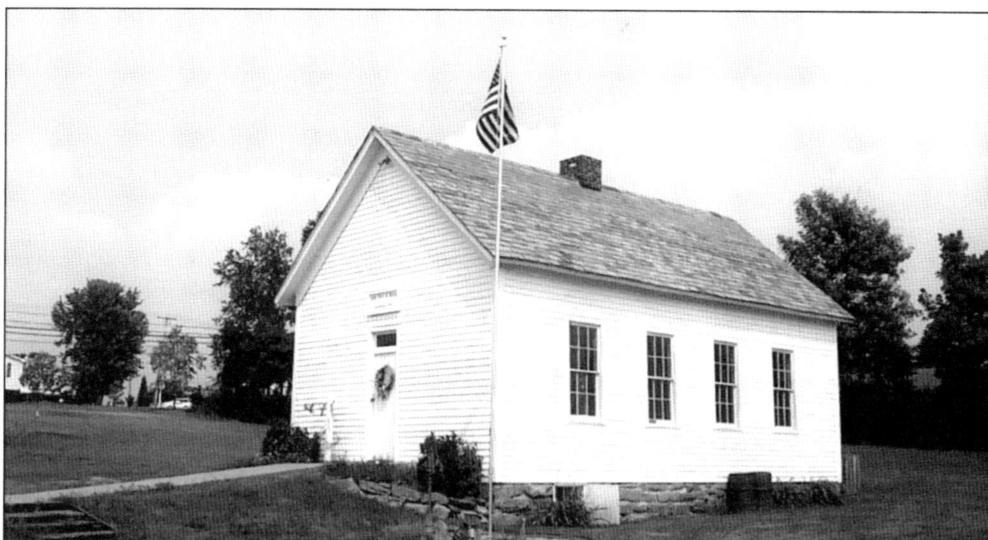

The New Era School was located on Missouri Run Road close to Pettyville. It opened in 1884 and closed in 1956. For several years it was used for community meetings. In 1991 a group of volunteers moved the school to the campus of Mineral Wells Elementary to use as a living heritage museum. Every year fourth-grade classes spend a half-day in the school learning what it was like to go to a one-room school. Also, the New Era school is a repository for Wood County School history. (Photograph by Fred Cornwell.)

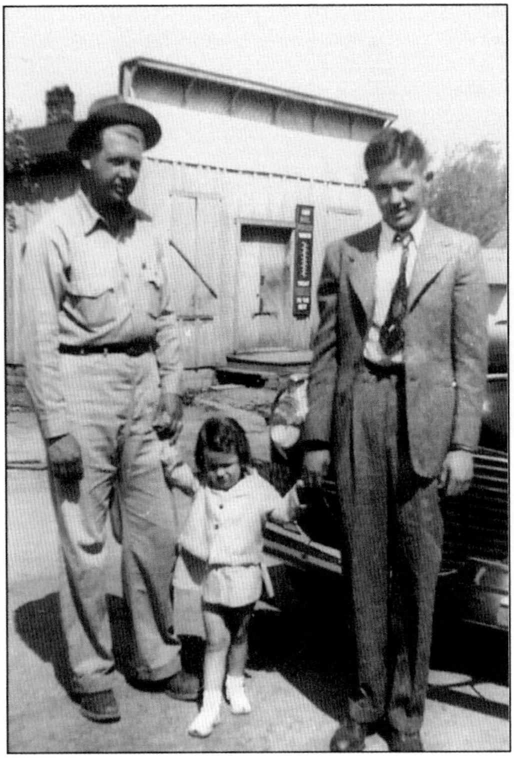

Arden Marshall, Betty Lee Marshall, and Clarence Hackett stand in front of the Hackett Store in Pleasant Hill (now Deerwalk) c. 1941. Steve and Ida Hackett purchased the store building and land surrounding it from K.W. Goodwin around 1890. The store has been relocated twice, once when the original Route 50 was constructed and again when Route 50 was rerouted. The Hacketts operated the store until the early 1950s. Today the store has moved once again—it is now on old Route 50 in Pleasant Hill. It served as a community center until it was leased to the Deerwalk Chapter of the Veterans of Foreign Wars. (Courtesy of Gladys Marshall.)

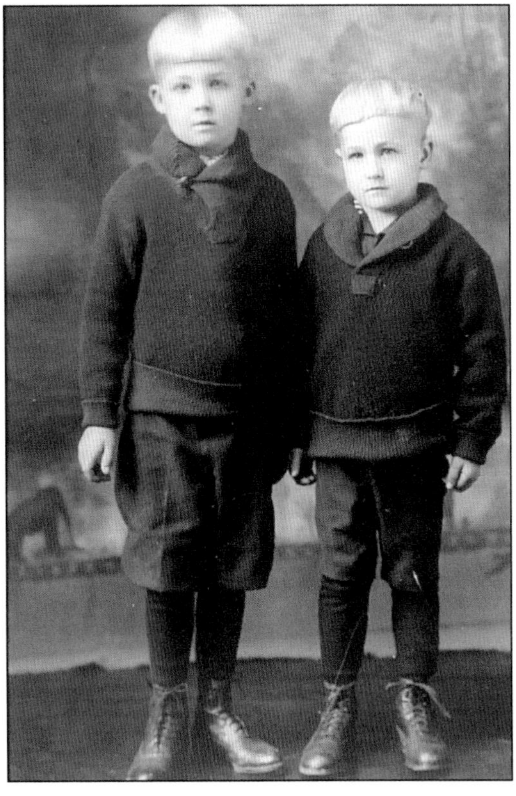

Brothers Arden and Paul Marshall of Pleasant Hill are dressed in their Sunday best knickers as they pose for the photographer, c. 1925. In those days, boys wore dresses until the age of six, when they converted to knickers. Arden worked as a surveyor and made the first surveys for the Wood County Airport. He was instrumental in starting the West Virginia Association of Land Surveyors, which established statewide standards for surveyors. Paul served in the army air corps in World War II and later became a surveyor. He served as Wood County surveyor for many years. (Courtesy of Gladys Marshall.)

The congregation of the Pleasant Hill United Methodist Church stands on the steps in front of the church for a group photograph in the 1940s. The church stood high on a hill above the community, and getting to services meant climbing a long flight of steep stairs. The church pictured is the second of four churches that have served Pleasant Hill. Built in the early 1889, it replaced the original log church built in the 1870s. The church was dismantled in 1957. A new cement block church was built later that year, only to be torn down when the four-lane Route 50 was built in the late 1960s. Still another church was built on old Route 50. It was dedicated in 1968 and is still in use today. (Courtesy of Ruth Gearhart.)

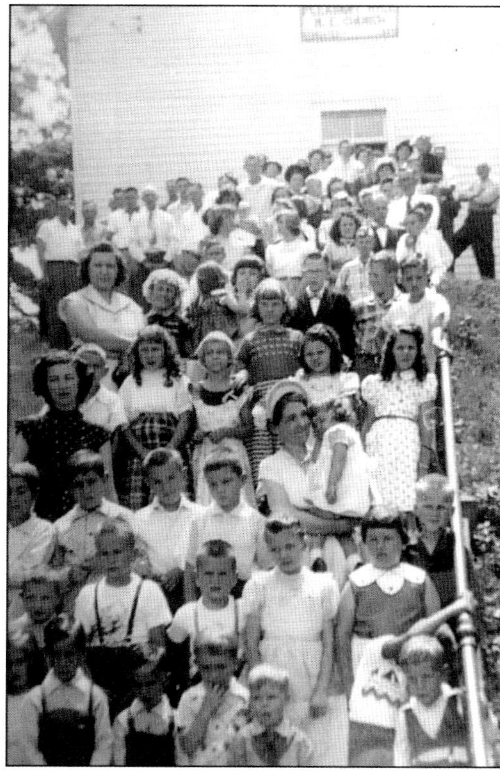

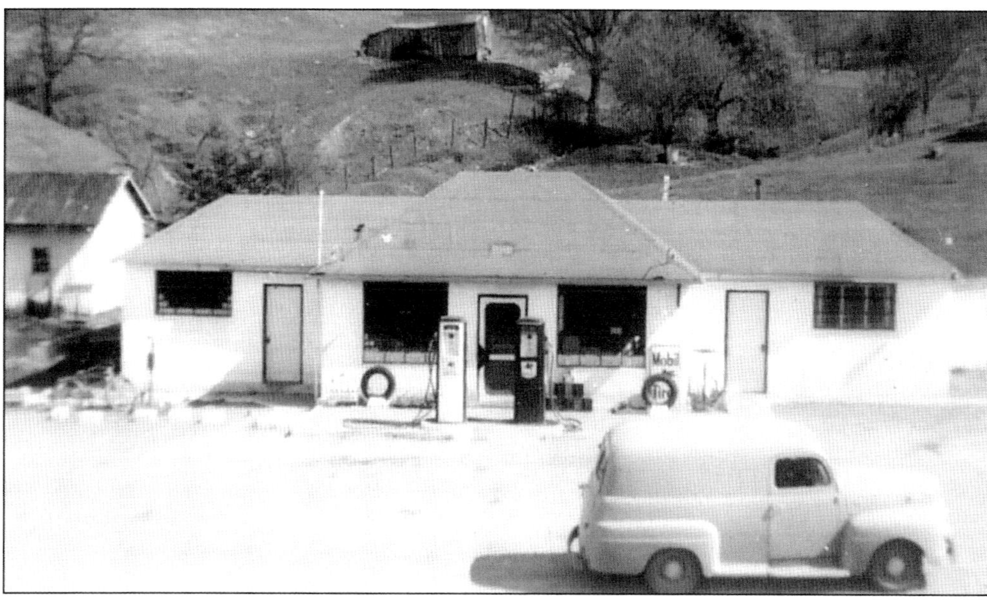

Arden and Gladys Marshall built the Pleasant Hill Grocery in 1948. Located 15 miles east of Parkersburg on Route 50, the store became the gathering place of the community. Customers remember the beautiful flower beds tended by Gladys and the full service station. Arden, Gladys, or their daughter Betty filled the tank, checked the oil and tires, and cleaned windshields. Today the Pleasant Hill Grocery, now called Reese's Country Store, is owned by Dale and Roger Park. (Courtesy of Gladys Marshall.)

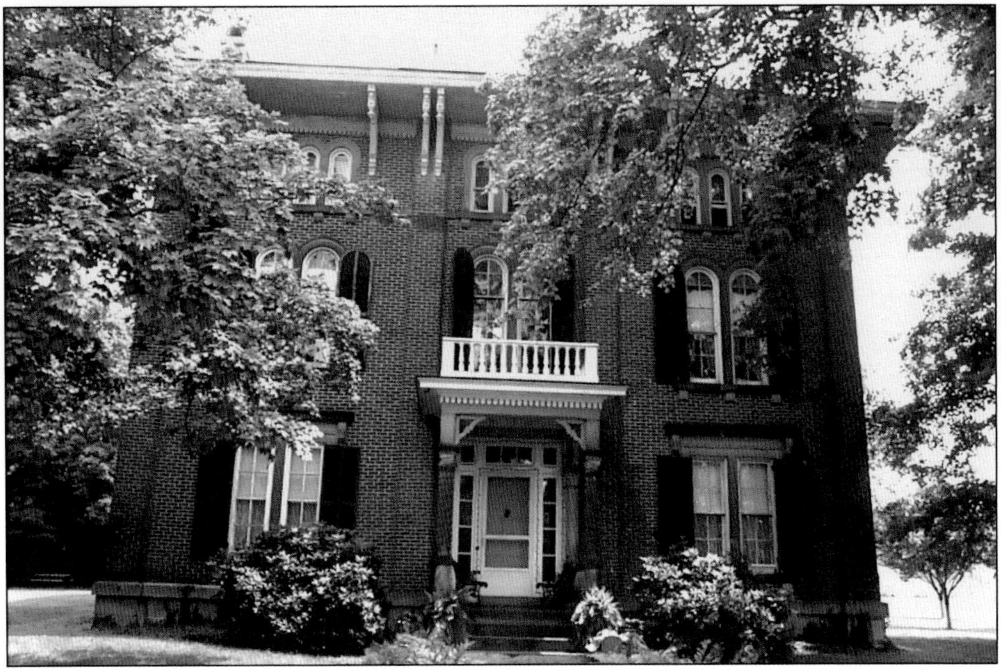

George Washington Henderson built Henderson Hall, two miles south of Williamstown, from 1856 to 1859. Construction materials used, including brick, timber and stone, were produced entirely on the Henderson plantation. The 17-room mansion overlooked the Ohio River and the extensive fields of Henderson's 2,000-acre plantation, and has been continuously occupied by descendants of the Henderson family. (Photograph by Fred Cornwell.)

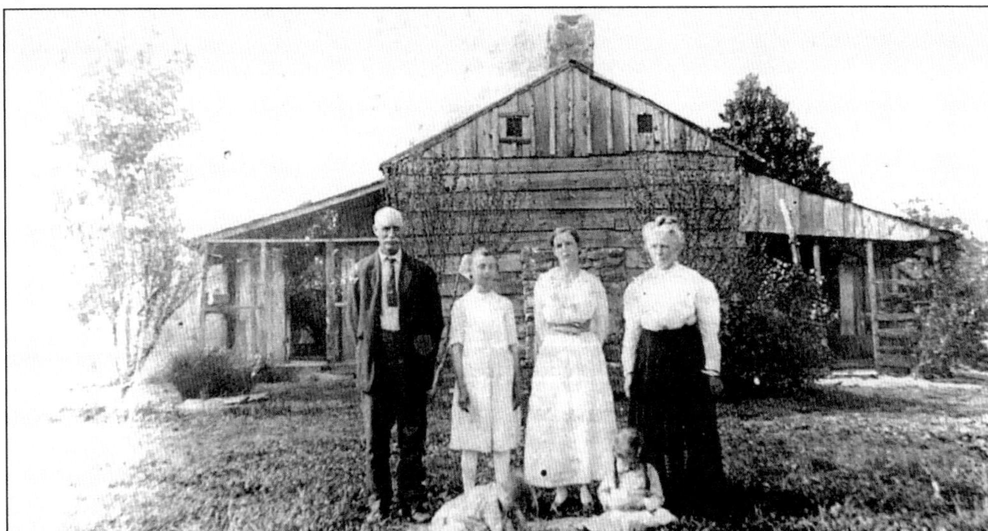

Settlers moved in the fertile land south of Boaz in the early 1800s. They lived along the banks of the Ohio River, raising crops and grazing cattle. Their homes were log cabins much like the home of Thomas and Victoria Deem Hoover, pictured above. They were quite a contrast to Henderson Hall a few miles upriver. The settlement soon became known as Boaz, named, as the story goes, by an early postmaster who was quite religious. Boaz was the husband of Ruth of "whither thou goest" fame. (Courtesy of Jacquelyn Goodman.)

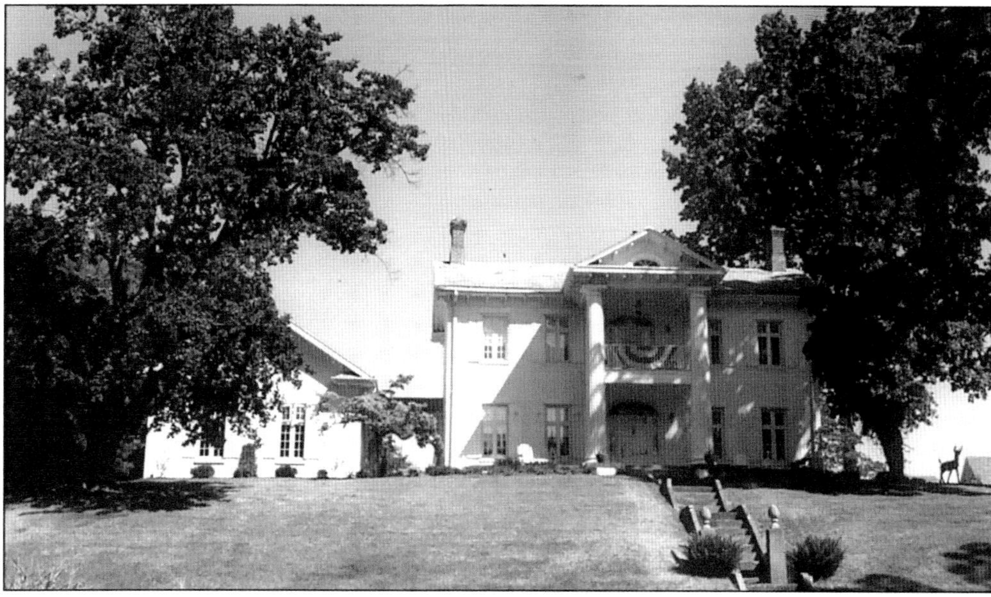

Dr. Joseph Spencer, his wife Deborah, and their nine children emigrated to Wood County from Connecticut in 1794. He settled on a 5,000-acre land grant that he received from the federal government for his services in the Revolutionary War. He and a partner, Austin Nichols, marked off half-acre lots on 100 acres and petitioned the Virginia General Assembly to establish the town of Vienna, which it did on January 21, 1799. Their attempts to sell the lots were not successful and Vienna remained essentially the plantation of Dr. Spencer. It was not until 1935 that Vienna was incorporated. The house pictured above was built by Dr. Spencer's son, David, in 1839. (Photograph by Fred Cornwell.)

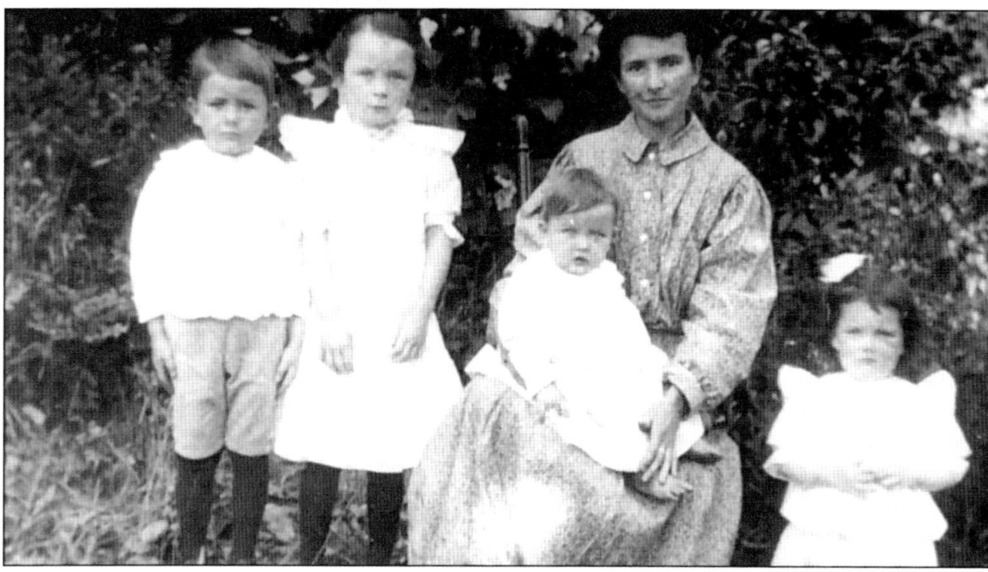

A Parkersburg photographer, Leland Davies, rode the train from Parkersburg to Volcano to take photographs around 1908. Pictured above, from left to right, is the Taitt family: Walter, Ethel, George (baby), Maggie (seated), and Marie. Walter, now 99 years old, has lived in Volcano all his life. He worked in the oil field for 46 years, having begun at age 14 as a pipeline walker looking for leaks. (Courtesy of Walter Taitt.)

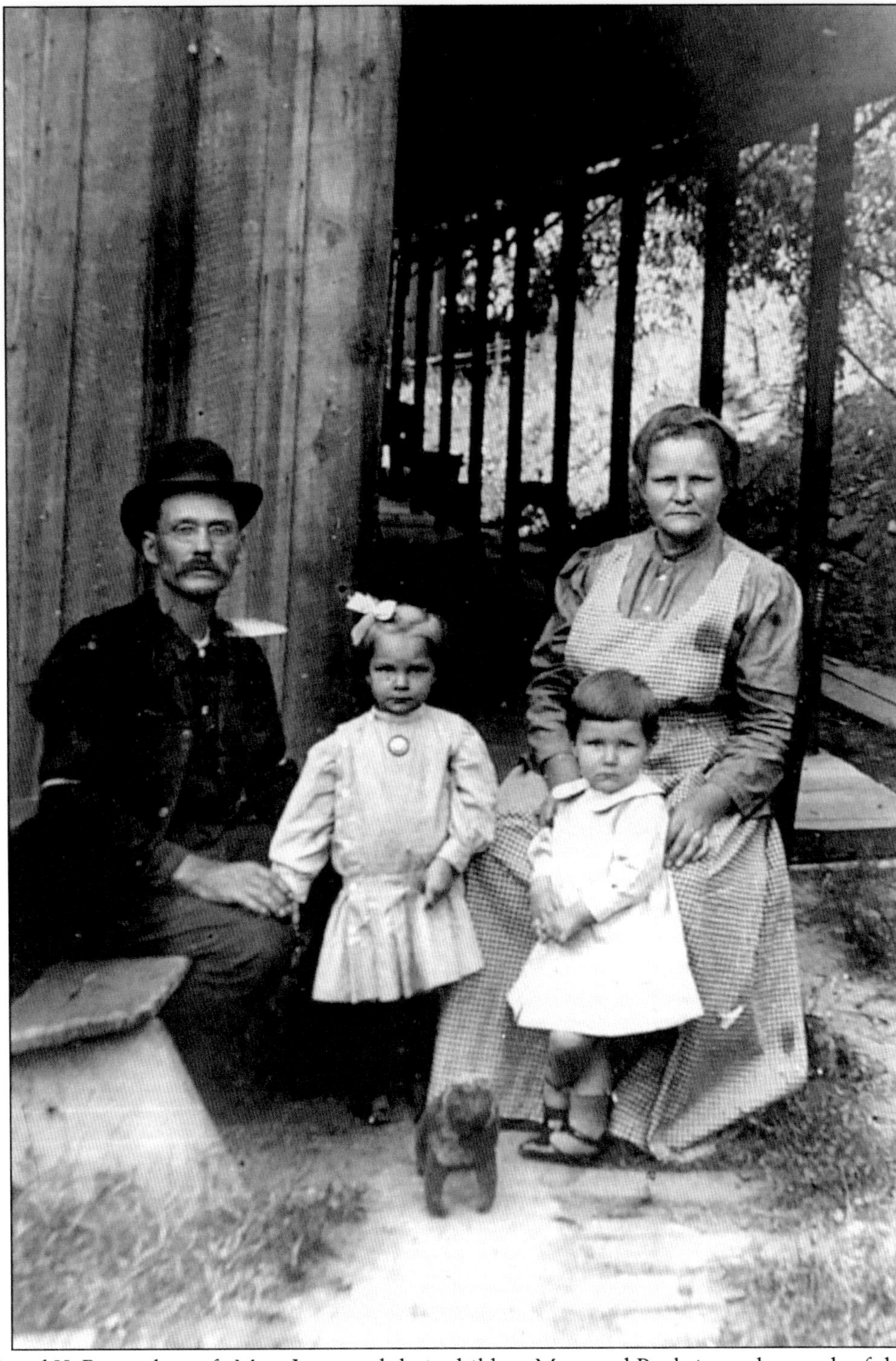

David K. Reece, his wife Mary Jane, and their children Mary and Paul sit on the porch of their home in Volcano around 1908. The house still stands today; it is the home of longtime Volcano resident Walter Taitt. Reece owned the general store in Volcano for many years. Prior to this he was superintendent for W.C. Stiles Jr. (Courtesy of the family of Mary Reece Dunlap.)